LORDS OF THE FLY

LORDS OF THE FLY

MADNESS, OBSESSION, AND THE HUNT FOR THE WORLD-RECORD TARPON

MONTE BURKE

PEGASUS BOOKS
NEW YORK LONDON

LORDS OF THE FLY

Pegasus Books Ltd.
148 W 37th Street, 13th Floor
New York, NY 10018

Copyright © 2020 by Monte Burke

First Pegasus Books edition September 2020

Interior design by Maria Fernandez

Library of Congress Cataloging-in-Publication Data is available.

ISBN: 978-1-64313-558-8

10 9 8 7 6 5

Printed in the United States of America
Distributed by Simon & Schuster
www.pegasusbooks.com

For Charles Gaines

For there is no folly of the beast of the earth which is not infinitely outdone by the madness of men.
—Herman Melville, *Moby Dick*

We live and spawn and want—always there is this ghastly wanting.

—Joy Williams

CONTENTS

INTRODUCTION

At daybreak, the cloudless sky was a deep dark blue. The water rippled gently in the light westerly breeze. Tom Evans, a stockbroker from New York City, and Steve Huff, a fishing guide from the Florida Keys, sat side by side in the stern of a sixteen-foot, shallow-water skiff, their shoulders slumped slightly forward. They were embarking on their twenty-fourth straight day together on the water.

Huff manned the tiller, slowly idling the boat out of the mouth of the Homosassa River toward the Gulf of Mexico, keeping the wake to a bare minimum, trying to maintain this fleeting moment in a world that felt reset and peaceful after a few hours of being left undisturbed by the disharmony of humans. Quail whistled in the gathering light. The roots of the mangroves on the shorelines gripped the river bottom like the fingers of witches. On previous mornings, they'd seen a herd of whiskered manatees lying on their backs, sound asleep, and dolphins had playfully swum beside the boat like dogs greeting a car in a driveway.

On this day—May 24, 1977—the little commercial fishing town some seventy miles north of Tampa, known as Homosassa, was little changed from seven decades prior, when Winslow Homer had captured it and its surroundings in some of the most tranquil of his watercolors. Unbeknownst to Evans and Huff at the time, this day would also mark the beginning of the end of that era.

Though Evans and Huff sat just inches apart from each other, they didn't speak. They'd dispensed with the usual pleasantries—asking after each other's families, gossiping about mutual acquaintances—weeks before. Now, they saved their words as if to conserve energy. The suffering, which both men withstood and even seemed to relish as it happened, would begin again soon enough. Today, just like the twenty-three days preceding it and the twenty-one days yet to come, they would be on the boat for more than twelve straight hours—and on their feet for eleven of those hours—in the glare of an oppressive sun, their eyes trained on the water. Their focus was singular, honed in on a dream they believed could become reality. Any wayward thoughts that happened to enter their minds were discarded quickly. They were acutely aware that any one mistake during the day—a noisy, errant *plunk* of the push pole used by Huff to move the boat, a blown cast of the fly or missed hook-set by Evans—could be ruinous. Even while on the water, they spoke to each other only when necessary, when fish were spotted or when the time came to reel up and run the boat to another spot. Otherwise, communication was wordless, transmitted by some familiar sixth sense developed during the 150 days they had spent together on the boat over the years, never more than sixteen feet apart. They were teammates, in a sense, but each had to rise to the occasion when it came to his individual role. And each sought to execute that role without flaw.

The world-record tarpon caught on a fly rod at the time was 170 pounds. In their four weeks of fishing in Homosassa—spread over two years—Evans and Huff had seen hundreds of fish they believed were much bigger than that. Evans had even hooked a few, only to lose them when the fish spat the hook, snapped the line, or shattered the rod. For now, the world-record tarpon, which they'd come to call "Rocquetta," was still only potential and not actual.

These tarpon they were seeing in Homosassa, by Evans's reckoning, were 50 percent bigger than any he and Huff had seen anywhere else. This presented the duo with something that had once seemed unimaginable, an explosive new reality that they had to figure out.

Over the course of two seasons, they'd spent countless evenings in the motel, forensically recounting each of the fish they'd lost, talking over the different ways in which they could have changed the outcomes. They'd found, after considerable research, new, stronger, laser-sharpened hooks from Japan, fly lines that didn't disintegrate after hooking and fighting one fish, and a one-piece fiberglass rod that refused to be broken. Huff had also insisted that Evans fight every tarpon he hooked to the boat to be released, even a "Rocky," which was what they called a fish that was well below the record weight. Huff argued that doing so was a way of respecting the tarpon. He also argued that it served as practice for the big show if and when that moment came. Evans balked at this idea at first, not wanting to waste time on lesser fish. But he eventually did as Huff requested, and through the process, he learned exactly how much pressure he could exert on the light tippet, and figured out how to work the leverage and angles during the fight. And, in short order, he was routinely getting a hooked tarpon to the side of the boat in under a half hour, three to four times faster than it took most tarpon anglers to do the same.

By that point in the 1977 season, the duo believed they had finally refined their techniques and tackle to the point where actually landing one of the true Homosassa beasts was a possibility.

⁓

Evans and Huff, physically and temperamentally, appeared to be a mismatched pair. Huff, then thirty-one, weighed around 160 pounds, with long arms, taut as cables, hanging from his lean, compact body. He was born and raised outside of Miami, and had lived in the Keys and worked as a fishing guide since his early twenties. He was easy with a smile but quiet and philosophical, moral without being preachy. The then-thirty-eight-year-old Evans, a former collegiate football nose guard and heavyweight wrestler, was all bulk and mass in body and in spirit. He had a growly voice, and was direct and opinionated and lacked any signs of serious introspection, a bull always very pleased to find himself in a china shop.

They did have some similarities, though. Both had serious issues with wretched fathers—Evans's father had kicked him out of the house for good when he was fourteen, and Huff's had abandoned his family when the boy was ten. Both men were stubborn to the point of exasperation. Both seemed to enjoy and even welcome pain.

Through quirks of fate, they had found each other, and then found *the thing* in the fishing world that animated them. And now they were completely in sync, matching both the yearning desire and the prodigious talent it took to pursue, and hopefully catch, Rocquetta.

∽

On this particular May morning in 1977, Evans happened to be feeling awful, though. Yes, the twenty-three straight days of fishing had taken a toll, on both body and mind. But for Evans, the bigger issue was his diet. He still had the capacious appetite, if not the metabolism, of a collegiate football player. The sleepy town of Homosassa didn't offer much in the way of dining options back then, and the nearest grocery store was a forty-five-minute drive away, a trip neither he nor Huff was willing to endure at 7:30 at night after twelve hours or more on the water. So Evans had ended up eating—and eating a lot—at the same local fish shack every night. The fried food had finally caught up with him and made him sick. Staying in the motel during the day to recover was not an option for Evans, not with just a few weeks left in prime tarpon season in Homosassa. So he went out on the water despite the discomfort.

At one point during the day, as Huff was poling the boat near an area known as Chassahowitzka Point, Evans's sickness became overwhelming. He made his way to the stern, pulled down his pants and then hung off the back of the boat. Huff anchored the boat and moved to the bow, giving Evans every inch of space he could, and continued to scan the water for fish. Almost immediately, he spotted something in the distance. *Tarpon.* A school of perhaps twenty fish was headed at the boat, fast.

Huff told Evans to hurry up. Evans reported back that there was no way he could do that, and that Huff should take a shot at the fish. Huff told Evans that he could not do that, that he was a guide, after all, paid by the client to get the client into fish. The school of tarpon was now swiftly gaining on the boat.

"Goddammit, Steve, just do it," Evans yelled.

Huff looked down at the fly rod on the bottom of the boat. He paused for a moment, paralyzed by indecision. Then he grabbed the rod and started to quickly strip out enough line to make a cast.

It turned out he had waited too long. By the time he worked out a cast, the fish had seen the boat and flushed off, their giant tails creating whirlpools in the water, propelling them instantaneously out of sight. Huff felt both disappointed and relieved. He began to reel in the line. Evans still hung off the back.

But just then, Huff spotted two new fish coming in, tracking along the same route as the previous school. Without any hesitation this time, he made a cast at what appeared to be the larger of the duo, placing the three-inch fly—made with chicken feathers and a large, two-inch hook—five feet ahead of it. As the tarpon neared, he made one long, slow strip of the line. The fish veered toward the fly, engulfed it, and leapt, its body lurching completely out of the water, before crashing back in. It was, as Huff would later recall, as if someone had dropped a Steinway piano into the ocean from a helicopter.

Though much smaller than Evans, Huff was equally adept at fighting fish, and after twenty minutes, the tarpon lay in the water beside the boat, exhausted and defeated. The fish was utterly enormous, bigger by some degree, Huff says, than any tarpon he had ever seen. Huff turned to Evans, who was finally back in the boat, finished with his business, and asked him to gaff the fish. Huff believed he would never catch a bigger tarpon in his life, and he wanted to have it mounted. Evans wanted to gaff it, too. He needed to see exactly how big the fish was so he'd know, definitively, where the mark now stood.

With that settled, Evans picked up the eight-foot-long kill gaff, with its massive barbed hook, reached it out over the tarpon, and violently yanked it back with all his force into the fish's massive silver flank. It was the first and last fish that Evans would ever gaff. With two hands and all of his strength—and with some help from Huff—the tarpon was hauled into the boat, where it lay, motionless.

"That's Rocquetta," Evans said, in barely more than a whisper, and then went silent. Water lapped onto the sides of the rocking boat. The two men drew and expelled heavy, adrenalized breaths. After a few moments, Huff picked up his push pole and started moving the boat and searching the water for fish. Evans took to the bow. The men were each going through emotions that veered from one extreme to the other, ones that would, at some point, need to be hashed out. And yet they fished for another four hours, speaking only when necessary (Huff: "Fish coming in at one o'clock." Evans: "I see them."), all the while trying, but failing, to ignore the giant dead tarpon splayed across the boat's bottom.

They didn't hook another fish. And finally, as the sun sank into the Gulf and the translucence of the water grew dull, Huff cranked up the motor and vectored the boat toward the commercial fish house onshore that had a certified scale. The two men sat next to each other in the back of the boat in silence, ending the day just as they'd begun it, even though everything had changed.

At the fish house, the scale read 186 pounds. Huff's tarpon had bested the standing world record by sixteen pounds.

"Well, you did it, Steve," Evans said.

"No," replied Huff. "I didn't." His feelings about the giant fish had left him vexed. Catching it had proved exhilarating. And yet, he bore a slight sense of regret for even picking up the rod and making the cast in the first place.

Over Evans's protestations, Huff had decided that he would not submit the tarpon for official certification as the new world record. He was a fishing guide, and he had been paid to do precisely that job on that day. By Huff's unwritten code, that disqualified him and the fish for world-record consideration. Evans quickly realized that Huff was too stubborn to be dissuaded on this point.

But even though Huff never did submit the tarpon, and nothing was ever official, Evans knew that the new level had been established. The potential had become actual.

After the fish was weighed, the two men finally talked through what had transpired, to sort of put on record and keep it all aboveboard—how Evans had insisted that Huff make the cast, how Huff had decided not to submit it for official certification. Evans tried not to let his disappointment show, at least in front of Huff. He extended a hand and congratulated him.

And yet, as Huff stood outside the motel room door that night, waiting for Evans to come out so they could go to the fish shack—that same fish shack—for dinner, he overheard Evans talking to his then-wife on the phone.

"Honey, that was the worst dump I've ever taken," he said.

1

THE BABE

Forty-two years after Huff's catch, I am sitting in the stern of a boat that was designed, constructed, and sold by a prominent Miami gangster, who is now deceased. We are floating off of Homosassa on an enormous white sand flat that's nearly thirty miles long and interrupted here and there by piles of dark black rocks. The flat is known to anglers and guides as Oklahoma. It is eleven o'clock in the morning. The sky is clear, the wind light, the sun blazing hard enough to induce a squint behind your sunglasses.

The boat is being moved, quietly and with purpose, by a man named Al Dopirak, a fishing guide who hails from nearby Pinellas County. He stands above me, on the platform on top of his boat's motor, rhythmically, and without any evident effort, placing his eighteen-foot graphite push pole in the water until he finds purchase on the sea's floor, then pushing it, gloved hand over gloved hand to its top end, then pulling and sliding the pole back up through his hands and doing it all over again. He never once takes his eyes off the water—in front of the boat, beside it, and, occasionally, behind it. Dopirak, sixty-three, is blue-eyed and deeply, and seemingly permanently, tanned. He has a cotton-white goatee and blonde-streaked hair that nearly reaches his shoulders. He looks like a younger, leaner Jeff Bridges, a South Florida cowboy of the flats. He prefers to address everyone and anyone as "dawg."

In the front, standing on the bow and gazing out over the sea with his hands monkishly clasped behind his back, is the Australian, Dean Butler. He is one of the world's finest deep-sea fly-fishing guides, despite the fact that he lost the use of two fingers on his right hand—the pinky and the ring—when he fell through a transom door while trying to land a marlin and had two tendons cleanly cleaved by the boat's propeller as he surfaced. He is here in Homosassa as a quasi first mate—a potential gaffer, a manager of rods, a tyer of knots and leaders and flies, another set of eyes on the water, a chef, a bartender, and a grocery-getter. Butler is fifty-six and sports a perpetual grin under his salt-and-pepper goatee. His blue eyes contain within them an unmistakable hint of mischief. He rarely utters a sentence without using the word "fuck," in some form. Presently, he turns to us, behind him in the boat, and says, "It feels like it's going to happen today," and turns back around to again watch the water. Then, with only a slight turn of his head this time, he adds as an afterthought, "I base that on fuck-all, of course."

He is addressing Dopirak and me, yes, but the main intended audience for the comment is the eighty-two-year-old man sitting in a lawn chair that's been placed just in front of the steering console. This man is tall and weighs somewhere north of three hundred pounds. An orange hat rests upon his white hair. His dark sunglasses are held onto his head by a pair of Croakies that read "Life is too short to drink cheap wine." He has on a purple long-sleeved T-shirt with printed pictures of his numerous world-record tarpon on the back. His feet, swollen and covered in liver spots, are propped on the elevated bow area in front of him.

This man is Tom Evans. And he did not hear Butler's comment because he is currently sound asleep, his chin on his chest—a state in which he has been for the past half hour, interrupted only twice by identical guttural utterances: *"C'mon, poon."*

It's been forty-three years since Evans first came to Homosassa in search of the world-record tarpon on a fly. Since then, he's returned every year and has missed only twice—once in the mid-1980s when he couldn't get away from work, and once again in 2015, when he had a mild falling out with Dopirak, and he and Butler went to the Panhandle to fish with one of the best young tarpon guides in the world in what would turn out to be a disastrous trip for all involved. The vast majority of Evans's Homosassa trips have been a month long in duration, meaning he's spent somewhere between 1,200 and 1,500 days here, or close to three and a half years of his life.

They haven't all exactly been glorious years, either. In fact, it's all been a bit mental, something he readily admits. "If I really think about it, it's crazy. I come down here and fish, and every six or seven years, I get a victory," Evans says. "The rest of the time, I've gotten my ass kicked."

The "victories," as he sees it, are the times when he has hooked and landed a record-breaking tarpon. Evans has set seven tarpon fly-fishing world records, as his shirt indicates. The first of these was a 177-pound tarpon he landed on Memorial Day in 1977, exactly a week after Huff caught *his* 186-pound tarpon. That it was a full nine pounds lighter than Huff's fish never sat well with Evans, but this one counted, nonetheless.

As for getting his ass kicked? According to Evans, that's all of the time he's spent in Homosassa *save* for those seven days during which those record fish were caught. The ass-kickings include days when he landed fish that weren't big enough to break the record or lost a big fish that might have, or spent eleven hours bobbing up and down in a boat without seeing a single fish, or had to spend the day stuck on land because of the weather.

And now, in early May 2019, he's back again for another season in Homosassa, another shot at victory. Or, more likely, another opportunity to get his ass kicked.

∽

The prior winter, I found myself driving around the almost implausibly quaint town of Grafton, Vermont, a place known for its exquisite aged cheddar cheese. I was looking for a driveway or a mailbox or anything that might have been a sign that I had arrived at my destination.

Grafton, in the southeastern part of the state, is just rural enough to render any mapping apps useless. I had already passed through the center of town and over the pretty Saxtons River a few times. The three feet of fresh, damp snow that had fallen overnight made the town seem even quainter, but it wasn't helping matters at all. That I had come to talk to someone about tarpon fishing here among the cows, the trout streams with their six-inch native brook trout, the snow—all of it some thousand miles away from the tropical climes in which tarpon swim the flats—made the entire endeavor feel even more out of whack.

Eventually, though, I did find the driveway, which snaked between rows of dark pines and led me to the house of Tom Evans.

⁓

The home, a converted 19th-century farmhouse, is one of two houses owned by Evans and his second wife, Tania (the other is in Jackson Hole). Inside, it was warm and cozy. A robust fire burned in one of the house's six fireplaces. Tania, an eighty-two-year-old former ski instructor and owner of a decorating business (the two of them met when she gave Evans a ski lesson at Stratton Mountain), loves it here in southern Vermont, and that's why they stay. She grew up in Connecticut and proudly describes herself as an "inveterate Yankee." She's trim and straight-backed, and exudes the healthful glow of a person who has spent a good portion of her life outdoors, skiing and hiking.

Tania gave me a brief tour of the house. It is filled with the fruits of Evans's collecting life. The first floor is constructed from salvaged 19th-century wood and decorated with American art and furniture from that period. In the basement, there is a room done in the same way, but modeled on American art and furniture from the 1680s. Perched throughout the house are priceless wooden duck decoys. And below it all is a cellar with thousands of bottles of wine.[*]

---

[*] Evans is known as "the White Tie Collector" in the wine world, and is considered a top collector of French wines. He has since sold much of his collection.

One room, on the second floor, is decidedly different from the others. It is thoroughly contemporary. On the walls are dozens of pictures of huge, glassy-eyed, dead fish hung by hooks or ropes on the docks of various sunny locales around the world. Standing next to these fish—tarpon and marlin and all of them, at one time or another, world records—is Evans, decades younger and a hundred pounds lighter, holding a fly rod in one hand and what might pass as a smile across his face.

It was in this room—a study—that I found Evans. He was sitting in a big modern chair, red and built for comfort, not aesthetics, and had one leg propped up on an ottoman. It was clear from first glance that Evans is broken. He can barely move, and when he does, he winces and sighs in pain. His present physical state is mostly the result of the years of football and wrestling and a bad bike crash in 1996 and the surgeries needed to alleviate the damage done by them. But all of those days on the water fishing for tarpon and billfish—up to eighty days a year for more than four decades—have certainly not helped matters.

Though he occasionally goes out for dinner or to visit his stepchildren and their families or to fetch the newspaper at the general store in town, Evans is now, for all intents and purposes, a shut-in for all but one month of the year. He spends his time in his study trying to read books (the author C. J. Box is one of his favorites), but the days are long, and the flickering lure of the giant television in his room is usually too hard for him to resist. He watches *Fox News* or *Fox Business* for long stretches at a time, and doing so appears to leave him agitated and aggrieved. He is now pretty sure that the world is going to shit. He has put all of his wealth into hard goods—real estate, art, furniture, wine, and silver bars, no longer trusting that the global economy in its present form will hold. (He might have been onto something here.)

But all of that pain and agitation and aggrievement is temporarily put aside, and the muscles in his face ease up a bit as he turns down the anchors on his television.

"Let's talk about tarpon and those great years in Homosassa," he says.

Back in the boat, Evans awakens with a grunt and shake of his head, just as Dopirak has nudged us to within shouting distance of the four other boats floating the Oklahoma flat today. The nap is over. It's time to get to work. Which means, really, that it's time to hurry up and wait.

As we approach the other boats, I detect a subtle shift among them, an ever-so-slight moving out of the way. Maybe I'm seeing something that's not, in fact, there. Maybe it's only something I *expect* to see. Or maybe not.

After all, Tom Evans is back in Homosassa, back on the water for another day. His presence on the flat today, forty-three years after he first visited and after all of his records here and his demonstrations of sheer will (or lunacy), is something the anglers and guides in the other boats can't help but notice. He is, by the book, the greatest big tarpon angler alive. The old king has arrived in his court. Some of the anglers and guides in the other boats don't much like the old king, but they grudgingly acknowledge his majesty anyway.

I have Babe Ruth on my mind today, so again, maybe I'm just projecting something onto this scene that's not there. But again, maybe not. There are two reasons I've been thinking about the Babe. The first is that I've been told the cast-iron tub tucked back behind the shed in the yard of the house in nearby Aripeka that Evans has rented for the tarpon season was once used by the Babe, who visited the area in the 1930s to fish. The second is that the night before, when I hopped on a plane to fly to Tampa, rent a car, and drive north to Homosassa to spend some time interviewing Evans, I received a text from Andy Mill, the former US ski team member who has become a renowned tarpon angler.

> Good luck w Tom down there. As you well know, you'll be with
> the Babe. He may not be able to walk, but he's still the Babe!

Evans is certainly Ruthian in his appearance and accomplishments. And, in a sense, his presence on the Homosassa flat today is akin to some alternate universe where the Babe never got sick and withered and died and, instead, somehow continued to show up at Yankee Stadium every year into his eighties, hobbling into the batter's box with the assistance of a cane, remaining in the Yankees' lineup because of his ability to still occasionally knock one out of the park.

There is one way in which Evans is not like the Babe, though, and that has to do with fame. Despite the fact that he is undoubtedly one of the greatest tarpon fly rod anglers who ever lived (and, perhaps, *the* greatest billfish fly rod angler), Evans is not nearly as well known as some of his contemporaries, like Stu Apte, Billy Pate Jr., and Bernard "Lefty" Kreh. Those three men are among many who found within the world of angling a method of self-promotion, who fished for records but also for adulation, and had newspaper and magazine features written about them, authored autobiographies, and starred in fishing films. Evans did none of that. That he can be a grump is part of the reason he has not received adulation and fame. But it's more than that. Though he readily admits that seeking records is, to a degree, about seeking attention, he says his main focus has always been on the records themselves and not what those records can do for him in a bigger, more promotional sense.

That said, those deep within this sport have always kept tabs on their fellow anglers. Those who know, *know*. The anglers and guides in those other boats today on the flat, who appear to have granted passage to Evans, are among those who know. Evans is a man who was here in Homosassa during the frenzy of its heyday four decades ago, a man who kept coming back during the dolorous decades when it later fell apart, and a man who keeps coming back now, though he is in no condition to do so.

Dopirak and Butler are part of all of this now, too, part of the recognition, the king's courtiers, the men who help Evans into the batter's box and help him round the bases when he connects. They are the all-star support team that's been assembled around him as he works on the coda to his life as a world-record tarpon hunter, like mountain Sherpas who play an indispensable role in reaching a summit. Dopirak has been one of the best—if not *the* best—guides in Homosassa for thirty-plus years now. His eyes, his patience, his historical and contemporary knowledge, his hunches, his sleight of hand, his knowing how to fish the other anglers on the water as much as the fish, and his ability to put his boat in exactly the right spot for his sport to cast are just a few of the things that have set him apart. Butler has gaffed more big world-record fish than perhaps any man alive, most of them marlin, which are larger, more dangerous (because of their bills), and harder to gaff than tarpon. With Dopirak finding the fish and maneuvering the boat, and with Butler preparing the rods and tying leaders and readying the gaff, everything is done for Evans save for the casting, the feeding, and the fighting of the fish.

Evans describes himself as the "weak link" of the team, but the three aforementioned tasks that he is responsible for are all still incredibly difficult to do well. He is still a fine caster, with a forthright stroke that might not be a thing of beauty but is uncannily accurate. He still manipulates the fly well enough to elicit a strike. His weaknesses have everything to do with his lack of mobility and stamina, which have come with age and injury. Fighting the fish—just staying upright long enough to complete the demanding task—is the biggest concern.

Evans has undergone eleven orthopedic surgeries, starting with a knee operation at the age of thirteen. He has two artificial hips and one artificial knee. He has survived a bout of prostate cancer and has had three worrisome melanomas removed from his skin. He's nearly blind in his left eye.

The biggest problem, though, is his back. Of those eleven surgeries, seven have been on his spine, and the two most recent ones—especially his last one in 2015, which resulted in a devastating hematoma that went untreated for days—have been botched to the point where he cannot stand upright now for more than a few minutes at a time. The battery that's been installed in his back, meant to inspire his nerves to fire correctly, "doesn't do a damn bit of good," he says. His rapid weight gain in recent years has to do with his lack of mobility, along with his robust appetite for food and fondness for good wine. And though the pain in various parts of his body can be excruciating, after a bad experience with opiates, he takes nothing stronger than Advil for relief, and even that sparingly. Despite it all, or perhaps because of it all, his pain threshold remains high, even in his eighties.

The lawn chair is in the boat to help alleviate some of this discomfort. Dopirak's skiff has been jury-rigged to help Evans in other ways, too. On the bow, on top of the three-foot-high platform that's found in nearly every shallow water skiff in the world (it's where an angler traditionally stands to cast), is a cage, with three-foot-high metal legs attached to a circular metal bar with a small opening on the stern side that provides the entry-and-exit way. A thick blue rope is attached to the cage so that Evans can pull himself out of the lawn chair and up onto the platform. The cage allows Evans to lean rather than stand. He hates the cage, which he calls a "baby carriage," and he curses it with regularity. "Fucking thing," he says. "I can't fish with it [it hinders the retrieval of his fly], but I can't fish without it."

Next to the cage is a tall bucket, meant to collect Evans's fly line as he retrieves it so it doesn't get wrapped around a bar on the cage or scattered about the boat. The bucket also serves as a holding place for Evans's rod when he's not in the cage. Butler makes sure that the line is already pulled out of the reel, and that the fly is notched securely in the cork handle of the rod so that Evans can easily just grab the rod and go.

Ideally, a shot at a tarpon works like this: Dopirak spots the fish and tells all in the boat the direction from which it/they are coming down the flat, something like, "Dawg, we have three coming at twelve o'clock." (The face of a clock is traditionally used by guides to point out the location of oncoming fish, with twelve o'clock being straight off the bow, three o'clock being perpendicular off the boat to the right, nine o'clock perpendicular to the left, and so on.) Butler then clears anything out of Evans's way as Evans gets out of his lawn chair and into the cage. Butler does not touch the fly or the rod, since doing so is against the rules of the International Game Fish Association, the body that keeps angling records; the angler is to angle by him or herself. When finally in the cage—a process that takes some time—Evans tries to locate the fish. Once he's done so, Dopirak will move the boat into position (Evans likes an 11:30 shot directly into the wind). And then Evans makes a maybe thirty- or forty-foot cast and begins retrieving the fly, trying to tempt a silver-plated, prehistoric-looking creature into biting it.

On a typical tarpon skiff, the angler is already standing on the platform and ready (in theory) to cast at a moment's notice. That's obviously not the case with Evans, but he's compensated very well for his shortcomings by Dopirak, with his excellent eyes that are able to spot tarpon from a great distance away, and Butler, with his overall preparedness for anything Evans may need. On occasion, Dopirak will spot fish that he knows Evans will never be able to cast to—tarpon often seem to appear out of the blue, behind the boat or to the side or even in the front. "There are some sliding by," Dopirak will say rather quietly, quickly turning his attention elsewhere, keeping his focus on potential fish in locations that he feels Evans has a decent shot at.

All of this may seem like a lot of work and sort of crazy, like attempting to roller-skate in deep, soft snow. All of it, really, makes something that is already challenging to the point of being nearly impossible—that is, fly fishing for giant tarpon—even more challenging. And the entire endeavor is made even more difficult by the fact that the number of tarpon that swim in Homosassa each season is but a tiny fraction—maybe a tenth—of what it was thirty to forty years ago. But every once in a while, and just enough to validate it all, everything comes together, and the Babe proves he can still swing it. The day before, Evans had enticed two fish to bite, which was more action than the other boats on the water had had combined. And just a week from today, he will have a very good shot at yet another victory.

∽

But, why?

Why does Evans, in his physical state, keep going back to Homosassa and attempting to do something that was nearly impossible to do when he was young and strong and mobile?

Nostalgia certainly plays a role in all of this. All of that collecting Evans has done in his non-tarpon-fishing life—the art, furniture, decoys, and wine—has something to do with it. His home in Grafton, at least outside of his study, has a museum-like quality, as if something, some past, is being preserved. Evans is the foremost collector of the wooden decoys made by a carver who was regarded as the master of the form, Elmer Crowell, a man from East Harwich, Massachusetts, whose prime as a carver lasted roughly from 1912 to 1922.* Evans collected the decoys because of what they represent: a time in America when a gentleman sportsman living on the Cape could, right from his doorstep, be easily and fully consumed with sporting and other outdoor pursuits, like fishing and bird hunting and clamming. This period came and went quickly—it lasted a decade or so before development engulfed and despoiled everything. The decoys are the only thing that remain.

Homosassa these days is, in some ways, also a museum, a place that really only exists now in Evans's mind, where there was once a golden era that is now long past and will never happen again. Nostalgia, though, is not only a longing for some lost past but also a mechanism for coping with the present reality. And it is merely part of the story, part of the answer to the "why."

∽

And here's where we enter the museum and go back in time and return to 1977, for it was that year that ignited Homosassa. Something significant happened when Huff and Evans caught their respective monster tarpon that year. Some perceived limit, both theoretical and actual, was expanded. Those fish set off a singular era that turned Homosassa into the epicenter of the fly-fishing world, an era that lasted maybe six years.

Those fish at Homosassa also would, as both men gradually came to understand years later, partially lead to the dramatic and heartbreaking change to the fishery. Word got out about Homosassa and its stupendous tarpon after Huff and Evans caught their fish, and with it came

---

* Two Crowell decoys have sold at auction for $1.13 million apiece, part of an overall sale of thirty-one of his birds that went for a total of $7.5 million.

the masses of anglers and guides. Some of them parachuted in for a few days or a week at a time, hoping for some magic. Others were more hard core, coming year after year in the spring for a month or more at a time, joining Evans and Huff in the pursuit.

Lefty Kreh, perhaps the most famous fly fisherman to have ever lived, and the sport's greatest carnival barker, was early to Homosassa and unable to keep its secret, playing a large role in the greater fishing world's discovery of its tarpon.

Stu Apte, a former boxer and pilot of both fighter and commercial jets, is the Muhammad Ali of the tarpon world, a braggart who has backed up his words with incredible fly-fishing feats. He pioneered many of what are considered to be the seminal techniques and tackle for tarpon, and he remains, at ninety, a living legend. He twice held the world record for tarpon with two fish caught in the Keys—a 151-pounder in 1967 and a 154-pounder in 1971—and he headed to Homosassa in the late 1970s to try and retake his crown.

The athletic Jimmy Lopez, an orphan raised by a judge in Miami, could have been, some contend, the world's greatest fly angler had he not run off the rails. He, too, once owned the world record for tarpon, with a 162-pound, 8-ounce fish caught in the Keys in 1974. One year in the early 1980s, he attempted to fish for tarpon for 125 days straight, spending much of that time in Homosassa. But that trip, like the rest of his life, was derailed by the personal demons and drugs that would eventually do him in for good.

Then there was Al Pflueger Jr., a gentle giant and the son of a famous taxidermist, who spent years in Homosassa after the record and was among the best at spotting and hooking fish but among the least when it came to fighting and actually landing them.

Carl Navarre Sr. owned Coca-Cola bottling franchises in South Florida. He was a top tournament angler in his day and would, for a time, also own Islamorada's Cheeca Lodge, long the center of the flats-fishing world in the Keys. He frequently fished with his son in Homosassa. He sometimes sent up a helicopter over the flats, searching for schools of tarpon, and would have one of his guides in the helicopter drop floats in the water to mark spots. Though the technique worked well in the Keys, it was not as successful in Homosassa.

After retiring from baseball, Ted Williams put much of his vast energies into fly fishing for tarpon, bonefish, and Atlantic salmon. He is thought of as one of the all-time greats in the fly-fishing world, his supernatural eyesight and hand-eye coordination coming in handy in that pastime, as well. He was intrigued by Homosassa and its big tarpon—the favorite of his "big three" fish, as he would tell anyone who cared to listen—and fished there as he neared his sixties. But the scene, with all of the people and the competition, left him more crotchety than he already was. He eventually retreated back to his hermetic life in the Keys, but he would return to the Homosassa area to live out his final years.

Billy Pate Jr., of Greenville, South Carolina, annually took up residence in Homosassa and would break many tarpon records there, including one that lasted for twenty-one years. At age thirty-five, the redhead sold his father's carpet business for millions of dollars, then dedicated the rest of his life to the pursuit of world-record fish—and women. A Southern gentleman who craved attention, Pate made a film about himself in Homosassa that brought in hordes of new anglers to the area and angered his fellow record chasers.

Others, like Flip Pallot, Norman Duncan, Chico Fernandez, Guy de la Valdène, Jim Harrison, and Russell Chatham, dropped in during those early years to see what all the hubbub was about.

During that era, these anglers were, of course, accompanied by fishing guides, vital cogs in the pursuit of tarpon. Huff, Dopirak, Hal Chittum, Eddie Wightman, Jim Brewer, Bill Curtis, Billy Knowles, Dale Perez, Nat Ragland, Harry Spear, Gary Ellis, Eustace and Mike Locklear, Neil Sigvartsen, Ray DeMarco, Freddie Archibald, and Jim Farrier were just a few. These men would never reach the level of fame of the sports they poled around, but they were no less deserving of it.

And so, for a relatively brief period that lasted from the late 1970s until the early 1980s, something unique happened in Homosassa: the best fly anglers and guides in the world at the time all gathered together in the same spot at the same time with the same goal—to break the world record, and possibly the mythical two-hundred-pound mark, for the world's most glamorous and sought-after fly rod species, the tarpon.

They came together in the mornings at breakfast. They were all on the water during the day, in competition. They ate dinner together at night, and socialized and partied, some harder than others. The world record fell nearly every year during these heady years. But records weren't the only things that were broken. Hooks, lines, rods, reels, hearts, and marriages didn't survive, either. The egos involved made the atmosphere electric. The difficulty of the quest made it legitimate. And the drugs and the women that were swept in with the tide made it all veer out of control. It was something, a period of time, a gathering, that had never happened before in the world of fly fishing and will never happen again, a collision of the top anglers and the top species of fish, which led, eventually, to smashed lives for nearly all—man and fish—involved.

∾

Fishing—the sport, the pastime, whatever you want to call it—is, in the end, about stories. The storytelling begins well in advance of the act of actually casting for a fish. It starts with the daydreams that can sneak up on any committed angler at any random time—during a business meeting or when a piece of water is glimpsed on a long drive. It goes into the planning of a fishing trip, the thinking through of what you will bring, the conditions you will face, who will be there with you, all of the strategizing and the preparatory tying of flies and leaders.

It happens before you hit the water, when you pull your fly rod from its tube and join the blanks, and then hold it up to your eye to sight it through the big snake guide, when you attach the reel and thread the fly line through the guides and tie a fly on the leader and then lean the rod against the car and gaze at that ensemble of equipment that to some of us is achingly beautiful in its potential energy.

It also happens with the silent internal monologue that takes place in your head throughout a day on the water, the questions, the answers, the self-castigation, self-correction, and self-satisfaction, for fly fishing is very much a sport of the mind. Even when fishing with a guide or someone else in a boat or on a river, you are mostly within your own head, constructing your own narrative, perhaps even thinking ahead to the obligatory stories you must give voice to at the end of the day, the big one that got away, the big one that didn't.

Fishing is often employed as allegory. Jesus told his fishing apostles, Peter and Andrew, to cast aside their nets and follow Him and become fishers of men. The ancient Chinese proverb warns, "The fish sees the bait, not the hook; a person sees the gain, not the danger." There is the dignity of Hemingway's aging Santiago and Melville's "grand, ungodly, god-like" Ahab.

Stories about fly fishing have been told for nearly two thousand years. Trout and Atlantic salmon fishing, the oldest varieties of the sport, make up a good bit of the literature, sort of in the way that baseball dominates the literary world of spectator sports in the United States. But pretty much anything you can catch on a rod and reel has been celebrated in writing. Some numbnut I know even wrote an entire book about large-mouth bass.*

Tarpon are fairly well covered when it comes to "how-to-catch-'em" books. But the story on the following pages—about the glory years in Homosassa, but also about what led up to that point in time and what has happened since in this world—is what intrigued me the most. It has to do with the "why" in fishing. Everything within it is linked, "an unbroken chain of events flowing one out of another," as Chekhov wrote, connecting the past to the present. When one end of the story is touched, as Chekhov continued, "the other end quivered." It contains joyous discovery, furious competition, over-the-top obsession, incredible

---

* That would be me.

willpower, and heartbreaking falls from grace. It details an uncertain future. It sheds some light on the motivations of Man, and possibly reflects, in some refracted way, something larger about our current state.

∞

But what about that "why"? Why so much fuss over a fish, then and now? Why does this story warrant this telling?

I think it starts with this: tarpon are an easy thing to become obsessed about.

2

GOD'S GREAT FISH

We skid turns through the labyrinth of backcountry mangroves. A few stars are visible in the pale early-morning light, but they are fading, soon to be hidden again. I'm sitting in the back of the skiff next to Steve Huff, who holds the tiller under his armpit. He is a man completely within his element.

As all the scenery in the Everglades—the green vegetation on the banks, the blue sky and water—blends together, I can't help but voice the clichéd thought.

"How in the hell would I get out of here if you keeled over?"

Huff's smile straightens out his white mustache.

"You wouldn't."

I gaze at his hands for maybe the third time that morning. You might find this strange, but I can't help it. Stories are worn into those hands, maybe even Commandments. They are gnarled by calluses and deeply etched scars, parched by decades in the sun. They look like old mangroves, whited-out by the elements. They have handled world-record tarpon, bonefish, and permit. They have pushed boats with poles for thousands of miles across sand flats. They have built and rebuilt skiffs from the ground up, some of which are still in use even forty years later. They are the hands of a man who has never had an email address.

It is the spring of 2011, and I am on my first trip for tarpon.

The weather is perfect, sun with no clouds, a light breeze. The tarpon are in, Huff says. I am a bit too jazzed. Sleep the night before had proven nearly impossible. We come to a stop in the *boca* of a river, the engine cut, the wash *shoosh*ing against the stern.

Huff tilts the motor, grabs the push pole, and ascends his platform. I stand and walk to the bow, fly rod in hand. My knees scrape against the raised casting platform that I feel a bit too clumsy to ascend just yet.

This *boca* is where Bloody Watson, the real-life murderer and outlaw fictionalized by Peter Matthiessen, once lived. Huff tells me this as he begins to pole the boat, slowly and deliberately, never taking his eyes off the water.

He spots a tarpon. It's lying there, near the surface, a serene beast at rest. My mind empties, swiftly. It's something we all seek to achieve, this purposeful clearing of the brain. Some find it via alcohol, drugs, sex, yoga. Some of us fish for it.

The fish is facing left. I cast there, tentatively, aiming for a spot maybe a foot in front of her nose. I instead land it on her head. The fish flushes, pushing a boat-sized wake. It's no problem, Huff says. There are more around. We find another one again within minutes, and I screw up that cast, too. Then we find another, and I blow it again.

A few tarpon roll in the distance.

That I am here on the water with Huff at all is a bit of a fluke. I had written a story about him the prior winter, and we'd spent some time in the boat together. We'd hit it off. But for decades, he has had a static list of twelve people he fishes with each year. He once turned down a fishing request from former president George H. W. Bush. After a trip, a client once gave him a condominium as a tip. But this week, as fortune had it, one of his regulars couldn't make his appointed trip and suggested that I go in his stead. And here I am.

Huff describes tarpon as heroin. He has been now, for decades, perhaps the world's foremost dealer in this fish drug. A prominent magazine once described him as "The Best Fishing Guide Alive."* He is, even now, some

---

* I wrote that story for *Garden & Gun* magazine. And while I did not write the title (editors are in charge of that kind of stuff), I heartily agree with it.

fifty-plus years into his career, a legend among legions of guides, their DiMaggio, still in his prime. He says his only job is to make an angler's dream come true.

He plays the role of coach/mentor/psychologist, which all great guides must, with aplomb. I have now blown three great shots at tarpon. By all rights, I should be a slobbering mess, fit for the funny farm. But I am not.

"We're going to get one," Huff says. I believe him. Later in the day, I finally make a good cast, right in front of the bigger member of a brace of laid-up tarpon. I get no response from the fish but am buoyed by the act, like a golfer in the midst of a bad round who finally feels something click on one swing.

"To the left!"

I see it. A monster fish has gulped air and then remained floating near the water's surface. I make the cast immediately, without any thought, make one strip, and then feel a pull I will never forget. Before I can even process what's going on, the she-tarpon clears the water *behind* us.

Images of the moment come to me now, in bits and pieces. I see the water part when the fish bites the fly. I see Huff somehow duck his head under my fly line, avoiding a clotheslining as it slices through the air over him, as tight as a guitar string.

Half an hour into the fight, I realize that my face has been contorted into a rictus, the openmouthed grimace of the dead. I am pulling on the fish, trying to follow Huff's instructions. Yet I can't seem to get the upper hand. My back is numb, my shins and knees rubbed raw by the casting platform that I'm leaning into. I understand at that moment why people say they sometimes give up while fighting a big tarpon, that it's easier to get a few jumps from one like this and then break it off and call it a day. But I can't do that.

She pulls the boat and its two occupants upriver a mile or so, to a mangrove-lined feeder creek barely big enough to fit us all. This is maybe where she grew up. I notice that Huff has put on a pair of orange landing gloves.

The fight has taken two hours. I am embarrassed, but not enough to stop. The fly line has begun to come apart, its coating stripped off by submerged mangrove roots. Huff tells me that Billy Pate Jr. once fought a tarpon for more than twelve hours. Pate would have been a lousy fishing partner. I swear to myself that I will get better at this, someday.

She finally comes up, leading with her huge, prehistoric-looking mouth. Huff holds her for a moment and removes the fly. He moves her a bit in the water, reviving her. She shoots off with a kick of her tail. Huff removes his gloves to shake my hand.

"Congratulations," says the dream-maker.

Waves of relief and exhaustion nearly bring me to my knees. My lower back throbs in pain. My shirt is soaked through with sweat, and I feel like puking from dehydration. My right hand is grotesquely stuck in a curl, as if still holding the rod handle. I cannot wait to do it all over again.*

∞

In Philip Dray's book *The Fair Chase: The Epic Story of Hunting in America*, he relays a credible hypothesis that for 99 percent of prehistory, humans were hunters (we spent only 1 percent of that time as agriculturalists). He quotes two anthropologists, Sherwood Washburn and Chet Lancaster, who wrote in a 1968 paper that "in its total social, biological, technical, and psychological dimensions, [hunting] has dominated the course of human evolution for hundreds of thousands of years. In a very real sense, our intellect, interests, emotions, and basic social life—all are evolutionary products of [this] success."

The author and artist James Prosek has written much about the communication that takes place between the fisherman and the fish when angling, especially when that angling is done with a fly. The rod, line, and hook, he says, are the tools of that communication, but "the fly . . . is the ultimate translator between languages, between our world of names, structures, systems, and hierarchies and theirs of instinct, impulse, and experience."

---

* Portions of this opening segment were adapted from an article I wrote that appeared in the *Drake* magazine, as cited in the Selected Bibliography.

Perhaps it is the atavistic pull of hunting and, ultimately, the communication that we feel during the keen anticipation of a fishing trip, or when we cast a fly for a fish, or when we feel the tug of a take. All of it evokes something that's hard to put into words. It feels like something primal. A bit like lust.

And tarpon are at the top of the list when it comes to evoking such feelings. "If you were to sit down and design a fish, and write all of the best factors of a fish on paper, I think you'd come up with the tarpon," Huff once said. They are the biggest fish that fly fishermen target in shallow water. They live in a marine environment, where the water is constantly in flux because of elemental forces of the earth—the wind, the tides, the waves. The majority of fly fishing for tarpon is done on the stalk, which makes it akin to hunting. And, unlike most fish or even hunted animals, the tarpon, and especially the bigger ones, fight back, providing a match that seems, especially in the moment, tilted in their favor.

∽

Fly fishing for tarpon, with only a handful of exceptions, is done out of a boat. The angler typically stands in the bow of a sixteen-to-eighteen-foot skiff, often on top of a two- to three-foot-tall casting platform, which provides an improved sight line. The guide stands in the stern, on top of his or her own platform, which is taller than that of the angler's, and located over the motor. The guide uses a push pole to move the boat quietly while searching for fish. Though there are times when an angler might blind cast for tarpon, particularly when they are rolling or when the water is dirty, most traditional tarpon fly fishing is done by sight in clear water and on sandy-bottomed flats, where you endlessly scan the water, hoping to see something. When tarpon appear, it almost always feels like it's happened out of nowhere, like figments of your imagination have come to life. The experience of seeing these massive beasts coming at you is both knee-buckling and heart-stopping (sometimes literally, as we'll see). Anglers frequently choke when faced with such huge fish (I've

been there). Buck fever—that is, the feral, sometimes paralyzing excitement one feels in the presence of a large, hunted animal—can cause all
sorts of freak-outs, like a blown cast or worse. The Frenchman Pierre
Affre, fishing one day in the Keys while wearing only a Speedo, got so
excited about an approaching school of tarpon that he rushed his fore-cast
and lodged the hook of his giant, European-style hook in the middle of
his penis. "I could only see *zee* feathers of *zee* fly," he says.

Once the tarpon is within range of a cast (a subjective thing that
depends on various factors, such as the angler's skill level and the wind),
the angler generally has one shot to get the fly in front of the fish and
then manipulate the fly in a tantalizing fashion as it's retrieved. If you
are skilled enough or, let's be honest, lucky enough, the tarpon will take
the fly, along with gallons of water (and all of the air in your lungs), into
its bucket-sized mouth, which can open to the full diameter of its body.

All of that lead-up is immensely exciting in an anticipatory sense. But
now the action begins, the rubber meets the road. The pull of a hooked
tarpon is, simply put, otherworldly, like being suddenly hooked up to a
speeding eighteen-wheeler. Then there are the jumps. A tarpon does not
like to be hooked, and it demonstrates its displeasure by cartwheeling,
pinwheeling, and leaping up to fifteen feet out of the water. Affre swears
he once hooked a tarpon in Homosassa that ran right at the boat of the
guide, Bill Curtis, and then hurdled it.

The fight then ensues, putting an end to the fun part, unless you are
someone like Tom Evans or Andy Mill, who has mastered the art of
quickly subduing tarpon through the employment of angles and leverage.

One of the most interesting aspects of fly fishing for big tarpon is that,
well, it's kind of scary. The hookup and the succeeding few moments are
usually a blur. Everything goes absolutely haywire, and there is no time
for thoughts. But when the chaos subsides, reality sets in, and the angler
becomes suddenly cognizant of what he or she will have to endure in
order to actually land the fish.

On nearly every morning before going out on the water to fish for
big tarpon, I have been filled with a sense of utter excitement, but also
a touch of dread because I know what I—and the fish—may have to

go through. "Most honest and skillful anglers who love big fish do so because the fish whips them," Ernest Hemingway once said. Maybe. Or maybe it's more honest to admit that getting whipped inspires a whole host of uncomfortable thoughts and emotions. I know that if I hook a big tarpon (say, over a hundred pounds), the fight will exhaust me (and the fish) physically. I also know that the fight will push me mentally about as far as I'd like to go. There are times during the fight with a big tarpon when you wonder how much more you can take, when you wonder what it would mean for your psyche if you just gave up. The likelihood that you will feel shame and disappointment is usually enough to keep you going. "We are frauds," the author and tarpon angler Randy Wayne White once wrote. "*Megalops* [the scientific name of the tarpon] is not."

In nearly every other type of fly fishing—say, for bonefish, trout, or salmon—a hooked fish really only requires that the angler hold the rod steady, apply a bit of pressure, and reel in the line when the fish has begun to exhaust itself after a few runs. That is not the case with big tarpon. With these fish, the angler must fight, too, pulling on the rod—which is about five ounces of pliable graphite—and the fish nearly as hard as he or she can. Any time the angler pauses to rest, the fish gets a breather as well and, as often as not, will resume the battle with even more vigor. The tarpon is a fish that is in much better shape than the vast majority of its pursuers. Most every guide who has attempted to gaff a big tarpon has been pulled into the water by the fish. In his early guiding years, Huff once had a client who hooked a fish and started to play it very slowly, as if in a trance. "I told him he needed to bear down on the fish because there are only two things that could happen—he would land the fish, or he would lose it," Huff says. "Little did I know there was actually a third scenario."

With the fish still attached, Huff's client suddenly collapsed face-first onto the bow, unconscious. Huff broke off the fish and raced back to the dock at full speed. But the man was already dead. His aorta had ruptured.

Everything has to go perfectly—or very close to it—to actually land a big tarpon. The hook can pull or break. The leader or line or rod can, too. So can an angler's willpower, which is—along with some knowledge of how to employ angles and leverage—far more important than his or her physical strength.

This mixture of the mental and physical, of excitement and dread, is the high of tarpon fly fishing. Kant once described the sublime as beauty mixed with terror.

∽

When the pope enters the Sistine Chapel via his private passageway, the first thing likely to catch his eye, just above the altar, is a giant (roughly twelve-and-a-half-foot by twelve-and-a-half-foot) painting of the prophet Jonah, a work done, like the rest of the ceiling in the Sistine Chapel, by the Renaissance master Michelangelo. The prominent placement of this fresco was likely no accident: Jonah's story is an important one in the Bible, viewed as a foreshadowing—and promise—of the resurrection of Christ in the New Testament.

In the Book of Jonah, the main, eponymous character is portrayed as a man who is somewhat reluctant about the whole prophet thing. At one point, he is instructed by God to go to Nineveh, an ancient Assyrian city (now part of Iraq) that was apparently a fairly wicked place at the time. Jonah, reluctant as he is, views this assignment as a fool's errand, seeing no hope for the iniquitous denizens of the city. So he decides to try to get out of his duty by going on the lam, hitching a ride on a boat that's headed in the opposite direction of Nineveh.

At some point in the boat's journey, an extraordinarily powerful storm pops up out of nowhere. The vessel tosses and turns, and appears to be on the verge of breaking in two when Jonah finally confesses to the captain and his fellow passengers that it just might be his presence onboard that's put them in this pickle. Infuriated, they toss Jonah overboard, which immediately results in a flat, calm sea. Jonah is then, quite famously, swallowed by a whale and stays inside the beast's belly for three harrowing days. During this time, he has a distinct change of heart and prays to God and promises that he indeed *will* go to Nineveh and prophesize. For this, God commands the whale to puke up Jonah onto dry land. Jonah then walks to Nineveh, covered, one presumes, in whale vomit, and tells the people there that God wants them to shape up or else. Wisely, they comply.

In the Sistine Chapel painting, which was unveiled with the rest of the ceiling in 1512, Jonah is depicted with his head thrown back dramatically. Perhaps it is because he is looking above, where some important scenes of the Creation and of Noah's life are depicted. But it also might be the case that Michelangelo wanted to depict Jonah in some amount of pain. After all, there is within the painting a giant fish—and not a whale—about to chomp on Jonah's muscly left leg and, we assume, swallow him whole.

The fish attacking Jonah, as quite clearly seen since the massive restoration of the chapel's frescoes done in the 1980s and early 1990s, is a tarpon.

In the ancient Hebrew text of Jonah, the sea creature that swallows Jonah is described as a *dag gadol*, which, roughly translated, means "great fish." By the time the Bible was Anglicized for the masses in the King James version, which appeared in 1611, most readers assumed that the only type of great creature in the sea that could swallow a man, much less house him in its belly for three days, would be in fact not a fish but a whale. As such, for centuries, we have understood this particular biblical book, in the popular consciousness, as the story of Jonah and the Whale.

Michelangelo, though, very clearly painted a tarpon, a species that is not mentioned anywhere in the Bible.

The inclusion of a tarpon on the ceiling of the Sistine Chapel is not a subject that's been studied much by scholars. In fact, it has not been studied at all. Nevertheless, I was curious about it, so I reached out to a man named William Wallace. Wallace is a professor at Washington University in St. Louis and, as the author and editor of seven books about Michelangelo, one of the world's foremost experts on the painter.

After lengthy back-and-forth questioning via email, during which the professor's enthusiasm for the subject seemed to dwindle with each subsequent exchange, Wallace wrote, with a sense of finality:

You are dealing with a painter who knows Florentine eels and carp much better than Tarpon and then you have to come up with a

really good explanation for substituting a Tarpon for a Whale—of
which Michelangelo would be equally ignorant of the appearance
and physiology . . . and not too concerned for either in completing the
Sistine after four years of painting the ceiling. I am still interested,
but I feel like you are swimming upstream.

It appears that Wallace is implying that Michelangelo's feeling at the time was basically, *I just want to get this damn ceiling done, who gives a shit about the big fish?*

I dropped the issue with the professor but still continued on, upstream. And I wondered, would Michelangelo necessarily be ignorant of the tarpon species? After all, he did frequent the fishing docks on the outskirts of Rome, to marvel at the various sea creatures that the fishermen brought in. He even painted silvery, dare-I-say tarpon-like scales on a demon in what is believed to be his first painting, *The Torment of Saint Anthony.*

I am not the only one who has taken the deep dive down this particular rabbit hole. Norman Duncan, a former civil engineer and avid tarpon angler (whom you'll learn more about in a bit), and Mary McCulley, a photographer once based in Florence, have both gone there, too, and have written a bit on various internet sites about what they found. They both theorize that it's not out of the realm of possibility that Michelangelo could have laid eyes on a tarpon. The species is believed to range as far north as southern Europe. According to the University of Michigan Museum of Zoology, tarpon have been spotted in Portugal and southern France, likely making detours from the Gulf Stream, within which they are known to travel. Could Michelangelo have seen a big, dead adult tarpon that had been netted and brought into port somewhere? Or maybe seen a smaller, younger specimen, one brought back by Portuguese sailors who frequented the coast of West Africa—where tarpon also live—that had been well-salted to prevent rotting?

It is highly unlikely that we will ever have a real answer here, but whatever the explanation, a tarpon is there, right in the middle of the Sistine Chapel. The painting and its imagery work maybe better than

Michelangelo would ever realize. For, metaphorically speaking, the tarpon has swallowed many a man (as well as some women).

The whole story fits into the greater mystery surrounding the fish itself, too.

∽

Though some people in Latin America do, in fact, eat tarpon, the species has never been a commercially viable food fish. And because we are a consumer-focused species ourselves—and tarpon have no value in that sense to us—the species has never really been seriously studied. We know a lot more about, for instance, tuna, salmon, cod, and orange roughy.

We do know a few things, though. We know that tarpon are ancient. Fossil data indicate that the species, in its current form, dates back to fifty million years ago. To paraphrase Richard Powers in *The Overstory*, his great novel about trees, this is not our world with tarpon in it. It's the tarpon's world, and we—who've been around for a mere three hundred thousand years—have just arrived.

We also know, from radiometric dating, that individual tarpon can live for a very long time, close to the age of eighty. We have decent proof of this, too, from a famous tarpon that lived in Chicago. Yes, Chicago. Just after the infamous Labor Day hurricane in 1935, a team of scientists traveled to Florida and collected some tarpon, transporting them to Chicago's Shedd Aquarium via a custom-made Pullman car full of sea-water. One of those tarpon got the nickname "Deadeye" because of an injury to one of its eyes, sustained in an accident at the aquarium. Deadeye turned out to be quite the popular attraction to aquarium-goers over the years. The fish lived at the Shedd, seemingly content, until 1998, when it suddenly and mysteriously leapt out of its container in what appeared to be an act of suicide. Scientists believed that Deadeye was at least seventy-five years old.

The biggest gap in scientific knowledge about the tarpon has to do with the species' spawning. They are believed to perform the act maybe a hundred miles offshore, on a new or full moon. They've been tracked diving as deep as four hundred feet just days before these moons. The working theory on this pre-spawn dive, according to Aaron Adams, the lead scientist of the conservation group Bonefish & Tarpon Trust, is that the pressure at that water depth may force sperm and eggs from the tarpon's body. But we can't know for sure. No human, as of yet, has ever witnessed the spawning of a tarpon.

We have seen the aftermath of the spawn, though. A tarpon begins its life as a small, translucent, eel-like larva that actually grows smaller before it gets bigger. These larvae migrate, floating on currents, into lagoons and brackish, mangrove-lined backwaters, where they grow into the shape of a fish and eat worms and insects. Tarpon have a swim bladder, connected by a duct to the esophagus, which allows them to take in atmospheric air, almost as if they are the missing evolutionary link between fish and humans. They are facultative air breathers—meaning "optional"—and not obligate air breathers, as once commonly believed. That air bladder comes in handy, particularly when they are young. Juvenile tarpon live in low-oxygen waters, which serve to protect them from predators, like snook and jacks, which cannot survive under those same conditions. Juvenile tarpon roll on top of the water's surface to gulp air and get the necessary oxygen. After they leave these lagoons at the age of three, tarpon continue to roll and gulp air throughout the rest of their lives as a means of acquiring supplemental oxygen. They gulp air as they migrate. They gulp air while being fought by an angler. "It's a bit like football players getting oxygen on the sidelines during a game," says Adams.

Adult tarpon tend to do much of their rolling and gulping in the early mornings. They do so because the photosynthesis done by plankton and algae and sea grass has ceased overnight, leaving the water at daybreak somewhat depleted of oxygen. Tarpon are not the only ocean-dwellers that rise to the water's surface at dawn in search of oxygen. Shrimp and crabs do, too, which provides the tarpon with some breakfast as they get their oxygen hits. The tarpon's rolling and gulping, which sounds like a *bloop*, may also serve as a communication tool. Sound travels five times faster in water than it does in air, and it travels farther, too. The *bloop*ing noise is transmitted from one tarpon to other tarpon. It's theorized, too, that the thumping noise that occurs within their swim bladders when they get air may also be a method of communicating.*

Tarpon can grow to eight feet long. Adults range from 65 to more than 300 pounds (a 350-pounder was once caught in a net), with the females growing much bigger than the males (tarpon over 100 pounds are likely female). They have big half-dollar to sand-dollar-size scales on their sides. In the Keys, those scales look like the polished armor of a knight. In Homosassa, the silver flanks of the tarpon are thrown into relief by black backs. In the Everglades, tarpon look like a true jungle fish, their backs and sides reflecting hues of purples and pinks and greens. The large plates that cover their gills make a deep *whuff-whuff-whuff* sound when they leap and shake their heads. Tarpon have a pronounced underbite, the protruding lower jaw of a pugilist. The last ray of their dorsal fin is elongated into a filament that just hangs there, sometimes in a curve that, in the right frame of mind, can strike you as a simulacrum of the shape of the Florida Keys, that coral archipelago that arcs off the mainland United States.

When tarpon visit the flats, likely ahead of the spawn, they are often seen swimming in strings, following a lead tarpon, but they sometimes swim in singles or in pairs. As they swim, they roll on the surface, and they sometimes free-jump, appearing for a snapshotted, split second in the air like a fish mount in some dude's living room in Houston. Often, they swim together in a circle, which is called a daisy chain, a thrilling sight to behold. Adams says these daisy chains are likely a pre-spawning ritual of some sort and may also be the behavior they demonstrate when spawning offshore. (In some daisy chains, a large female tarpon sometimes sits in the middle of the circle, suspended in the water.) The daisy chain may also be a defense mechanism, a literal circling of the wagons when there is danger—a hammerhead or bull shark, or a boat—in the area. Adams says that scientists believe daisy chains may also be part of the tarpon's

---

* Not to make you feel self-conscious, Mr. or Mrs. Fisherperson, but when you see all of those rolling tarpon in the slick calm of the early morning, you should know that they are likely talking about you.

complex communications. They occur sometimes when tarpon move along a sandbar and come to a dead end (perhaps the sand bar is out of the water or too shallow to swim). The fish appear to circle up to get their bearings or even change out the lead fish in the migrating school.*

Tarpon also like to chill. In the backcountry and in various basins, or even, sometimes, in the open ocean, they will often fall into a semi-dormant state, and appear to sleep while floating high in the water column. Fishermen refer to this as a "laid-up" tarpon. Huff says he has seen laid-up tarpon actually yawn, like a fat man sitting on a bench, waiting for a bus.

Tarpon range in the Atlantic Ocean from Canada to Brazil, and, as mentioned, from southern Europe to West-Central Africa, though in most of these places, they stay in rather deep water. There are a handful of tarpon in the Pacific Ocean—off the coast of Panama (a population that likely squirted through the Panama Canal at some point) and off the coast of Costa Rica (perhaps conveyed there as juveniles during a hurricane). Tarpon are sometimes taken in the nets of deep-sea trawlers in the Gulf Stream in the northeastern United States. While fishing for striped bass, Paul Dixon, a fishing guide, and Tom Colicchio, a chef, have both, on separate occasions, seen a tarpon swimming the white sand flats off Long Island, New York (both men cast fruitlessly at their respective fish). The largest populations of tarpon, though, are concentrated in the Caribbean and the Gulf of Mexico.

The earliest written record of the fish dates back to 1444, which is nearly seventy years before Michelangelo completed the fresco of Jonah and the tarpon in the Sistine Chapel. Tarpon were given their scientific name by a French zoologist named Achille Valenciennes, who worked with Georges Cuvier on his volume *Histoire Naturelle Des Poissons*, a compendium published in the mid-19th century that listed and classified all of the world's known fish at the time. Valenciennes had seen a drawing of a tarpon done by his naturalist friend Alexander

---

* By the way, tarpon have no collective noun—like a "murder" of crows or a "smack" of jellyfish or a "parliament" of owls—that I could find, other than "school." They need a new one. My suggestion: an "implausibility" of tarpon.

von Humboldt, who had traveled for five years, starting in 1799, in the Americas. Valenciennes noticed the fish's large eyes and decided to name the species *Megalops* (big eye) *atlanticus*. Tarpon are also known as *grand-écaille* (big scale) in the French West Indies, *sabalo* (silver fish) in some Latin American countries, and, supposedly, *show-a-wee* by the native Florida Seminoles (who keep much of their language private). All of the tarpon in the world are of the same species.

What makes tarpon most interesting to humans, and particularly to anglers, is that they are denizens of the ocean's great deep water—which remains 80 percent unexplored—that periodically comes into the shallows (primarily in the Caribbean and Gulf of Mexico areas). There, we can see them and, as James Prosek says, even communicate with them through the act of angling. We are provided a glimpse of the great unknown. We are given the opportunity to intersect, however insignificantly, in their migration, which the author Thomas McGuane says "may be some spiritually embedded human impulse." Efforts to study tarpon have ramped up considerably in recent years, partially because of their rising economic importance as a gamefish to states like Florida. There may be a time soon when we know much more about them. This knowledge, the argument goes, would be good for the species, for their protection while spawning, or during their rearing, for instance. But for now, the mystery of tarpon, still held in this world overdone by explanation, remains a substantial part of their allure.

3

THE KNIGHTS OF THE
CORNER TABLE

n January 1959, shortly after deposed Cuban president Fulgencio Batista fled his country for the Dominican Republic, an eighteen-year-old boy named Chico Fernandez boarded a freighter ship in Havana that was headed for Key West. Up until that point, Fernandez's family, friendly with Batista, had been wealthy property owners in Cuba. But that wealth disappeared overnight. Fidel Castro, the revolutionary who would soon become Cuba's new leader, had seized all of their real estate.

Fernandez's parents had flown ahead to Miami. His mother had walked onto the small plane clutching her jewelry. Fernandez was also leaving Cuba with his most prized possessions. He boarded the freighter with a metallic blue Mercedes 190 SL, an Orvis Battenkill nine-and-a-half-foot bamboo fly rod, a Pflueger Medalist 1498 reel, and some flies.

Fernandez arrived in Key West in the middle of the night. The next day, he hopped in his Mercedes and made his way north on US 1, through the Keys to Miami, to meet up with his parents. While driving through downtown Miami a few weeks later, he noticed a store on the corner of Southwest 27th Avenue and US 1 called "The Tackle Box." Yearning for something that felt familiar in this brand-new country, he decided to stop and check it out. Inside, he marveled at the endless rows of lures and the stacks of shiny new fishing rods. In the back of the store, he noticed a boy who looked to be about his age standing by the shrimp bait tank. The boy walked over to Fernandez and said hello. Soon, the two of them were exchanging stories about their respective fishing exploits. The boy regaled Fernandez with stories about fishing for snook in the canals of Dade County and in the nearby Everglades. Fernandez, in turn, told the boy about Cuba's bountiful populations of snook, bonefish, and baby tarpon, about how he'd learned to fly fish from an American boat captain who had come to Cuba, and about how he believed that he was the very first fly fisherman in his home country.

The boy stuck out his hand and introduced himself. "My name is Flip Pallot," he told Fernandez. The duo quickly became inseparable, bonding over their shared love of fishing, forming a friendship that would have a profound influence on the history of the sport of fly fishing for tarpon.

⁓

Claudius Aelianus was a Roman author and teacher of rhetoric, who supposedly lived from 175 A.D. until 235 A.D. Somewhere along the way, he published an odd book called *Varia Historia* (*Various Histories*), in which he offers his thoughts, in a series of vignettes, on a range of subjects from Greek art to funeral customs to serpent worship. But for anglers, Aelianus's book is significant for one reason. Within it, he relates a story that he heard of some Macedonians fishing in a river. It is, many historians believe, the first-ever reference to fly fishing in print. Aelianus writes that the anglers:

> . . . *fasten red wool . . . round a hook, and fit onto the wool two feathers which grow under a cock's wattles, and which in color are like wax. Their rod is six feet long, and their line is the same length. Then they throw their snare, and the fish, attracted and maddened by the color, comes straight at it, thinking from the pretty sight to*

gain a dainty mouthful; when, however, it opens its jaws, it is
caught by the hook, and enjoys a bitter repast, a captive.

The quarry in the story is a brown trout.

∽

In various theological circles, it is believed that there existed a piece of writing, known as the Q Document, that contained the sayings and stories of Jesus and predated three, if not all four, of the Gospels found in the New Testament of the Bible. This document has never been found, only postulated, but the theory is that it is the primary source for the Gospels, the original text from which all others flowed.

If there is a Q Document—a primary source—in the sport of fly fishing, it is angling for trout.

In 1496, just four years after Columbus first reached the New World, a long essay entitled "A Treatyse of Fysshynge wyth an Angle" was published in England, and within it were instructions for fly fishing for trout. The essay, which was an addendum to a book that had been published ten years prior about hunting, falconry, and other gentlemanly pursuits, was supposedly authored by Dame Juliana Berners, the head of a nunnery north of London.

In 1676, 180 years after Berners's essay, Charles Cotton, a British aristocrat, added twelve new chapters about fly fishing for trout to the fifth edition of *The Compleat Angler*, a fishing book written by his friend Izaak Walton. That edition of the book, with all of its added information—a New Testament, if you will—became the Bible of the fly-fishing world. And the Word spread, eventually crossing the Atlantic Ocean to the New World.

The evangelists came in the form of British officers and gentlemen who traveled to the Americas in the mid- to late-18th century. They fished for trout and Atlantic salmon, as they had in their homeland, but they also cast flies for other freshwater species, like bass. They created converts. By the early 19th century, fly fishing had become an established sport in the northeastern United States, pursued mainly by the well-to-do in the corridor of large cities from Philadelphia to Boston. It was later in that century when fly anglers in the Northeast began to cast their gazes out over the sea and started taking their big Atlantic salmon rods out into the estuaries to fish for sea-run trout, and into the ocean for striped bass and bluefish.

Eventually those baby steps into the ocean became a full-on sprint, and the sport of saltwater fly fishing grew in popularity and found its way down south, to Florida, where it would find its apex with the fish that helped spur the rapid development of that state.

∽

In 1885, William Halsey Wood, a New York City architect who built the Yaddo artists' colony and whose client list included Andrew Carnegie, caught a ninety-three-pound tarpon using a baited mullet and a bamboo plug rod. It is believed, by some, to be the first tarpon ever landed with a rod and reel.

Halsey's catch caused a stir. Stories about his fish appeared in newspapers in New York City and Europe. He himself wrote a piece about the fish in the magazine *Forest & Stream* (which would merge into *Field & Stream* nearly half a century later), and he had his tarpon mounted and displayed for viewing in a popular fishing tackle store in lower Manhattan. The primary reason his fish garnered so much attention was that, up until that point, it was commonly believed that a tarpon, because of its size and general unruliness, could only be subdued by a net or a harpoon, not a rod and reel. The idea of trying to catch one on a fly rod was believed to be even more ludicrous.

But wait. As with a lot of things in the fishing world, the provenance of the first tarpon ever caught on a rod and reel is in some dispute. Though it seems fairly unlikely from an empirical standpoint, the feat actually might have been accomplished with a fly rod. James Henshall, a well-known late-19th-century angling writer, claimed in his 1884 book, *Camping and Cruising in Florida*, that he caught a tarpon of around ten pounds in 1878, seven years before Wood's fish. But even Henshall's claim of being the first to catch a tarpon on a fly is bucked by yet another writer, Frank Pinckney, who wrote in his 1888 book, *The Tarpon: Or Silver King*, that the first man to do so was a New York City doctor named George Trowbridge, who landed a one-pound, three-ounce tarpon on a fly in the spring of the year that Pinckney's book was published (not much of a fish to brag about, but . . .). So, who knows?

What we do know is that tarpon fishing, mostly on conventional tackle, was beginning to become quite the sensation by the late 19th century and early 20th century, especially among the well-to-do, who found themselves with the money and the time for recreational pursuits. Most of those recreational anglers who traveled to Florida to pursue tarpon were men of means from cities in the Northeast.[*]

And it is those folks and their zeal for tarpon fishing that Jack E. Davis, the author of *The Gulf: The Making of an American Sea* (which won a 2018 Pulitzer Prize), says is responsible, in large part, for the development of western Florida. He calls the tarpon "the wild fish that tamed the coast" and credits it with, among other things, starting the boom that created the city of Fort Myers. When William Halsey Wood caught his tarpon in 1885, the "city" of Tampa had only three thousand residents. That would change rather quickly. Henry B. Plant, the western Florida analogue to the eastern coast's Henry Flagler (who was, at various times, both his rival and his partner), began buying up bankrupt railroad companies and their lines in western Florida after the Civil War, then built a railroad system connecting that area with the rest of the United States. Plant complemented his railroad system with a series of luxury hotels (just as Flagler would do), building or buying them in Tampa, Punta Gorda, and Fort Myers. According to Davis, one of Plant's biggest selling points for his railroads and his hotels was the access they provided to tarpon fishing. (Plant himself was an ardent tarpon angler.)

---

[*] Jerry Gibbs, writing in *The American Fly Fisher*, and Randy Wayne White and Carlene Fredericka Brennan, in their book on tarpon (as cited in the Selected Bibliography), all did fabulous jobs writing about the history of the sport of tarpon fishing.

It's hard to overstate how popular angling for tarpon was among the elites back in that day. Thomas Edison and his second wife, Mina, had a winter home in Fort Myers (complete with a laboratory and gardens) and were said to be "agog over tarpon." (Edison once told a friend that the best tarpon fishing in the world was "right in front of my house.") Grover Cleveland had a winter retreat in Homosassa, where he enjoyed tarpon fishing. J. P. Morgan fished for tarpon in southwest Florida. So did Al Capone and Zane Grey. Ernest Hemingway and John Dos Passos were tarpon-fishing buddies in the Keys. Theodore Roosevelt once missed a presidential press conference because he was in the midst of a one-and-a-half-hour battle with a tarpon. The *New York Times* wrote a story about a 185-pound tarpon that President Herbert Hoover caught on conventional tackle in 1937.

Much of the tarpon zeitgeist of that time period was captured—and further encouraged—by a New York man who sported a brushy mustache and, in the preferred style of that era, pants pulled up to his belly button.

Anthony Weston Dimock was born in Nova Scotia in 1842. His family eventually moved to the United States, and Dimock was educated at Phillips Academy Andover and then Columbian University (later known as George Washington University). Dimock lived a varied professional life. He became a member of the New York Stock Exchange at the age of twenty-one, and by the age of twenty-three, according to his *New York Times* obituary, he "dominated the gold market of the country." A little later, he would own a steamship concern and run an eponymous banking and brokerage firm. He also managed to go bankrupt a handful of times.

At the midpoint of his career, Dimock abruptly left his professional life to seek out adventure. He ventured out to the Rocky Mountain West to hunt and fish, and he also went south, to Florida, to do the same. After a few years of the peripatetic sporting life, he came back to the East Coast and became a real estate developer, helping to construct many buildings in Elizabeth City, New Jersey. He later left the New York City metropolitan area for a little town in the Catskill Mountains, where he died in 1918.

Dimock wrote several books about his life and adventures, but by far his most popular one was *The Book Of The Tarpon*, which was published in

1911. It is the seminal book about the fish and was far ahead of its time, in both its prose and illustrations. Within, Dimock recounts his fishing expeditions on the west coast of Florida.

Dimock begins his book with the recounting of a tarpon that he hooked in February 1882 (three years before Wood's tarpon, it must be mentioned) in, of all places, Homosassa. He described the "twisting, gyrating" body of the leaping fish, "garmented in glistening silver and enveloped in a cloud of sparkling diamonds . . . unlike any denizen of earth." Dimock attempts to gaff the fish, but instead falls backward into the water. By the time he clambers back into the boat (a wooden lapstrake canoe), he finds a broken rod and a broken line and no fish.

What makes Dimock's book truly remarkable—and, likely, breathtaking to his audience at the time—are the photos. On his expeditions, Dimock brought along his son, Julian, who followed his father around in a separate canoe. Julian carried a camera, which weighed seventeen pounds, and documented his father's battles with tarpon. The resultant photos, though in black and white, are spectacular. In one, a tarpon in midleap hangs high above the seated anglers in the boat. In another, a tarpon appears to be jumping *into* the boat. In yet another, a giant tarpon has sunk Dimock's boat—only Dimock's head and brushy mustache, the bow of the canoe, and the tail of the tarpon are visible above the water's surface. There is even a photo of a smiling Dimock swimming with, and petting, a large manatee. The photos, because of their historical context, but mostly because of their arresting nature, retain their relevance to this day.

∽

Henry Flagler was not the tarpon enthusiast that his counterpart Henry Plant was. But he was every bit as influential to the sport, if not more. When he completed his railroad on the east coast of Florida connecting Miami—the mainland—to Key West in 1912, he opened up access to one of the world's great saltwater flats fisheries, whether he knew it or not.

The first true fly fisherman of the Keys flats was likely a man named Bill Smith, who would become a well-known early Keys fishing guide.

In 1939, he supposedly got curious about using a fly rod—one used for Atlantic salmon—on the flats to target bonefish. The famed New York City stockbroker and trout and salmon angler George LaBranche, who was visiting the Keys at the time, told Smith that there was no way he could catch a bonefish on a fly. Smith proved him wrong, landing what is commonly believed to be the first bonefish intentionally caught on a fly, a simple pattern made of feathers and squirrel hair.

Smith married a woman named Bonnie Laidlaw, one of three pioneering sisters who became guides in the Keys. One of the Laidlaw sisters, Frankee, married a man named Jimmie Albright, who would go on to guide Hemingway, Jimmy Stewart, and Ted Williams, among others. Smith and Albright were joined on the water by Jack Brothers, Cecil Keith, and George Hommell, who all started guiding in the Keys in the 1940s. A little later, a guide named Bill Curtis began working the flats of Biscayne Bay. All of them began their careers guiding for bonefish. But they would, after a time, turn their attention to that fish's bigger flats companion, the tarpon.

By the early 1950s, fly-fishing pioneers Joe Brooks and Stu Apte had begun pursuing tarpon on the Keys' flats in earnest. Williams, who had fished southern Florida beginning in 1947 while in spring training camp with the Red Sox, bought his first home in Islamorada in 1952. By then, fly fishing for tarpon in Florida was beginning to gain a foothold, yet it remained a sport only practiced by a few. That would begin to change a decade later with the serendipitous friendship of four men who would transform the sport and bring it to a greater audience.

⁂

Soon after their initial meeting in the tackle shop, Pallot introduced Fernandez to two of his friends, John Emery and Norman Duncan, whom he'd known since the first grade. The four boys became immediate friends, based primarily on their shared love of fly fishing. Fernandez came to think of the group as the Four Musketeers. Each of them played a distinct role. Even at a young age, the mannered and cultured Fernandez was a sensualist. He fished wearing a tweed jacket or with a tennis sweater tied over his shoulders. He enjoyed food and jazz and Cuban music, and appreciated the craftsmanship of a fine fly reel and the feel of a line loading on a good rod while casting. Pallot was a philosopher king of the outdoors, and he would later grow a full bushy beard that somehow gave his thoughts and words more gravitas. Duncan was the problem-solver, straightforward in his approach to everything. Emery, who was known as "little John," was the absent-minded professor, a messy genius distracted from some of life's more quotidian tasks by deep thoughts.

They took to hanging out in the city's fishing shops, at The Tackle Box (where Duncan worked for a time) and Captain Mac's Tackle Shop, owned by the irascible Bob McChristian and, later, at J. Lee Cuddy's, where Emery worked for years. There they met guides, like Bill Curtis, and fly-fishing legends, like Stu Apte, whom they worshipped, and Joe Brooks. "Miami was just so small back then," says Fernandez. "You could meet everyone who fly fished." The shop rats hovered near the older men in the tackle stores, listening in on conversations and soaking up any scraps of information they could get about tackle, fish, and, especially, about places to fish.

The Four Musketeers all enrolled at the University of Miami at various times, some overlapping with each other. (Fernandez sold his Mercedes to pay for his tuition.) They worked jobs during the day and took their classes in the evenings. Sometimes at night, after class, they would gather together in one of the school's parking lots and practice fly casting under the lights. And on Friday evenings, they would make their way to a restaurant off US 1, where they settled into the same corner table and made plans for their weekend fishing. "We barely had enough money to pay for dinner," says Duncan. "But we went there because we loved to talk about fishing. We were all so obsessed."

At first, those plans made at that corner table rarely involved going south to the Keys or east to Biscayne Bay. "There just weren't that many people fishing in the Keys then, and you really needed a boat to fish the Bay," says Pallot. Instead, they looked west, to the Tamiami Trail, otherwise known as US 41, which bisected the canals and marshes of the Everglades and connected Miami with Tampa. The Trail was the focal point of the saltwater fly-fishing world at that time. "There were real fly fishermen who fished the Trail," says Pallot. "They were giants. Rocky Weinstein, Homer Rhodes, Ted Williams, Stu Apte. They were all curmudgeons, but they were willing to at least acknowledge us. Even Ted did. We weren't kids, whom he always loved, but we also weren't quite yet adults, whom he loathed."

The Trail then was nothing like it is today. It didn't have much traffic, and it was still fairly wild, and the water on either side of it was easily accessible. The four friends sometimes fished the Trail out of a truck. They would take turns standing in the bed of the truck with a fly rod, scanning the water, searching for laid-up or cruising snook as one of them slowly drove the truck down the road. When the person standing in the back spotted a fish, he would tap on the truck's top, which was a signal to stop. "Then we'd cast for the snook right out of the truck bed," says Pallot, who pronounces the fish's name as "snoook," and still pronounces the name of the city he grew up in as "My-am-uh." They fished all day Saturday and then on Sunday until the evening, when they had to return to Miami for school and jobs.

The years went on like this, the friends hanging around tackle shops, meeting at the corner table, and fishing. The slate was clean back then. As they grew older, their horizons expanded. Duncan got a boat, and they used that to fish for bonefish in Biscayne Bay. They soon yearned for bigger fish and bigger challenges. They heard about the tarpon in the Keys, a fish that would hook them all, deeply, and push them to become better fly anglers, which resulted in innovations—in boats, rods, reels, lines, and flies.

Their first trips to the Keys took place after class at night. It was an easy drive from Miami back then in the early 1960s—the speed limit on US 1 was seventy miles per hour, and there wasn't a stoplight from Homestead down to Big Pine Key. They headed for the bridges, where the tarpon congregated at night.

The young men stood on the top of a bridge, on the up-current side. The tarpon would be lying in wait, on the edge of the star shine and the shadows made by the bridge. The men could hear the tarpon and see parts of them as they crashed the crabs and busted the mullet and knocked the pinfish into the air, bait that was washed under the bridge by the raging tide. "There is no way for me to describe it in a way that would be relevant to anything you could imagine," says Pallot. "The sheer number of fish and the amount of bait was like nothing I've seen since."

The excitement of seeing the fish was accompanied by an element of danger. The bridges on US 1 were narrower back then. When the men heard the growl of an oncoming truck and saw the headlights growing larger and brighter by the second, they pinned themselves against the bridge railing, bracing themselves as the truck *woosh*ed by with its concussive blast of wind.

They used the biggest fly rod available at the time, a bamboo cane rod that was the equivalent of an eight-weight in today's rods. It was impregnated with a fiberglass resin, which supposedly provided it with more strength but really only made it heavier. They believed that they had to throw flies that warranted the attention of the large tarpon, "flies as big as a chicken," says Fernandez. They cast the fly across the current into the star shine and let it wash into the shadows, and then stripped as hard as they could to keep the slack out of the line. As soon as the fly reached the shadows, the water would explode in a take, and the hooked tarpon would immediately jump and run and then go under the bridge and break off. They used 12-pound tippet and attached that to the fly, with no piece of 80- or 100-pound monofilament, known as "bite tippet," tied between the tippet and the fly to cushion the shock of the bite. Bite tippet had not yet been dreamed up. Or, at the very least, it wasn't yet in wide use.

"In the end, our fly lines would be gone. Totally gone. Everything gone," says Pallot. "You tried to break the tarpon off as soon as you could so you'd lose as little backing as possible because you didn't want to lose both the fly line and the backing. There was no winning. But it was worth it. It was truly worth it. We were on top of the bridge. You could see the strike, which was otherworldly. There was phosphorescence in the water, and when they bit there was this explosion and this huge visual of splashing, glowing water." If trout fishing was the Q Document of fly fishing, then tarpon fishing was decidedly Revelations.

They took to buying monofilament, which had recently been introduced to the United States from Europe with spinning rods and reels. They strung a piece of 200-pound monofilament between two clotheslines, then strung an actual fly line beside it. They used emery paper to sand down the monofilament to match the taper of the fly line. These became their bridge lines. Their fly reels couldn't hold all of it because of its stiffness. They'd go to the bridges with ten lines per man, and they'd hook ten fish each and lose everything anyway. "Those lines cost us about as much as a good date would, and we had to buy new ones every single time we went out, which was a lot," says Pallot. "And we didn't care."

Eventually, they started fishing the flats for tarpon, from the boats of friends and ones they bought cheaply and tinkered with. Everything about the fish raised a set of new questions. They sought the answers by trial and error. They eventually figured out how to actually catch them (on the flats, not from the bridges). They began using bite tippets and helped make them de rigueur in the tarpon fly-fishing world. They tinkered with new rods in Duncan's garage, using their own equipment. They tested and re-tested their creations, bending them into parabolas. They modified lines and reels. They built their own vise grips and tied new fly patterns. Those innovations—stronger rods and reels and clear fly lines (which came from their monofilament experiments)—would enter the mainstream as the fly-fishing fame and industry influence of these men grew.

By the time they were all out of college, the fun was over, at least that type of fun. The quartet split up, each man going his own way. "That was just life," says Duncan. He became a civil engineer and, later on, he'd work on the Seven Mile Bridge and the Long Key Viaduct in the Keys. Emery graduated with a degree in philosophy and worked in J. Lee Cuddy's store and guided, living a bit of a bohemian life with fly fishing at the center of it. Fernandez took a job with the then-young fast-food chain Burger King. He started as the assistant budget director, then was promoted to the top budget post. Pallot went into the Peace Corps and then the army, serving as a linguist. He later did a stint for an engineering company in Detroit, then returned to Miami to work as a commercial lender. He hated the job. "I was spending my days helping other people achieve their dreams while watching mine wither," is his oft-repeated line about the experience.

The fly-fishing supergroup was kaput, but each individual member went on to a spectacular solo career. Their fame and writings and innovations made fly fishing for tarpon more accessible—and desirable—to more people. Neither Fernandez nor Pallot lasted very long in their office jobs. "I turned to my wife one day and told her that I wanted to quit Burger King and somehow make fly fishing my livelihood," says Fernandez. "She just said, 'Okay. Make it work.'" He did, becoming a well-known writer, teacher, and designer and tyer of flies, as well as an ambassador for many of the major fly-fishing companies, for whom he tested equipment. Fernandez has traveled the world sharing his knowledge.

Pallot quit his job as a banker and started guiding fishermen and hunters in Florida and Montana. He hosted a local television show, which grew into a new career. From 1992 until 2006, Pallot was the host of *Walker's Cay Chronicles*, the most successful fishing series to ever air on television. He also helped start Hell's Bay Boatworks, which crafted boats that are still considered among the best shallow water skiffs ever made. He was a founding ambassador of Yeti, and his honeyed drawl is the voice of the Discovery Channel's *Sport Fishing Television* and various ESPN football documentaries. Later in his life, he would also play a role in launching the fishing career of one of Homosassa's most notorious anglers.

Duncan didn't leave his civil engineering job. Instead, he fished around it, using his analytical skills to build custom skiffs and rods and invent new knots and flies (one of which, as you will see, he believes was stolen by another well-known fisherman).

Emery continued to guide, building up his reputation on the flats of the Keys, and designing and building what was really the first heavy-duty tarpon fly reel (in a venture backed by Tom Evans), one from which all modern reels have descended. In the 1980s, he would develop an ominous-looking spot on his skin, which he refused to have checked out for some time. It turned out to be a melanoma. He died in 1985 at the age of forty-two, while sitting on the examination table in his doctor's office. "He was the best of all of us, for sure," says Pallot.

∽

By the dawning of the 1970s, thanks in large part to the innovations and promotion of Fernandez, Pallot, Duncan, and Emery, the sport of fly fishing for tarpon had made a giant leap in popularity. What came next were the artists, the men who attempted to interpret—in words and on film—what all of this meant, and had a helluva good time in doing so. Our lens now pans down through the Keys, to as far south as you can get in the continental United States.

4

BONE ISLAND

n late 1972, Guy de la Valdène, the French count-turned-tarpon-fishing-addict, tried for days over the phone to coax his friend, the writer and poet Richard Brautigan, into taking part in a movie he was making about tarpon fishing in Key West. Brautigan continually declined his invitation.

Brautigan was then five years removed from the publication of his first, and most popular, book, *Trout Fishing in America*, but he and his work were still very much a part of the cultural vanguard. *Trout Fishing in America* is often described as a novel, and I guess it does fit that description in that it is a work of fiction. But some of the other traditional guideposts that we expect in a novel—a plot is what I'm really talking about here—are nowhere to be found. As the title suggests, the book is ostensibly about fishing for trout, a sport and a pastime that Brautigan was very fond of. And it *is* indeed a book about fishing in another sense—the narrator and all of the other characters within are angling for answers and for meaning, for ways to survive in a country where the frontier and the wilderness are in retreat against an attack from rampant commercialization. But through its metaphors, vignettes, language head-fakes, playfulness, and surreality, it becomes much more than that. Brautigan was once described by a reviewer as "a Thoreau who cannot keep a straight face." His book is considered to be the connective tissue that binds the Beats and the hippies, and it sold two million copies. He palled around with Allen Ginsburg and Gary Snyder in San Francisco, not far from his home in Bolinas, California. Once, when the Beatles visited San Francisco, John Lennon made a side trip to meet him.

Brautigan was tall and quiet, and he dressed in a style that could be described as hippie-frontiersman, often donning a broad-brimmed hat over his long, stringy blonde hair. He frequently twisted locks of that hair in his fingers and also worried the tips of his Wyatt Earp–like handlebar mustache, as if always in a state of deep contemplation. "He was a sweet, generous and entirely odd person," says Thomas McGuane, who was his friend. "Otherworldly, really."

Though Valdène could not, at least initially, convince Brautigan to be in his movie, he did manage to get him to come down to Key West for a spell in the spring of 1973, to hang out with him, McGuane, Jim Harrison, and Russell Chatham, who were in the midst of their run as the Merry Pranksters of the tarpon world.

∞

Brautigan loved to fly fish, but he loved to do it in his own simple way, standing in the same spot in a mountain stream for hours on end and catching six-inch brook trout. He had never fished for tarpon and had pretty much predetermined that the big rods, big fish, and big action wouldn't appeal to him. Valdène dearly wanted Brautigan in the film, but he didn't push him after he arrived in Key West, and instead resorted to gentle persuasion. "Just come out in the boat with me," he told Brautigan. "I just want you to see this." That method worked. Brautigan went out and, though he didn't fish, he seemed impressed with the incredible setting—the cerulean sky, the emerald green water, and the giant, ancient fish. He signed on for a few more trips onto the water.

One evening after returning from one of those excursions, Brautigan turned to Valdène and said, "You know, if you want me in your movie, I'm going to have to jump a tarpon."

The next morning, Valdène poled through a basin as Brautigan stood in the middle of the boat, sporting a huge, childlike smile across his face. Valdène spotted some tarpon cruising slowly, half a mile or so away, and pushed after them. When he reached the fish, he put the pole down and picked up a rod and made a cast. One of the fish ate the fly, and Valdène handed the rod to Brautigan. "The fish went nuts," says Valdène. It surged violently, leapt completely out of the water three times, and then came off. Brautigan held the now lifeless rod in his hand, staring out over the still frothy water, then let loose a long howl. The entire episode had lasted maybe ten seconds. Brautigan handed the rod back to Valdène and sat down in the boat and didn't utter a word for an hour.

Later that evening, back at their rental house, Valdène and Brautigan shared a joint. Valdène then asked—for the last time, he'd determined—if he could interview Brautigan for the film. Brautigan finally said yes.

In the movie scene, Valdène appears clean-cut, wearing white jeans with a short-sleeved polo tucked into them, his medium-length dark hair combed in a part. He is sitting in a chair. Brautigan is wearing a long-sleeved shirt printed with a mix of light blues and whites, like a sky dappled with cumulus clouds. He rocks gently back and forth in a hammock. He is still a decade away from the raging alcoholism that would consume him all the way to the point when he would, as a final act, take his own life with a .44 Magnum.

Looking to the side of the camera, Brautigan describes his experience with the tarpon as "so extraordinary as to, uh, create immediate unreality upon contact." The clip lasts for about as long as his fight with the tarpon did. But it is my favorite scene in the movie (which would be called *Tarpon*). "Immediate unreality" is the single best descriptor I've ever run across to describe an encounter with a tarpon. It's fitting, too, that the phrase could also be used to describe what it feels like when an ingested drug hits your system.

∞

Key West has always had an outlaw, anything-can-happen vibe to it. The early Spanish explorers called it "Cayo Hueso," or "Bone Island," because when they first landed there, they found the land strewn with human skeletons. Its earliest industries were not the most upstanding ones. Rum running was rampant. Blackbeard was one among many pirates who frequented the island. And because of the treacherous coral reef that surrounds the key, "wrecking"—that is, salvaging the goods from a shipwreck—thrived as a local livelihood and was its own form of angling, as some of the wrecks were caused by locals who lured ships into the unsafe waters with false navigation lights lit on land.

Key West was among the first places in the country that was friendly to gays, and it has always been a refuge for those who didn't quite fit in on the mainland—the hippies, the dropouts, the anarchists—even after it was connected to it in 1912, when Flagler completed his railroad. In 1982, it seceded from the Union in a somewhat tongue-in-cheek fashion, calling itself the "Conch Republic" and declaring that it would use sand dollars as its official currency. The writer William McKeen once described Key West thusly: "It's as if God picked up the country at California and shook it, so that all of the loose pieces ended up in the reservoir tip at the country's southeast edge." The allusion to the terminus of a condom seems wholly intentional.

With time, the island became a haven for artists, though that didn't necessarily make it any more genteel. Wallace Stevens was one of the first to take up residence there, spending parts of the winters for most of the 1920s and 1930s, and he used the place as the setting for one of his most famous poems, *The Idea of Order at Key West*. The poem, as writer Jay Parini interprets it, is about the desperate battle that takes place between neatness and chaos during the creative process. The brilliant Stevens certainly went through some chaos during his years in Key West, much of it self-made. At a cocktail party he hosted, he drunkenly argued with Robert Frost, another poet who spent his winters in Key West at the time. The encounter so enraged Frost that he gossiped about Stevens's insobriety at a public lecture at the University of Miami a short while later.

And on another night, at yet another cocktail party, Stevens cornered a female partygoer and began to tell her how much he detested the work of Ernest Hemingway and, it had to be said, didn't much like the character of the man, either. The cornered woman happened to be Ursula, one of Hemingway's sisters. She told her brother, who by that time was also wintering in Key West and was at the same party, about the episode. Never one to back down from a slight, Hemingway waited outside in the rain for Stevens to leave the party. The ensuing fight was one-sided. Hemingway, then thirty-six, a full two decades younger than Stevens, knocked him to the ground three times. Stevens managed to land one punch—on Hemingway's jaw—but it didn't faze Hemingway and, in fact, broke Stevens's hand. One onlooker described both men as "pretty well lit."

Hemingway and his pregnant wife, Pauline, had first arrived in Key West on a ship from Havana, on their way back from France. Hemingway had been tipped off about the island by his friend John Dos Passos. The Hemingways only planned on a short stay, but their departure was delayed by car trouble. Hemingway fell in love with the island in short order. He rented houses in the winters during his first three years there, and then the couple was given a house by his wife's uncle in 1931 (this is the house that is now a museum with all of the famous cats). Hemingway wrote parts of *A Farewell to Arms* and *For Whom the Bell Tolls* while there. He also fished for tarpon around the island and on overnight trips to the nearby Marquesas Islands.

Hemingway crossed paths with the poet Elizabeth Bishop in his last year in Key West. Despite not being much of a catch-and-release angler, he was fond of her poem "The Fish," in which the narrator lands a big fish, "looks into his eyes," and then decides to let it go. Bishop became friendly with Frost, but she kept her distance from Stevens. She also overlapped with Tennessee Williams, who wrote all or part of *Battle of Angels*, *Night of the Iguana*, and *The Rose Tattoo* while living in Key West in the 1940s and 1950s (the last play was made into a movie and filmed in Key West). Truman Capote also lived in Key West for a spell, renting a two-bedroom trailer with a bamboo roof to work on his novel *Unanswered Prayers*, which, perhaps fittingly, was never finished.

∽

Thomas McGuane certainly knew of this long literary tradition when he arrived in Key West in 1970. A few years earlier, he had written his first novel, *The Sporting Club*, while completing a Stegner Fellowship at Stanford, and it had been published in 1969 to much critical acclaim and sold to Hollywood. But, McGuane says, the bigger reason that he rented a "sleazy house on a canal that looked straight out at Loggerhead Basin" and moved into it with his then-wife (Becky, a direct descendant of Davy Crockett) and their baby son was because of the tarpon.

He'd been to the Keys as a child, fishing with his father, and the place had made an impression on him that he'd been unable to shake. Throughout his teenage years, he says, he read about the great catches of tarpon in the Keys in *Field & Stream*. "As I was trying to start a career and finish graduate school, I thought that as soon as I had two nickels to rub together, I was going to go down there," he says. "I wanted to figure out the fishing."

He first rented a house in 1969, the year of Woodstock, on Summerland Key, then migrated down to Key West the following year. The only tide book available at the time was from Miami, some 160 miles away, so he had to reckon his tides from there. He became friendly with the guide Woody Sexton, and Sexton came over at night and sketched maps of the fishing areas for him. (McGuane even did some off-the-books guiding, taking some of Sexton's overflow.) In his Willy Roberts wooden skiff, McGuane fished a triangular zone, with Marathon, the Content Keys, and Sugarloaf Key as the three vertices. "It was so wild then," he says. And uncrowded. There was only a handful of boats on the water, and he knew the owners of them all. He says he pretty much had Loggerhead to himself for five years. "I mostly fished, though, on occasion, I'd feel guilty and try to write," he says.

That guilt produced some of his finest work. He wrote much of what turned out to be his third novel, *92 in the Shade*—which was nominated for a National Book Award—while in Key West. The book is set in the Keys, and the main characters are ones he knew well: fishing guides.

The novel opens with a line that feels entirely prescient, perfectly capturing the mood of our current time. Or, perhaps, its sentiment encapsulates every era.

> *Nobody knows, from sea to shining sea, why we are having all this trouble with our republic . . .*

At the time, McGuane also had a deal with *Sports Illustrated* to do a certain number of articles every year, under the legendary editors Ray Cave and André Laguerre. "They liked having literary types, and they didn't care what you did," says McGuane. "You could do two thousand words on the spotted alewife if you wanted." Instead, McGuane wrote his first fishing story, about permit, called "The Longest Silence." "Cave beat me like a Georgia mule," he says. "I wrote that story over and over. I learned a lot."

It was all worth it. The story might just be the finest ever written about fly fishing, or fishing in general. McGuane has always treated his angling pieces (the best of which are collected in a book that takes its name from his seminal story) as seriously as he did his novels, which means that we—anglers, readers, and writers—have permission to do the same, though most of us on the writing side have turned out to be mere pale imitators of the master of the form.

So much of McGuane's writing at the time was influenced by Key West, the place. Tennessee Williams, after reading *92 in the Shade*, asked him if he'd lived there all his life. "Key West was run-down, Duval Street was plywood," says McGuane. "You could live cheaply. It was a hippie Brigadoon. It didn't feel like America. I was intensely in love with it then." His enthusiasm for the place, and for its tarpon fishing, drew in some of his friends, who would join him there.

One of those men was Jim Harrison, the poet and writer and a friend of McGuane's since their shared undergraduate years at Michigan State University. Harrison was a grand, charismatic presence, a puckish man with a great, welcoming, oval face and a left eye that had been blinded by a broken bottle when he was seven. Though he had written two books of poetry, Harrison had not yet published the novellas and novels that would elevate him to literary fame. He had, though, helped McGuane get *The Sporting Club* published by putting him in contact with an editor at Simon & Schuster.

Russell Chatham was another friend who came down. He had a mane of dark hair and a great promontory of a nose and a generous laugh (and, also, a damaged eye). He lived in Bolinas, California, and knew Brautigan and had met McGuane when he was in the area while doing his graduate school fellowship at Stanford. Chatham was a writer and self-taught painter of large mural landscapes, who later in his life would be recognized for his artistic brilliance. He was a devoted outdoorsman and an accomplished steelhead fisherman who also once held the world record for striped bass on a fly rod. He would later move to Montana, near McGuane's home, and McGuane, in a story, would memorably describe him as "a man who has ruined his life with sport."

⁂

Guy de la Valdène was born in New York City but spent some of his younger years living in a 17th-century castle in Normandy, as some members of the French aristocracy do (his father was a count and a famous French flying ace). Valdène was sent to the United States before he was a teenager to attend school in Florida. There, he became friends with a fellow student named Gil Drake Jr.

In the late 1950s, Drake's father opened a lodge in Grand Bahama named Deep Water Cay, which became a premier saltwater flats fishing destination, primarily for bonefish. Valdène and Drake spent months there at a time, fishing, doing odd jobs, and hanging out with all the famous fishermen who came through the lodge, like Joe Brooks and Al McClane. In 1967, one of those famous fishermen—Stu Apte, then a guide—met the young Valdène and asked if he'd like to book him for some tarpon fishing in the Keys. Valdène said yes.

Apte was then in the midst of his ascendance as a well-known saltwater fly fisherman who specialized in tarpon. As a guide, he was "difficult," as

Valdène describes him, a stern taskmaster who yelled at his clients all day long when they didn't do things exactly as he—in the prime of his life as one of the best tarpon fishermen who ever lived—would have. Valdène at the time was "a mess as a tarpon fisherman," he says. "I had no idea what I was doing." Which made Apte yell even more.

One morning in the spring of 1967, Apte and Valdène were fishing a basin in the lower Keys. Valdène remembers it as a particularly appalling day for him with the rod. "I was nervous as hell and was pulling the fly out of every fish's mouth I saw," he says. After he missed three relatively easy fish in a row—and endured the verbal lashings—he handed the rod to Apte, who made just a few casts and smugly hooked a tarpon. The fish turned out to be 151 pounds, which broke the world record of 148 pounds, 8 ounces that had been set by Joe Brooks six years earlier (Apte was Brooks's guide that day). "I'm glad I didn't catch that fish," Valdène says now. "It would have been a farce."

The next year, Valdène asked Woody Sexton if he would guide him. Sexton, an educated, articulate man from the Pacific Northwest who spent five months of the year guiding in the Keys, was wary about breaching etiquette, of "stealing" another guide's client. So he declined. Valdène, who by this time had begun to publish some pieces of writing, spent 1968 fishing with a handful of different guides, including Cal Cochran and Harry Snow. The next season, with the etiquette statute of limitations apparently passed, Sexton took Valdène on—well, sort of. Valdène was hungry for knowledge and improvement. He wanted to book Sexton for sixty days straight, and he suggested that they both fish, and that he would pay Sexton thirty dollars a day (half the price of the standard guiding wage at the time) and provide lunch. Sexton agreed to the deal, and the two men fished together like this for years.

In the spring of 1969, Sexton told Valdène that there was someone he wanted him to meet, a fellow writer named Thomas McGuane. He thought the two of them would get along. Sexton took Valdène to a small rental house occupied by a tall, prepossessing man with longish dark hair, who was accompanied by his wife and their eight-month-old son. Over a cup of coffee, McGuane told Valdène about the permit story he was working on for *Sports Illustrated*. Valdène happened to be also working on a magazine piece, a story about fly fishing for billfish for *Field & Stream*. Months later, after both men had left the Keys for their respective homes, Valdène read "The Longest Silence" and sent McGuane a letter complimenting him on the piece. McGuane responded by inviting Valdène out to his place in Montana that autumn to fish for trout, and a friendship was born.

The next year, Valdène and McGuane got together in Key West, where they were joined by Harrison and Chatham. And that's when the fun began.

∾

Valdène began renting a house every year for the months of May and June, hosting Harrison and Chatham (McGuane continued to live with his wife and son). They never locked the doors of the house, and they never had any idea of what they would find within it when they got back after a day on the water. "Every night, all hell would break loose," says Valdène. "It was unbelievable, really." Usually what they walked into was a revolving door of women, alcohol, marijuana, and mescaline.* If there was no party at the house, they took the show on the road, usually to their favorite bar the Chart Room, which was located inside a Key West hotel. "The whole scene was beyond anything you could imagine," says Chatham. "Key West was an open town. The authorities, if there were any, didn't seem to care what went on. It was wild, the fooling around after dark. That's what it seemed like the town was there for, that misbehaving. Ordinary people never get the chance to act like that."

The party attracted others. In subsequent years, Jimmy Buffett, still some time away from prominence, came down. He busked on the street

---

* Some of the early Keys fishing guides freelanced as late-night weed smugglers, using their intimate knowledge of the backcountry to avoid detection by the authorities while delivering bales of marijuana, which were known as "square groupers" in the local vernacular.

in shorts and a T-shirt, making twenty dollars a night, or played for beer at the Chart Room. Hunter S. Thompson also began making annual appearances, roaring into town with his infectious, kinetic energy, and sometimes staying with Buffett. Neither man fished for tarpon (Buffett would later in his life), but they both had a multiplying effect on the nightlife.

At first, McGuane didn't partake in the partying as much as the others. "I lived there and had a child in school and was involved in the community," he says. (His wife, Becky, started the Montessori school in Key West that's still operating today.) "Guy and Russ and Jim were there without their wives. They were like conventioneers. They had a great time. I had just a good enough time to be decent." McGuane would succumb, though, eventually.

Throughout it all, the four men—McGuane, Valdène, Harrison, and Chatham—stayed true to the fishing. They never missed a fishable day, no matter what had transpired the evening before. McGuane wrote about that time in his story "Southern Salt":

> *Closing time left four hours for the sleepy quiet of backyards and old streets before the sun came up, and once the engine of the skiff went down and several waves of sickness were fought back, we again were up and running—lust and booze banked down—off looking for fish in the glare . . . I remember the special horror of fighting wild tarpon with a bar-life muzziness on my face and my clothes revealing beer stains, cigarette burns, and head-shop perfumes.*

Valdène and McGuane, the most serious tarpon anglers of the bunch, had the boats and would take turns fishing with Harrison and Chatham, neither of whom ever really learned how to pole a skiff. The men fished for fun and not for records. There wasn't much competition for spots on the water—there were only two full-time Key West guides at the time—so the water world was theirs to explore: Garrison Bight, Man and Woman Keys, Archer Keys, the Sisters, the Eccentrics, Mule Key, and basins and banks that had yet to be named. The fishing they experienced was almost implausible. And the discovery and the fishing—all of it, really—felt like an extension of their respective practiced arts. "It *was* creative work," says McGuane. "We were kind of inventing it as we went along. The shallow water fishery was really blank paper. That excitement you feel when a piece of writing is going well, that was very much the feeling when things came together on the flats, with the wind and the tides and the fish."

One morning during Harrison's first year in Key West, McGuane took him out and poled him around. Harrison had never hooked a tarpon, and had been making a mess of himself on the boat. ("A hilarious clusterfuck," as Chatham describes it.) Valdène was poling Chatham around nearby. McGuane spotted some fish and told Harrison to cast. "Jim made the cast, but it was a horrible one," says Chatham. "The wind caught his fly and it sailed over the back of the tarpon." But there happened to be another tarpon right behind the intended target, and that fish ate the fly and took off. "Jim was terrified," says McGuane. "His knees started buckling and he actually sat down in the middle of the boat and said he couldn't go through with it. I told him I was going to beat the shit out of him if he didn't."

Harrison stood back up and fought the fish—a small one, around fifty pounds—for a while, until he had it ten feet or so from the boat. And then the hook pulled free. "We called that a Palm Beach release," says Chatham.

Later that night, when McGuane, Valdène, and Chatham walked into the Chart Room, they spotted Harrison sitting at the bar holding court, surrounded by a group of admirers who were hanging on his every word. He had a cigarette in his hand and was using it to emphasize his points, pausing his monologue every once in a while to take a dramatic drag. "He was lecturing people like he was some expert on tarpon fishing, telling them how to cast, how to hook them, and how they should really try the Palm Beach release," says Chatham. "It was vintage Harrison."

∞

In 1972, Valdène invited his sister's boyfriend, a Parisian filmmaker named Christian Odasso, to join the group in Key West and do some tarpon fishing. Odasso immediately fell in love—with the place, the dramatic fish, the light on the water. He told Valdène they should make a movie.

The next year, Odasso came to Key West with a French film crew in tow. For three weeks, camera crews in boats followed Valdène and Gil Drake and Woody Sexton around on the water. They shot scenes from Duval Street of the buskers, the hippies, and the general cultural diaspora of the town back then. Jimmy Buffett did the sound track, recording it all in one day in a studio in Nashville. Brautigan had his cameo, of course. McGuane and Harrison had brief ones, too. They, along with the other anglers, all give off an *Easy Rider* vibe in the movie, sporting bandanas and cut-off jeans and yards of facial hair. In one scene, three guides—Drake, Sexton, and Steve Huff—are interviewed. They are far more clean-cut than the anglers, the only facial hair among them being Huff's neat mustache, which had not yet gone white.

The stars of the movie, though, are the tarpon. The movie features what is still some of the best footage of jumping tarpon, complete with the audible gill flutters and the spectacular crashing flops back into the water. The film is loosely plotted. What we see is a funky town and an incredible fishery, and there's a sense that the world is a good-hearted place. One scene, however, throws that notion into question. It was shot on a party boat, and the small sharks caught by the people on the boat are brutally and senselessly clubbed to death, a stark contrast to the ethereal beauty of the tarpon shots.

At the end of that tarpon season, Valdène and Odasso took the raw footage to a famous editing house in Paris. Jacques Cousteau and Orson Welles were editing films there at the same time. The soft-core pornography film *Emmanuelle* was being finished there, as well. In September of 1973, Valdène and Odasso had completed *Tarpon*, and they showed it a few times to some small groups in the Keys. Valdène then set out to try to sell it. He shopped it around for a year and a half, getting meetings with the presidents of ABC, CBS, and NBC. No one bit. "It was too hippie-ish for the big networks," says Valdène. He did sell it in Japan, but for a very small sum of money, nothing close to the hundreds of thousands it cost to shoot and edit it. Valdène eventually gave up and put the film, stored in metal canisters, in a barn in Normandy.

Here and there, though, there were whispers among those deep in the fishing world about the film. A few bootlegged copies floated around the country, and it achieved a cult status. I watched what must have been a copy of a copy with a friend in the 1990s. The picture jumped every couple of minutes, and the sound was tinny. I remember feeling giddy the entire way through, regardless.

Nearly three and a half decades after the completion of the movie, Valdène's sister called him one day and told him she'd come across the film canisters in the barn. She wondered if he wanted them. Valdène had the canisters sent to a film house, and there it was discovered that though the film had been exposed to the heat and cold for more than thirty years, it was mostly intact. Valdène decided that he wouldn't try to sell it again, and instead gave it to his niece to do with it whatever she pleased. She had it remastered as a DVD and released the film, officially, in 2008. Fishing geeks like me gobbled it up.

∽

There was another movie filmed partly in Key West during that era, this one a year after *Tarpon*. It was McGuane's movie, the film adaptation of his novel *92 in the Shade* (some of which was shot in England). McGuane had signed on as the writer and director of the movie, which attracted a notable list of actors and actresses—Peter Fonda, Warren Oates, Margot Kidder, Elizabeth Ashley, Burgess Meredith, and Harry Dean Stanton. It was during the filming of the movie that McGuane finally joined in on the fun that his friends had been having in Key West, and he went all in. "Buffett and I were running the streets," says McGuane. "I was probably tired of working all the time and being left out, so I really blew it out for a few years." McGuane wouldn't write another novel for five more years. Instead, he focused on writing more scripts for Hollywood and partaking in that scene, which was, decidedly, in the fast lane. During this period of time, he earned the nickname "Captain Berserko."

During the filming of *92 in the Shade*, a sort of musical chairs took place among couples. The affairs turned into marriages. Peter Fonda would eventually marry McGuane's first wife, Becky. McGuane married Margot Kidder. After he and Kidder were divorced three years later, McGuane married Laurie Buffett, Jimmy's sister (to whom he is still married). McGuane lasted only a few more years in Key West after the movie, and then he left, pretty much for good. He quit drinking and drugs, cold turkey, in 1981. "My issues with those substances were always more behavioral than addictive," he says.

Brautigan had stopped visiting Key West by then, too. He fell out of touch with the rest of the men, save for the occasional incomprehensible, late-night drunken phone call. In October 1984, he was found dead in his home in Bolinas, of a self-inflicted gunshot. He was forty-nine.

That left Valdène, Harrison, and Chatham, who kept making the annual pilgrimage to Key West, even without McGuane, the man whom Valdène had called "our leader." They collectively became known as the "Fat Boys." They only had four good eyes among them, but they maintained a nearly bottomless appetite for fishing and fun.

By the late 1970s, though, the setting had begun to change. Gone was the Key West as Valdène had first discovered it, "sultry, magnificent, and suspicious," with the hippies and the loads of pot and the acoustic guitars. In their place: Cubans in dark sunglasses and cocaine and guns. The young, carefree hippie women had been supplanted by hardened professionals. (Valdène says a Madame once asked the Fat Boys if they wanted to be "testers" for women she was planning on bringing down from Miami.) T-shirt shops sprung up on Duval Street, and cruise ships did daily dumps of T-shirt customers onto the shores of the island. In 1977, Buffett released the song that would become his anthem, *Margaritaville*, which crystalized the notion that Key West was a drunken tourist destination.

Valdène, Harrison, and Chatham still went out fishing on any clement day, no matter what, but it all began to get a little sloppy. The wild nights began to leak into the daytime. They sometimes drank Cuba libres while on the water. One day, some fishermen spotted Valdène's skiff drifting out to the ocean, unmoored and seemingly unmanned. When the fishermen approached the boat to investigate, they found Valdène, Harrison, and Chatham dead drunk, passed out asleep in the bottom. "It became a real fucking mess," says Valdène.

The coup de grâce came in 1982, when Harrison, flush with some money he'd made from his work (McGuane had returned Harrison's earlier favor and helped *him* get published), showed up in Key West with a quarter ounce of cocaine. The trio finally ran out of it a few weeks into their trip. "And we looked at each other and said, 'If we ever do this again, we are going to fucking die,'" says Chatham. After that season, they all went their separate ways. And that was that.

∽

Valdène went back to Palm Beach and, later, to a quail plantation outside Tallahassee. Every decade or so, he has produced a new little gem of a book. He continues to fish for tarpon, but not in the Keys. McGuane lives most of the year in a beautiful, unpretentious ranch house on a trout stream in Montana. He has remained productive, publishing more novels, as well as collections of short stories and nonfiction.* He still fishes for tarpon every year, mainly in Boca Grande, where he owns a house. Harrison would escape back home to Michigan, and then to Arizona and Montana, producing along the way the novels and novellas, including *Legends of the Fall*, that brought him critical acclaim and fame. In March 2016, at the age of seventy-eight, Harrison died, his heart finally succumbing to the punishment of decades of hard drinking and smoking and overeating. When his heart stopped, he was in the midst of writing a poem. Left on his desk was a piece of paper. On it was the unfinished poem and a streaked line made by the pen in his hand as he collapsed. Chatham moved to Montana, and then back to California. By the 1990s, he'd finally received the deserved recognition for his epic

---

* McGuane is a member of the American Academy of Arts and Letters *and* the Fly Fishing Hall of Fame.

landscape murals of the Rocky Mountain West, which were collected by the likes of Jack Nicholson and Robert Redford. Declining health and finances made his final years difficult. He never fished for tarpon again after turning fifty. He died in November 2019, in a nursing facility at the age of eighty.

In the immediate years after the four men left Key West, they stayed in touch. When they saw or talked to each other, they reminisced about how lucky they were to partake in that spectacular fishing and to imbibe in the pleasures of Key West at the time, and to emerge from it all somewhat intact. But time and work and life moved on, and in the subsequent decades, they started to fall out of contact, except for McGuane and Harrison, who wrote letters to each other every week for fifty years. "I feel an empty channel with his passing," says McGuane. "He was breathtakingly intelligent."

∽

"The tarpon fishing is what brought us to Key West," says Valdène. "The women and the partying came later and that was all part of the fun. But it was the tarpon fishing that kept us there."

Perhaps tarpon fishing with a fly rod attracted these artists because of a basic artistic premise—that yearning to understand, to express and reveal something that defied any easy description. That "immediate unreality."

Perhaps tarpon fishing with a fly rod was the perfect representation of Stevens's artistic conflict between neatness (the perfect knots, the perfect cast) and chaos (the bedlam of the hookup and the fight). Maybe the fishing itself—explosive, beautiful, and tremendously difficult—was the art form, that struggle against limitations that, as Kurt Vonnegut once put it, "is what you respond to in a work of art."

Much art came out of this period of these men's lives. McGuane wrote his novel about fishing guides and his nonfiction fishing stories. "There's a part of fishing that's kind of like looking into a fire, a place where a sort of alpha wave activity can go on where creative ideas can begin," he says. Harrison used angling as a metaphor in much of his writing, and also used it as a form of respite when he needed a break from his work and his hard-living ways. "Fishing makes us less the hostages to the horrors of making a living," he would say, many years after Key West. Chatham wrote a few books about fishing, and his western landscapes incorporated elements of the vastness and wildness of the Key West sky and flats. And Valdène—though less prolific and less well-known than his contemporaries—has produced some beautiful writing, which include some pieces about his time in Key West.

∞

I think now of the artists who moved into the SoHo neighborhood in New York City in the latter half of the 20th century. In that former industrial wasteland, in those cheap, high-ceilinged lofts, artists lived together and created and showed their work. They made SoHo hip. And once that was established by the artists, then the more commercial and competitive and richer set came in, following the artists' wake—the high-end boutique and chain stores, the lawyers, the hedge funders. And they made the neighborhood theirs.

Because of who they were becoming as artists, because of their look and their joy and their creativity, McGuane, Harrison, Chatham, Brautigan, and Valdène brought a sense of cool to fly fishing for tarpon.

And then the world-record chasers—commercial, competitive, and rich—entered the scene and descended upon the little Florida town of Homosassa, making the sport theirs.

5

HIDDEN IN
PLAIN SIGHT

Upon seeing Homosassa for the first time in the late 1970s . . .

"I'm in the boat with Stu [Apte]. It's my first day there. Jim Brewer is in another boat. Eddie Wightman is out there. So is Bill Curtis. We haven't seen any fish. It's slick calm, maybe ten o'clock. I'm standing in the bow, looking out over the Gulf when I see them. It looks like a rain shower hitting the water. The fish are two hundred yards away, rolling, coming at us. I'd never seen a population of tarpon like that, and never will again. There were thousands and thousands and thousands, as far as you could see. The fish came right through the boats, as happy as they could be. Everyone was just standing there, mouths wide open. I took a cast and hooked one. I looked around and everyone was scrambling to get their rods."

—Al Pflueger Jr., angler

"There were thousands of fish, five hundred in a school. They'd push a wake like you couldn't believe. You could see it from six hundred yards away. I got so excited about the tarpon that I had to get my doctor to prescribe me some sleeping pills."

—Dale Perez, guide

"There were thousands and thousands of tarpon. Ten thousand of them. I'm serious."

—Steve Huff, guide

∽

Tom Evans was named after his father, Thomas Mellon Evans Sr. As the middle name indicates, the Evans family is related to one of the wealthiest families in American history. The relation is distant, though: Evans Sr.'s grandmother was Andrew Mellon's first cousin. So while Evans Sr. got the name, he did not receive the inheritance. Instead, he made his own fortune.

In the mid-20th century, Evans Sr., according to Diana Henriques's book about him, used cash, debt, and a few loopholes in the tax code to gain control of some eighty American companies. He was the forefather of corporate raiders, like Carl Icahn and Nelson Peltz, who would flourish in the latter stages of that century. Among the elder Evans's businesses were a railroad company and the Crane Co. of Chicago, one of the nation's largest plumbing supply manufacturers. Evans Sr. would typically buy a company that was foundering, significantly cut costs by firing many of its employees, then build it back up to a point he found suitable before selling it.

Evans Sr. was ruthless during a somewhat genteel time in American business. *Forbes* described him as "the man in the wolf suit." During an antitrust hearing on Capitol Hill, a New Jersey senator called him "a corporate embodiment of Jaws, the great white shark." One of his former employees once told the *Wall Street Journal*, "He'll call somebody a dumb bastard or an ignorant son of a bitch, and the guy has no choice but to put up with it—until he can find another job."

Perhaps unsurprisingly, Evans Sr. was also a horrible husband and father. Tom Evans was born in 1938. He, along with his two younger brothers, was raised outside Pittsburgh. His mother was musical and painted and wrote autobiographical short stories, some of which were not very flattering to her marriage. She and her sons saw very little of Evans Sr., and she would later testify during divorce proceedings that her husband "had more concern for his business than he did for me."

Despite not having much contact with his father, Evans had moments of idyll during his childhood. Most of those moments came at his family's country home in Ligonier, Pennsylvania, where he had the run of the place, wandering the woods and learning to fly fish the trout streams. That idyll was cut short, though, when his parents began to argue with regularity. As those arguments progressed from the merely verbal to the physical, Evans stood up for his mother.

On Christmas Eve when Evans was fourteen, his father returned home from work with alcohol on his breath and the threat of violence in his demeanor. He began to yell at his wife. Evans, by this time, was growing into the body that would eventually earn him a college scholarship as a football nose guard and heavyweight wrestler. He realized what the yelling would inevitably turn into, so he picked up his father, threw him out of the house, and locked the doors. The cops came but no charges were pressed, presumably because of Evans Sr.'s stature as a nationally known businessman. Evans Sr. showed back up at the house, apologetically, on Christmas morning. But he'd had it with his interfering son.

Evans was sent off to the Brooks School in Massachusetts. While he was there, his parents got divorced, and his father took his two younger brothers to live with him in New York City. His mother was completely cut off from the family then, and Evans would only see her on rare occasions from that point on for the rest of his life. More than fifty years later, a cousin would send Evans some pictures of his mother. "I'd forgotten how pretty she was," he says.

During his second year at Brooks, Evans was dismissed for drinking and sent home to New York. Before he could unpack his bags, his father handed him a train ticket and told him that he'd been enrolled at Admiral Farragut School, a military school in Pine Beach, New Jersey. The train left the next day.

Evans recalls walking to the school's entrance the next afternoon, his duffel bag slung over his shoulder. It was cold and rainy. He saw a guard standing at the gates, a kid about his age, with a hard look of resignation on his face. Evans turned around right then and there, and got back on the train to New York, arriving back at his father's that evening.

His father was enraged. "Goddammit, I'll teach you a lesson," he told his son. Two days later, he sent Evans to a boardinghouse in Williamsville, New York. Evans moved in with a group of steel workers, all of whom were at least a decade older than he was. He swept the floors in the local mill, which his father happened to own. In the evenings, he joined his housemates at the local bar for "dimies" (ten-cent beers). "I was lonely and terrified," says Evans.

One weekend day, he spotted some kids his age playing football in a park, and he asked to join in. The kids happened to play for the local high school team. They introduced Evans to their coach and, for the next two years, Evans attended that high school and played football and wrestled. He was a very good football player but an even better wrestler—at one point in high school, he won eighty matches in a row. He moved out of the boardinghouse and into the home of a local family.

After a postgrad year, Evans applied to Yale—where his father had gone to college—and was accepted. In the summer of that year, he went to New York to visit a friend. He stopped by his father's apartment, mainly to see his brothers. His father, without saying hello, told him that Yale had rescinded the offer of acceptance.

"I don't have anywhere else to go," Evans said.

"That's your problem," his father replied.

Evans learned later that his father had called Yale and used his influence to get the school to withdraw his son's acceptance. Evans left that night and would have no meaningful contact with his father for the next three decades.

Before he'd been accepted at Yale, Evans had attracted some interest from the football coach at the University of Virginia. So he called the Virginia coach, who offered a scholarship for football and wrestling. Evans went there for a few years and left in 1960, before graduating.

He borrowed some money from a family trust to get a seat on the New York Stock Exchange as a specialist trader who maintained markets on a specific set of stocks, becoming one of the youngest specialists ever on what's known as the Big Board of the exchange. He paid the borrowed money back quickly and soon had a couple dozen people working for him at his own firm.

Evans continued to play football on the weekends for his first few years on Wall Street, making $250 a game for the semi-pro Stamford (Connecticut) Golden Bears. When some of his elders on Wall Street suggested that showing up for work on Mondays with cuts and bruises on his face and arms might not be the best look for business, he quit the game for good.

Because his firm made its own markets, it carried all the risks and the rewards of its bets. There were big highs and big lows. Evans did very well, making the equivalent of $4 million a year in 2019 dollars. But it was stressful work. He got his airplane pilot's license and flew a Piper Aztec to try to relieve the stress. He discovered, though, that that wasn't enough. Something was missing from his life, something that he'd once found on the football field and on the wrestling mat. He craved competition. He wanted to be the best at something. He wanted to get out from under the shadow of his name and his father. The money, as nice as it was, didn't provide him with the buzz he sought, and he knew he'd likely never have more of it than his father did.

He fished on the weekends, out of his second home in Old Lyme, Connecticut, which he flew his plane to on Friday afternoons, taking off from the old Flushing Airport near LaGuardia. He caught boatloads of striped bass and bluefish, and while they were fun to catch, they weren't much of a challenge. In the summers, he went north to Canada to fish for Atlantic salmon, the silvery, leaping gamefish that topped out at around twenty-five pounds. He loved Atlantic salmon and still does to this day. One summer, though, the salmon failed to show up in the rivers, part of a larger downward trend for the species, and Evans decided he needed a new fish to target.

This was around the time that Fernandez, Pallot, Emery, Duncan, Apte, Ted Williams, and others were bringing attention to tarpon fly fishing in the Keys. Evans read about the sport in an outdoor maga-zine. In the spring of 1968, he flew down to Marathon in the Keys and booked a guide named Harry Snow for three days. On his last day of fishing, Evans hooked his first tarpon, feeling that sudden, heavy pull. The fish broke him off after a jump. But it had caught him. He'd found his purpose. He stayed down in the Keys for an extra day and booked the legendary guide, Jimmie Albright, in Islamorada. And it was with Albright that Evans landed his first tarpon, a fifty-six-pounder.

The next season, Evans tried to book Albright again, but the guide had no openings. Snow was booked up, as well, but he suggested that Evans call his neighbor in Marathon, a young guy who was just starting out as a tarpon guide. A young guy named Steve Huff.

∽

Huff, too, was the product of a dysfunctional family. He was born and raised in Miami. His father was an alcoholic and a gambler. He would periodically go on fishing trips. Huff would always ask to tag along, but his father always said no. Huff learned later that these "fishing" trips were really just extended drinking binges, anyway.

When Huff was ten, his father gave him a spinning rod, in what was likely a plaintive, last-ditch effort to do *something* right as a father. It was the first piece of fishing tackle that Huff ever owned. The very next day, his father left. Huff neither saw nor spoke to him ever again.

With that rod, though, his father had actually done some good. It was the tool that unlocked what would become Huff's abiding passion in life. He immediately took the rod to a canal in Miami, made a cast, and caught a two-pound snook. "And that was it," he says. "I was done."

Huff's mother, like Madame Loisel in Guy de Maupassant's "The Necklace," was someone who always wanted to impress the society people whose company she craved but could never afford. Her husband never came close to providing her with any social or economic advancement. So she wanted her son to fill in, to become something she deemed worth-while, like a businessman or a lawyer. But Huff was already hardheaded and single-minded at a young age. After he graduated from the University of Miami with a degree in marine biology, he told his mother that he was going to become a fishing guide. "She didn't like that idea at all," he says. "She said that fishing guides were a bunch of drunks and bums and that I would never amount to anything."

Huff is unsentimental about the impact his parents might have had on his life. "I think we grow up to be whatever we want to be," he says. One can't help but wonder, though, about how it all fits into that pain on the water that he not only endures but seems to welcome. ("Steve is a pain freak," says his fellow guide Harry Spear.)

Huff does seem to have learned at least some things from his mother, some negative and some positive. He's always been wary of the gossipy moneyed set, and he is distasteful of any pretense. But he also learned some lessons about working hard from her. Huff's mother worked as a seamstress, making dresses and other clothing for those same wealthy women whose company she yearned to join. After her husband left, she was forced to work overtime to make ends meet for the family. Huff remembers, as a child, waking up at 2:30 A.M. and hearing the clicking of the sewing machine. He tiptoed into the living room and saw his mother sitting at the table, sewing, her eyes filled with tears of exhaustion or despair or pain.

In the end, despite her misgivings about his career choice, Huff's mother did cosign a bank loan so that Huff could buy a skiff after college. He moved to the Keys and got his captain's license. On November 1, 1968, he took out his first client. The day was windy and cloudy and fishless. The guy never came back. "Poor bastard," Huff says. "I had no clue what I was doing. I didn't even know what I didn't know."

But he was a quick study. By the spring of 1969, when he first met Tom Evans, he was ready.

∽

The guide-client relationship in tarpon fishing is a fascinating one. It can all get a bit fiddly. "A skiff can get really small really quick, to the point where you can't negotiate yourself out of it," says Pallot. One reason that sudden shrinkage can happen: fly fishing for tarpon is an expensive sport. It often requires travel. With only a few exceptions, it requires a boat and a guide (who will cost around eight hundred dollars per day nowadays). It is a sport done largely by elites, the captains of industry. The "elite" is standing in the bow of the boat, rather than in the back, and is paying the guide. But there can be some tension that arises, tension that's unusual in our service economy, because of the knowledge and control that guides have (they pick the spots, they work the boat) and the subservience—which some might find odd—that the clients willingly take on. Jack Brothers, Jimmie Albright, Bill Curtis, and many of the old-time flats guides were notorious for yelling at their clients, like old-school football coaches.* But the curiously imbalanced relationship goes beyond just yelling. At the dock one day, two overweight men once asked Brothers if he could take them fishing. "If you think I'm going to pole your fat asses around all day you're crazy," he replied. Harry Spear used to fish with Lou Gerstner when Gerstner was the CEO of IBM. "Lou would get on the boat and start telling me what to do," says Spear. "I'd stop him after a minute or two and say, 'Lou, you know what to do in a boardroom. You're now in my boardroom, and I'm in charge here.'"

Huff once fished in the Keys with a big-time executive from Procter & Gamble. He poled to a point off a bank and staked off the boat. The executive kept looking at another point, a half mile away. "I think we should move up to that point," the executive said. Huff didn't respond. The executive repeated his thought, and Huff remained silent. When the executive said it a third time, Huff turned to him and said, "Wild horses couldn't drag me away from this spot. There is only one captain on this boat, and that's me." And the man went meekly silent. Asked years later if there just might have been more fish at the executive's preferred spot, Huff replied, "Yeah, maybe."

---

* Most of the newer generation of guides do not yell at their clients, but there are some exceptions.

The best tarpon guides are so good, so rare, and so in demand—and so likely to have built up a static list of returning clients—that they are impervious to the whims of our service culture. There have never been any Yelp reviews of Steve Huff.

∽

Huff says he thinks a guide is a bit like a bird dog, that he wags his tail and runs around working his ass off to find his sport a "bird," which is, in this case, a fish. All the guide desires is to point one out and then, hopefully, retrieve it once his sport has held up his or her end of the deal. Huff says that if a guide has spent the day pointing out fish after fish for the sport, and the sport fails to catch one, "like a good bird dog, you can start to get a little batty, a little cuckoo and start gnawing on things. The guide, like the bird dog, needs to be rewarded every once in a while."

I thought about this analogy one day while on the water with another guide. I'd been led to many fish, and I'd screwed them all up. I'd failed to spot fish that he'd pointed out, I'd thrown inaccurate casts, and I'd broken the tippet on the two fish I had managed to hook. At the end of the fishless day, after the guide told me it was time to reel up and head for the dock, I turned around and stared at him.

"What?" he asked.

"I'm just making sure you weren't back there gnawing on your elbow," I said.

"Huh?"

Many have likened the guide-sport relationship to that of a golfer and a caddy. And while that analogy—and the mountain Sherpa one—works on many levels, a better one might be that of a pitcher and a catcher in baseball. The sport is doing the "pitching" of the fly. The guide, like the catcher, is calling the pitches and playing a physical role in the game, as well. And while the sport will ultimately get credit for the fish landed (the "win"), the guide, like the catcher, deserves more credit than is usually offered. (This works in the opposite way, too. A guide can blow a call or not position the boat correctly, and he will usually not be blamed too much for any angler screwups.) When both guide and sport are on the same page, "there's a bond that can form, an alchemy," says Pallot.

Evans and Huff found that alchemy. They formed a great battery, at least early on, before it all went to hell. They were at the same stage of their tarpon-fishing careers. Both were intent and obsessed with learning all they could about the sport. Both were intense, and there was tension, but it was an athletic tension. "When we were in the boat, it was like a pressure cooker," says Evans. "So much was expected from the back of the boat, and so much was expected from the front of the boat."

Huff was what people call "fishy." He had the right gut instincts about where the fish would show and on which tide cycle they would best bite. Part of it was intuition, but a bigger part of it was how hard he worked at it. He was a true student of the game, spending hours studying tide and navigational charts and tying flies and knots (he invented the Huffnagle knot, which allowed heavy shock tippet to be tied to smaller, thinner tippet without losing any strength). He was always ethical about the sport and anal about the condition of his boat, his leaders, and tippets and the rest of his equipment. He even kept his hair and mustache neatly trimmed.

Evans, at this time, was still an athlete, in body and in mind, barrel-chested and competitive as hell, his mop of brown hair just starting to grey slightly at its edges, like a tip of a lit cigar. Unlike 99 percent of tarpon anglers, Evans's favorite part of the sport was the fight, and he was constantly refining his technique to get better at it. His brute strength helped, yes, but he would discover that doing it well was more about angles and leverage and keeping the fish off balance, knowing when to pull and when not to. Fighting big tarpon makes most anglers miserable because the fish dictates the game (part of the dread I spoke about earlier). Evans was different. "I loved getting into the box and talking to him and tugging on him," he says. "The faster I could settle the thing, the better." He was playing football. He was dropping his shoulder to get under the pads of the center, trying to get to the running back.

Evans and Huff started out unknown and un-respected in the Keys. When they entered their first tarpon tournament, no one bid on them in the Calcutta, which is the betting pool in which competitors place wagers on each other, based on perceived levels of skill. That perception would change over time.

Evans and Huff fished together in the Keys, during the months of May and June, from 1969 until 1976, fishing for a few weeks at a time in the early years, and then expanding that to forty-five days a year. As they got better at catching tarpon, their focus began to shift. They were aware of Fernandez, Pallot, Duncan, and Emery in the upper Keys, of McGuane, Harrison, Chatham, and Valdène down in Key West, and of what had been unlocked when it came to tarpon fishing, from the innovations to the freedom and romance (Huff knew all the players fairly well). "But we weren't fun fishing," says Evans, who was stockpiling all of his vacation days and leaving his firm in charge of his lieutenants so he could fish for a month or more a year. "We were trying to catch the biggest tarpon in the world."

The typical "big" Keys fish was around 100 pounds. There were some larger fish to be found, a few in the 150-pound range and a handful bigger than that. Evans and Huff caught tarpon up to 120 pounds, huge fish by most people's standards, but it soon became clear to both men that they wanted something more.

✢

One more digression before we really get into it. We must talk a bit about rules and records and, in particular, about the keeping of rules and records when it comes to the biggest fish ever caught.

The impulse to record who caught the biggest fish likely goes back to the origins of fishing itself. Back in early human history, in those purely subsistence days, the biggest fish fed more people, and it was probably the case that the anglers who consistently caught the biggest fish were venerated within their given societal/familial group.

Humans would eventually settle into more agricultural-based societies, which made them a little less reliant on hunting and gathering. By the 15th century, as evidenced by the Dame Juliana Berners essay, fishing had taken on a bit more of a recreational bent. It's likely that most anglers still killed what they caught, but they probably didn't need all of the fish they kept to survive. By the late 19th century, trout and salmon fishing clubs and syndicates had sprung up around the UK. In the United States, the wealthy men who fished recreationally started some clubs in the 20th century. One of the first on the saltwater side was the Long Key Fishing Club, founded in 1908, which was based halfway between Islamorada and Marathon in the Keys. It boasted among its membership the likes of Zane Grey, Herbert Hoover, and Andrew Mellon, but it was completely destroyed by the Labor Day hurricane of 1935. More important to the history of tarpon fly fishing, though, was the 1929 founding of the Miami Rod & Reel Club, which was followed in later years by the Tropical Anglers Club and the Miami Sportfishing Club. These clubs established rules and regulations for the fishing done by their members (which would include, eventually, Pallot, Fernandez, Apte, and Brooks, among others), based on the principles of "fair chase"—that is, that the fish could only be taken under certain rules that made it possible for them to get away.

This is one of the most beguiling aspects of fly fishing. It is a true "sport," in the sense that it has evolved not to make things easier for the angler but to make them more difficult. If the goal is just to catch fish, a net or dynamite is a far more effective tool. Using conventional tackle (a spinning rod and reel and either a lure or bait) adds some sport to fishing. But fly fishing—the small flies, the wispy rods, the light tippets—swings much more of the advantage to the fish. And nowhere in the fly-fishing world is the advantage for the fish greater than in tarpon fishing, provided one uses a light tippet. (One of the most significant rules established by the South Florida clubs at the time was that twelve-pound tippet was the heaviest allowed). This impulse toward making fly fishing more sporting stems from the same impulse that allows us to "accept the net in tennis," as McGuane once wrote. In tarpon angling with a fly rod, that net is made taller.

The clubs eventually started engaging in tournaments so they could compete with each other. That competition led to improvements in tackle, like the shock or bite tippet, which was pioneered, Apte says, by the same J. Lee Cuddy who owned the store in which John Emery worked, and made the landing of big tarpon a possibility. Those inter-club tournaments eventually led to something called the Metropolitan South Florida Fishing Tournament (MET), which would, at one point, be headed up by a gap-toothed man named Bernard "Lefty" Kreh, a writer, raconteur, veteran of the Battle of the Bulge, anthrax poisoning survivor, casting instructor, and convention presenter, who would become the world's most famous fly fisherman and the sport's Apostle Paul.

Around the time of the founding of those South Florida clubs, a man named Michael Lerner hit the scene. He had founded, along with his father and brothers, Lerner Shops, which sold women's clothes (and is now known as New York & Company), and made a mint for himself and his family. Sometime in the early 1930s, Lerner decided he'd had enough of the corporate life and went fishing, primarily for big pelagic fish, like tuna and marlin. He traveled on months-long expeditions for the American Museum of Natural History, catching fish and collecting scientific data. In 1939, he decided he wanted to codify that data—and the size of the fish he was catching—so he founded the International Game Fish Association (IGFA), which was initially housed in the upstairs offices of the American Museum of Natural History.* The IGFA, in its first four decades of existence, didn't bother with fly-fishing records. But that changed in the late 1970s, thanks to a man named Mark Sosin and his fear of getting sued into oblivion.

∞

In the early 1960s, "back when people looked at you like you were crazy if you fished in saltwater with a fly," says Sosin, the idea for a nationwide saltwater-fishing club was proposed by a tackle store owner from the northern New Jersey coast named Elwood "Cap" Colvin. The group, which would call itself the Saltwater Fly Rodders of America, had its inaugural meeting—which included the likes of Joe Brooks, Lee Wulff, and Charley Waterman—in 1965. During the meeting, Sosin, the rare

---

* Hemingway was one of the organization's first vice presidents, a post he'd later vacate because he didn't do much more than bitch about his fellow members and their angling abilities.

outdoor writer who had a degree from the Wharton School of the University of Pennsylvania, suggested that the group come up with rules and keep records. "They said, 'That's a marvelous idea, why don't you do it?'" says Sosin. "That's the last idea I ever had."

Sosin spent a year collecting information, which included talking to the South Florida clubs. And in April 1966, the rules and records of the Saltwater Fly Rodders of America were officially published. Sosin ran that side of the organization for many years until he ran into a problem. "I had to disqualify the records of two millionaires for cheating," he says. "One of them had used a bucktail [a conventional lure] on a fly rod and claimed she'd been fly fishing. I was in my thirties and had two young boys. It dawned on me one day that if one of these folks ever wanted to ruin my life, all they had to do was call their lawyer."

So, in 1978, Sosin invited Elwood Harry, who ran the IGFA at the time, to lunch. "I said, 'I have a deal for you. You need to start keeping saltwater fly fishing records, and I'm going to give them to you,'" says Sosin. And he did. That same year, the IGFA also collected all of the salt- and freshwater records from *Field & Stream* magazine[*] and truly became the world's authority on fishing records of all kinds.

The world-record application has morphed over the years, but these days the IGFA requires a membership, the weighing of the fish on a certified scale, the tippet that was used for the catch, pictures, witness testimony (if available), and a signed affidavit by a notary who attests that the information in the application isn't falsified. The process, as involved as it is, hasn't stopped some anglers from trying to deceive their way to a world record. The largemouth-bass world record has been a recurrent target for conmen and conwomen.[**] In recent years, one angler's application for a tarpon fly-fishing world record was tossed—along with the applicant from the IGFA—for submitting a different, and smaller, tippet than the one he actually used (he was ratted out by his friends). Jason

---

[*] Those records had been meticulously kept by a woman named Mary Ball, who went by the name "Mike" Ball on the magazine's masthead.

[**] These men and women are known, collectively, as "bassholes."

Schratwieser, the head of the IGFA and its longtime conservation director, has, in recent years, been in charge of testing tippets on the organization's Instron tensile machine (plenty of world records are disqualified when a submitted tippet "over-tests" to a heavier weight). He says the organization does all it can to prevent cheating, but "at the end of the day, a lot of this process is predicated on angler integrity."

For fly fishing for tarpon, the IGFA—which now has around eight thousand members—has what's known as tippet classes. A quick note on these, because they are complicated unless you are *waaaay* into it. The basic tippet classes for fly fishing are two-, four-, six-, eight-, twelve-, sixteen-, and twenty-pound tests (the "test" is the breaking strength), and there are records in each of these categories. In 1998, women saltwater anglers got their own set of records, in an attempt to get more people involved in the IGFA. An angler must have at least fifteen inches of tippet (measured inside of the connecting knots) and no more than twelve inches of shock tippet in his or her leader. With its myriad complicated knots, like the Bimini Twist, the Huffnagle, the nail, and the Rizzuto, a tarpon leader is a beautiful, mysterious thing that is very difficult to master.

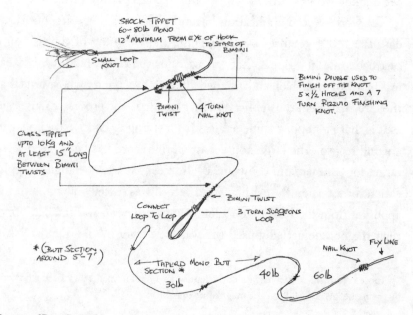

Courtesy of Dean Butler

The tippet classes have shifted all over the place in the past decades. There was once a ten-pound class. There was also once a fifteen-pound class. These are no longer, and some of those records were shifted to the appropriate higher classes if they qualified. Making it all even more complicated, the tippet classes are officially recorded in kilograms, which means the sixteen-pound class, which is officially eight kilograms, has an actual breaking strength of 17.6 pounds.

But forget all of this. Erase it from your mind. For our purposes, we will concentrate mainly on the twelve-pound (remember, the original heaviest tippet), the sixteen-pound, and the twenty-pound classes, with some mentions of the eight-pound class.

All of this is to say that around the time that Evans and Huff started seriously considering, and then going after, the world-record tarpon, record fever was in the air. Suddenly, more and more anglers on the water were aware of the world records, and there was recognition—a mix of admiration and jealousy—among the peers of the holders of those records. In freshwater, the large mouth-bass world record was the most hallowed one. For fly anglers, that designation quickly became the tarpon. In 1976, a Canadian angler fishing near Islamorada landed a 170-pound tarpon. Given the outlier size of that fish, that world record seemed like an impossible one to top.

In late May 1976, seven years into their partnership, Evans and Huff were fishing in the Keys, using Huff's house in Marathon as their base camp. They were nearing the end of a 45-days-straight run, and the fishing had been decent but unspectacular, and they certainly hadn't seen any tarpon that would have come close to the record. And then a tropical depression hit, complete with gobs of rain and wind, and the two men were forced off the water for two days. Restless, Huff mentioned to Evans a spot up on the west coast of Florida, this little commercial fishing town with an odd name that supposedly had a run of some absolutely giant tarpon. "I'd never heard of Homosassa, but we had nothing going on in the Keys," says Evans.

So they packed up Huff's station wagon, trailered the boat, and drove a miserable nine hours upstate, through the rain and wind, with no idea of what they would find when they got there.

The tropical low hung over Homosassa, too, so for the next few days, Evans and Huff were confined to a room in the only real motel in the area, the Riverside Villas, on the banks of the Homosassa River. They fiddled with fly lines and leaders and tied flies. They read books, including *The Eiger Sanction*, an espionage/murder mystery in which a trained assassin is contracted to climb the imposing Eigerwald and "sanction" (that is, murder) a man who is a national security threat while, of course, spending a decent amount of time drinking beer and sleeping with beautiful, coquettish women.

At some point, Evans and Huff decided that though the Gulf was still rough and the light still poor, they couldn't stand the inaction for one more moment. In Huff's skiff, they ventured out, navigating the six and a half miles from the Riverside to the mouth of the Homosassa River, where they were greeted by nauseatingly large swells in a Homeric "wine-dark sea." They steered south, where they found the slightest of wave breaks between two rock piles. They anchored the boat in three places—from the stern and bow and middle—but it still heaved to-and-fro. They called the spot the Eiger Rocks, after the thriller they'd read in the hotel room.

And then they saw them arcing through the waves. Tarpon. Almost too large to believe. Evans says that in the odd light emanating from the bruised sky, the fish took on an ethereal golden hue. It was an atmospheric condition he'd never seen before and hasn't seen since. The tarpon made a hissing sound as they swam and rolled past. Only one group of fish came within range of the anchored boat. Evans made a cast, stripped his fly once, and felt a convincing pull. The fish leapt. The hook dropped out of its mouth. The incident took all of five seconds. Both men had trouble sleeping that night. By morning the front had lifted.

∾

And here's where things get a little tricky, from a storytelling point of view, anyway. The end of Evans and Huff's 1976 trip and the beginning of their 1977 trip are recalled differently by each man. These types of diverging memories happen more often than we'd like to admit. We age. We conflate. We tend to stick up for our favorite recollections. "History is that certainty produced at the point where the imperfections of memory meet the inadequacies of documentation," says the main character of the Julian Barnes novel *The Sense of an Ending*. In fairness to both Evans and Huff, I've indicated where their memories differ.

After seeing the golden tarpon in 1976, Huff says they left because they were expected back in the Keys. Evans remembers that they went out again the next day, back to the Eiger Rocks, and sat there for hours without seeing a thing. Evans says Huff lifted the anchor and began to pole the giant flat, which would become known as Oklahoma. At an average of six to eight feet, the water was deeper than the typical Keys flat by about double. The depth made the poling difficult, but Huff went for miles. They were out until nightfall. They never saw a fish. Evans says they left Homosassa the next day to return to the Keys to participate in a tournament (they were well-known enough at this point to have at least a few people place bets on them in the Calcutta).

What they both remember about the end of the 1976 trip is that they kept their mouths shut about what they'd seen in Homosassa. They'd found their fish. And their lives would never be the same.

∾

In 1977, Huff met Evans in Homosassa, at the Riverside, in the beginning of May. Evans had booked him for a month. The trip did not get off to a good start. After their first day on the water, Evans received the news that his father's second wife, Josephine, had committed suicide at their Virginia horse farm in a rather gruesome manner—after three attempts to shoot herself in the head with a shotgun, she shot herself in the neck and bled out all evening, not expiring until the following morning. Evans flew up to Virginia one morning a few days later for the funeral and flew back to Homosassa that same evening. And then a cold front shut down the fishing.

Huff says that after Evans returned from Virginia, the fish still hadn't shown up. "We went out for ten days straight," Huff says. "We'd pole around all morning, have our lunch, and then pole around a bit more. We didn't see a thing in those ten days. But we weren't leaving. Not after what we'd seen the year before."

Huff says Evans began to get antsy. "We need to get in the plane," Evans said. They went back to the dock and then to the airport in nearby Crystal River. In Evans's Piper Aztec, they flew low, looking down over the flat, brightened to clarity by the sun and the white sand on the sea floor.

"Tom, is that what I think it is?" Huff asked. He pointed down to a string of moving objects, which looked like a giant unhooked necklace of fat, black pearls.

"My God," Evans said. Below them, streaming over the flats, were tarpon, in groups of one hundred to two hundred per string.

"How fast can you get this plane down?" Huff asked Evans.

And then, as they were eating lunch on the water the next day, Huff thought he saw a tarpon roll a hundred yards away. "We poled over, and there were fifty fish just lying there," Huff says. "And then they began pouring in. And all the friggin' things were giants. We thought every one of them was two hundred pounds compared to what we'd seen in the Keys. They were in strings and in daisy chains, just swimming. We saw one giant school of tarpon, of probably a thousand fish, that broke into five different daisy chains, looking like the old Ballantine Beer label. And we had fishing so extraordinary that you couldn't even begin to describe it."

Evans doesn't remember the airplane, though he was a pilot at the time. He does remember that they enjoyed fabulous fishing during those three weeks in Homosassa. Or, at least, fabulous hooking. "We broke everything—rods, lines, hooks. Everything was getting destroyed," he says. "We'd never hooked tarpon that big." The average size of the fish they hooked was around 120 pounds, they guessed, but the size went up to 180 pounds. Every one of the fish felt like a new milestone. "Tarpon are like humans. Most are within a size range. But every once in a while, you get an outlier, some sort of glandular mutant, like the guy they have to get out of the house with a backhoe," says Huff. "Homosassa happened to have a lot of those guys." They managed to land a few fish, with Huff, of course, insisting that Evans bring even the smaller ones to the boat.

On the twenty-fourth of that month, Huff caught his 186-pounder while Evans was hanging off the back of the boat. One week later, on Memorial Day, Evans and Huff started the day at what's known as "Black Rock," an area north of the giant flat, and a part of the channel of the Chassahowitzka River, which empties into Homosassa Bay. As the name indicates, the area had a dark, rocky bottom. Evans and Huff had figured out by then that Black Rock was, for whatever reason, the place where the tarpon all congregated, spent the night, and stayed until mid-morning, when they would leave to swim south to the flat. Evans, the great nick-namer, took to calling the place "the Cock Hole" (for the male tarpon that overnighted there, which are sometimes referred to as "cocks").

That morning, in the space of just a few hours, Evans hooked fifteen tarpon. One of them jumped so high in the air that it appeared to clear the pale moon that was sinking over the Gulf. ("The poon that jumped over the moon," he called it, "poon" being a tarpon.) Evans got six of those fish to the boat, all of which were more than 140 pounds, an astounding morning of tarpon fishing. By the time the fish started to move south to the flat, Evans says, "we'd emptied the fly box." He had one fly left (the others had been broken off by fish). At 3:30 that afternoon, Evans cast to a fish swimming in a string and hooked it. It was a giant. True to form, he got the tarpon to the boat in twenty minutes. Back at the commercial fish house, they weighed the fish. The scale read 177 pounds, which was seven pounds larger than the standing record.

"We have the world record," said Huff.

"No we don't," said Evans. "You have the 186 and it's going to look like I bought you off or something."

"I made the decision myself, Tom, and I didn't enter it and I'm not going to," Huff said, for probably the tenth time.

When Evans's submission was accepted a few months later, he officially had the world record. He knew it wasn't the biggest tarpon ever landed on a fly, though. He'd seen the one that was. That fact gnawed at him almost daily for the next four years.

On both the day that Huff caught his fish and the day Evans landed his, the men had not seen another boat on the water. "We had it all to ourselves," says Huff. "We had to pole through two miles of laid-up and daisy chaining fish just to get back to the dock with Tom's fish." Evans and Huff believed that by weighing these fish—and another 162-pounder that had died on them when they'd landed it—at the commercial fish house, word wouldn't get out. "We were dumber than a post," says Evans.

At the end of their stay in Homosassa, Huff put the three giant fish—now frozen solid from being stored in the giant, commercial fish freezer—in the back of his station wagon, wrapped in shower curtains from the Riverside. He was going to have them mounted by Al Pflueger Jr.'s taxidermy shop (Huff still has the mount of the 186-pounder in his garage to this day). As Huff was driving through Islamorada, he was met by the guide Woody Sexton.

"Ho-lee fuck!" Sexton said upon seeing the fish.

Evans and Huff would never again be the only boat on the water in Homosassa.

∽

In 1977, Homosassa was not really known to the greater fly-fishing world. But the place had never exactly been a secret. You'll remember that A. W. Dimock hooked his first tarpon in the mouth of the Homosassa River in 1882, and that Grover Cleveland spent some winters fishing for tarpon there. Throughout much of the early and mid-20th century, local bait-fishing guides, though they preferred fishing for redfish, would occasionally hook a tarpon and gleefully watch their clients flail around trying to fight them. Evans and Huff weren't even the first fly fishermen to visit the area. Former guide and current boatbuilder Hal Chittum says he went to Homosassa in his late teen years and hooked a tarpon on a fly but wasn't really aware, at that age, of the significance of that find. A man named Gary Maconi started fly fishing there in the late 1960s, and invited Norman Duncan to fish with him in Homosassa in 1970. And Carl Navarre Jr. says his father, Carl Navarre Sr., the Coca-Cola bottler, and his father's guide Eddie Wightman went there in 1973.

So there were fly fishermen there, darting in and out, nibbling at the fishing. But, for whatever reason, none of these early Homosassa fly-fishing pioneers brought attention to the place. They managed to keep it a secret.[*]

The first real blast of attention for the Homosassa fishery would come from none other than Lefty Kreh.

In 1973, Kreh left his position as the head of the MET to take a job as the outdoor writer for the *St. Petersburg Times*. At that time, the Homosassa fishery was primarily the province of three men: Harold LeMaster and Kirk Smith, the duo who founded and ran the L&S Lure Company outside Tampa, and their friend, a doctor named Dee Mitchell.

The L&S Lure Company was best known for its fishing plug, called the MirrorLure. LeMaster and Smith, using spinning gear and said plugs, mainly fished for tarpon near Tampa, close to their office. One day, though, when the fishing was no good in their spot, they decided to do some exploring and rode north. When they got to the town of Bayport, at the southern end of Homosassa Bay, they started seeing giant tarpon. They couldn't believe what they'd found. The spot became their shared secret. They eventually brought Mitchell into the fold, and for years they pretty much had the place and its extraordinary tarpon to themselves.

All fishermen are liars, as the saying goes, and that's likely true to some extent. But it's also sometimes the case that fishermen are the most foolish

---

[*] Maconi and Duncan once believed that they had hooked the world-record tarpon by Pine Island, a spot on the Oklahoma flat. They let the fish go, but they had decided that had they entered it, they were going to claim that it had been caught at the Pine Island near Tampa, which was two hundred miles to the south.

of truth-tellers. They discover a new spot, a secret place that teems with fish, and they find that they just *have* to tell someone else. It's human nature. People like to brag, to tell others of their good fortune. It's also a bit like the tree falling in the forest with no one around to see it, that philosophical thought experiment about reality. They want the place to *exist*.

When Kreh moved to the Tampa area to take the newspaper job, LeMaster and Smith invited him to fish with them in their special spot. To their credit, they did ask Kreh to keep Homosassa and its fish a secret. To their debit, they were pretty naïve about whom they were talking to. Kreh was the mouthpiece of the fly-fishing industry. For him, information was currency. It was his job, in fact, to spread the word and promote good fishing. "I knew never to tell Lefty a damn thing," says Huff.

Kreh went out with LeMaster and Smith and took along a fly rod. He hooked and landed a massive tarpon. There is a picture of Kreh standing next to LeMaster while holding this fish. One can see the exertion on Kreh's face and almost hear the expelled breath whistling through the gap in his upper front teeth.

And a short while later, on May 25, 1973, an article appeared in the *St. Petersburg Times*, authored by Kreh, about some big tarpon in Homosassa Bay. It wasn't a huge story, but it was enough. To be sure, tarpon fishing off the coast of Homosassa had been mentioned in local papers for years before then. But they were mostly tiny stories, and none of them had been written by someone as famous as Kreh. Kreh also told a few influential people about the fishery. He told Apte about it, and he was the one who clued in Carl Navarre Sr., mentioning it to him as a thank-you for the many years of Coca-Cola's sponsorship of the MET tournament.

The not-totally-secret place was no longer a secret. And yet, Kreh's article didn't immediately bring in hordes of anglers. This was the pre-internet age. Local news, even in a big paper like the *St. Petersburg Times*, was just that: local. It took some time for word to spread beyond southwestern Florida. And Kreh wasn't the only vector of information about Homosassa, anyway. Another was Norman Duncan, who also, in the end—and quite understandably—couldn't keep the lid on it. That Kreh and Duncan were mortal enemies adds another layer to this. Duncan has long accused Kreh—online and in a torrent of letters to the editors of many magazines—of stealing a fly pattern of his and renaming it the Lefty's Deceiver. That multiuse fly helped establish Kreh as a fly-fishing star and even ended up on a U.S. Postal Service stamp. Kreh vehemently denied the accusation until his death in 2018 at the age of ninety-three. This sort of thing—accusations of people stealing fly patterns or ideas—happens all the time in the hyper-derivative world of fly fishing.[*]

One morning in 1975, when Duncan was doing some engineering work on the old Seven-Mile Bridge near Marathon, he went to a restaurant named Ted and Mary's (now the Wooden Spoon) for breakfast. There, he ran into two fishing friends, Huff and a guide named Dale Perez. Huff and Perez mentioned to Duncan that they'd heard that a man named Ray Donnersberger, a Chicago businessman who fished for tarpon in the Keys, had had a trip planned to a place called Homosassa, but the trip had been canceled by weather. They wanted to know if Duncan knew anything about the trip or the place, which neither of them had heard of.

"I've been there," Duncan said. "And I have pictures."

Duncan went out to his car in the parking lot and retrieved some photos of massive tarpon he'd caught in Homosassa.

"Their jaws dropped to the floor when they saw them," Duncan says.

Huff would first go up the following year with Evans, chasing the fish in those pictures. Perez wouldn't be too far behind. Word was out. And just a few years later, Homosassa would be buzzing.

---

[*] Actually, it happens everywhere. New inventions are rarely the product of a single person, as the sociologist Robert K. Merton has argued. There are many instances, in fact, when they happen simultaneously. Charles Darwin and Alfred Russel Wallace thought of natural selection at roughly the same time. Gottfried Wilhelm Leibniz and Isaac Newton argued until their respective deaths about which one of them had invented calculus.

INTERLUDE 1
MORAL EXAM

Back in the day—even up to the early 1990s—the killing of any fish that you caught, even ones you did not intend to eat, was completely condoned, if not encouraged. Hanging up fish at the dock after fishing was a simple way of doing the math on the day's catch, of displaying prowess and of avoiding lies.

Those attitudes have changed, and there is much less senseless killing of fish these days. We have more knowledge and data now. We are mindful of finite resources.

And yet, the central problem with tarpon when it comes to world records is that, in order to submit one, the fish must be killed. With other species, like largemouth bass or trout, the killing of the fish can be avoided—smaller fish can be kept alive in the water or in a livewell on a boat, weighed on land (as per the IGFA rules), and then returned to the water. A tarpon is simply too big to weigh on land and then be safely returned to the water. All world-record tarpon die, and none of them are eaten (tarpon are not considered to be an edible fish by most people in North America).

So the question we must confront before we go any further into this feverish chase for the world-record tarpon is this: Is it ethical or moral to kill an animal for a world record, especially an animal that one does not intend to eat?

The simple, quick answer for me is no. But it is a complicated issue if you take a little time to delve in.

If you're a tarpon, the good news these days is that government agencies have put some of these more modern sentiments into law. The Florida Fish and Wildlife Commission (FWC) made tarpon officially a "catch-and-release" species in 2013, recognizing the fish's worth to the state's economy and, perhaps, recognizing the pointlessness of killing them. Anglers are not even allowed to bring any tarpon of more than forty inches into a boat, for doing so is sometimes fatal to the fish.

The FWC did include an exception to that law: if you want to target an IGFA world-record tarpon, you can buy one tag per season for that purpose. But even within this exception, there is a reflection of popular attitudes about killing tarpon: the number of tags the FWC has issued per season has dropped from seventy-seven in 2013 to forty-three in 2019, and most tags go unused these days.

∽

Despite the popular attitudes, there are complications with this issue. The first has nothing to do with ethics or morality: killing a tarpon for a world record is still a legal right. The second is that fishing, whether it's catch-and-kill or catch-and-release, remains a blood sport. Catch-and-release fishing is, for many, a blind behind which one can hide, or not think about, what one is actually doing, a bit like buying meat from the grocery store without a thought about the slaughterhouse it came from. It can provide a false sense of moral superiority. No fish wants to be hooked, played with, and then released. A hooked and played tarpon, whether it's released after twenty minutes or two hours, is not a happy tarpon. "You wreck a fish's day either way," as Huff puts it.

It must be noted, too, that there is a lot of unintentional killing that goes on with catch-and-release fishing. A landed tarpon, or even one that is not landed but played for an extended duration of time, is a weakened tarpon. Released tarpon are savaged and killed by sharks all the time, and some just die from being overstressed. Is fighting and releasing a tarpon that much morally cleaner than killing it? Evans, in his fifty-one years of fishing for tarpon, has intentionally killed around fifteen tarpon. He has certainly unintentionally killed many more, but so have I, and I have released every tarpon that I've landed.

∞

So, should we fish at all? Is it a moral endeavor?

I'm biased as hell because I love to fish, but my answer is yes. The biggest reason, for me, anyway, is the giant role that fishermen play in conservation. Put simply, without fishermen, there would be fewer fish. Bonefish & Tarpon Trust (BTT), an organization started by, and consisting of, fishermen, is the world's leading conservation group when it comes to tarpon, bonefish, and permit. They fight—through science and advocacy—for an abundance of fish, clean water, and protected habitat. The IGFA also does critical conservation work, particularly when it comes to research involving pelagic species. I think it's safe to say that there would be far fewer Atlantic salmon left in North America without the advocacy work done by the angling conservation group, the Atlantic Salmon Federation. And Trout Unlimited, an organization made up of anglers, has restored ten thousand river miles in the United States since the organization's founding in 1959.

There is a paradox here that is hard to wrap your head around but is nonetheless true (again, for me, anyway): those most apt to fish are those most apt to work hard to save said fish. (This holds true for true hunters—and not those who do "canned hunts"—and their game, too.) It is, in some way, a natural relationship between predator and prey. "We protect what we love," Aldo Leopold supposedly once said. In an ideal world, we wouldn't need anglers and hunters to preserve our fish and game and the habitats in which they live. We'd do it because it's simply the right thing to do. But, I think you'll agree, we don't live in an ideal world.

∞

No matter where you fall on the "kill or no kill" spectrum, one thing is for sure: Evans and his world-record-chasing cohorts are not the real problem that tarpon face these days, anyway. There is still some commercial harvest of tarpon in Brazil and Mexico, and it is likely that some of those Mexican fish are part of the population that visits the Florida coast each year. Though almost all tarpon tournaments have moved to a strictly catch-and-release format, there is a popular one in Louisiana, the International Grand Isle Tarpon Rodeo, which still allows the killing of tarpon. A tournament that's held annually in the Boca Grande Pass, while nominally catch-and-release, has killed hundreds of tarpon over the years.

That pass is controversial for more reasons than just the tournament, though. It happens to be a place where tarpon congregate, a pre-spawning staging area (it's like a much bigger Black Rock at Homosassa).* During the height of the tarpon season each year, the pass is mobbed with boats and anglers, and hundreds, if not thousands, of tarpon are caught on bait and conventional tackle. Those fish are all (supposed to be) released, which means they have around a 90 percent chance of survival, according to the BTT. But that percentage drops drastically when there are sharks in the area. And there are days when sharks show up in the pass by the legions. "You can hook and release twelve fish during those days and all twelve of them will be eaten by sharks," says Aaron Adams, the BTT's director of science and conservation. That can mean that up to, say, three hundred tarpon are killed a day when a lot of sharks are around. With an estimated twenty-two thousand tarpon that congregate in the pass at any given time during the season, losing three hundred a day has an impact on the population and, given that this has been happening for a long time now, perhaps a significant one.**

---

* It is believed that many of the Homosassa tarpon spend some time in the Boca Grande Pass.

** There are many anglers and conservationists who strongly believe that the Boca Grande Pass should be declared a sanctuary for these pre-spawn tarpon, and that the fish should be left alone and fished only when the tarpon venture out of the pass to the backcountry or ocean. A similar argument could be made for Black Rock at Homosassa, as well.

But even all of that killing pales in comparison to the biggest issue facing the tarpon population as a whole, which is habitat loss. This problem is intertwined with many other issues affecting Florida and the rest of the world. Tarpon need brackish backwaters for rearing habitat. But Florida's freshwater reserves have been severely depleted by development and golf courses and agriculture. At the same time, sea levels have risen. This one-two punch has led to far saltier backwaters. That, combined with rampant coastal development, has killed off mangroves, to the point where the state now has half of its historical count of these shrubs, which happen to be an integral part of the coastal ecosystem and juvenile tarpon habitat. "The overall population of tarpon will never be as big as it once was because of this habitat loss. We've lost entire year classes of tarpon," says Adams. "If we don't reverse the course of habitat loss, it makes every other measure we take rather pointless."

∞

All of that said, there is a fundamental question for the world-record chasers: Why intentionally kill any tarpon?

The issue was complicated, too, for the most notable of our earliest tarpon scribes. Near the end of *The Book Of The Tarpon*, Dimock advises, "Don't carry a gaff. Don't murder your game. To object to taking a tarpon for mounting or other rational purposes would be fanatical, but wantonly to slay the beautiful, harmless creatures that have contributed to your pleasure is not only cruel, but is unfair to your fellow sportsmen."

It's a nice sentiment, one that was well ahead of its time. It's also full of baloney, for Dimock gaffs a good number of tarpon in the tales he tells in his book. Perhaps he believed those killings were done for "other rational purposes"?

In the end, we are left with something that's likely unsatisfying: the question about intentionally killing tarpon, as well as the moral questions around catch-and-release angling, are ones that every individual angler must ask of, and answer for, him- or herself.

6

CHARACTER SKETCHES

By 1978, all of the players were in place in Homosassa . . .

Stu Apte was born in Miami on Mother's Day in 1930. He pronounces the name of his hometown as "My-am-uh," in the same way that Pallot does. Apte's voice is, at once, deep *and* nasally—almost like he has a persistent head cold—which provides it with a peculiar sort of authority, one he has earned and one he is unafraid to let you know about.

Apte's parents moved to Miami from New York City. His father was in the produce business until he took up a side hustle gambling on the ponies, which ultimately cost him his livelihood. Apte's mother took to doing the majority of the raising of her son. Apte boxed a bit in high school. He went to the University of Miami and then into the military, where he became a fighter pilot. Though he was on active duty during the Korean War, and says he was "gung-ho to get over there," he never left the training base in Virginia and didn't see any action. After his military service, he became a commercial pilot for Pan American World Airways.

Apte, now ninety, is the hub from which all of the spokes on the tarpon fly-fishing wheel emanate. He knew—and knows—everyone, from the early tarpon guides, like Brothers and Albright, to the big shots of the 1970s and 1980s, like Evans, Billy Pate Jr., and Al Pflueger Jr. He also personally mentored and trained both the young man who would catch the world's largest recorded tarpon on a fly in 2001 *and* his guide. No one in the tarpon world is more than a degree or two away from Apte.

He started fly fishing in saltwater at the age of sixteen, with a three-piece, South Bend bamboo rod. Joe Brooks was among his first real fishing partners. At the age of eighteen, while in college as a zoology major, Apte routinely cut his botany labs to go snook fishing on the Tamiami Trail. He was driving home on one of those days when he saw "this big dude casting a fly," he says. He pulled his car to the side of the road, got out, and asked the man if he was having any luck with the snook. The big dude ignored him. Apte asked a second time and was again ignored. After the third try, the big dude finally turned to him.

"WHAT DO YOU KNOW ABOUT CATCHING SNOOK, BUSH?"

"I know enough that I caught three fifteen-pounders this morning," Apte replied.

The big dude reeled up and walked over.

"YOU'RE NOT BULLSHITTING ME, ARE YOU, BUSH?"

Apte told him he was not bullshitting him, and they chatted a bit and then fished together the next morning. The big dude, who had a pretty cast, fished well. After the tide ran out and the fishing slowed down, the big dude wrote down his name and number on a piece of paper and gave it to Apte. "I don't follow spectator sports, and had no idea who this guy was until a friend told me later," says Apte. And that's how Stu Apte and baseball immortal Ted Williams became fishing buddies.

Apte started guiding in the Keys after he was laid off by Pan Am in 1956. He was later rehired by Pan Am, and then laid off again, but by 1960, he had a house in Little Torch Key and was fishing and guiding full-time.

Well, almost full-time. Much of this era in his life is detailed in his autobiography, *Of Wind and Tides*, which is really the story of Apte's aptitude for the three F's: Fishing, Flying, and, to put it rather indelicately, Fucking. There are pictures of a young Apte in the book. He is indeed quite studly—wiry with muscular forearms. In some of the photos, he sports a tightly trimmed mustache, which he wears to this day, one that seems ironed onto his upper lip. He tells stories of his fishing exploits and his flying career. And he talks about the many flight attendants who took their layovers at his love shack in Little Torch. He writes that he was "scoring like Shaquille O'Neal at a basketball dunking contest . . . surrounded with never-ending groups of lovely ladies, coming down to visit whenever they so desired."

Modesty has never been Apte's strong suit. "Stu does not possess one molecule of humility," says the guide Harry Spear. Adds Sandy Moret, angler and owner of a fly shop in Islamorada, "Stu's very easy with a good story about himself." Apte was not pleasant to fish with, stressful even, as Valdène has noted. He was aggressive and pushy and a constant yeller. For many years, he had an RV that had an enormous picture of his face on the side, under which was written, in large letters, STU APTE, WORLD'S GREATEST FLY FISHERMAN. He drove that RV from the Keys to Montana and back every year, and he used to park it in front of his home in Islamorada.

But as Dizzy Dean supposedly once noted, "It ain't braggin' if you can back it up." Apte is the real deal, to some the best pure tarpon fly angler who ever lived. "He was a predator," says Moret. "People used to gather at the dock to watch him launch his boat." Much of his aggressiveness and self-promotion were rooted in his hard work and perfectionism. He spent his nights rigging his tackle, tying and re-tying knots until he got them just right. "There are knots, and then there are Stu's knots," says Doug Kelly, an outdoor writer from Florida who knows Apte well. Apte once wrote that he "caught most of his fish before he went fishing." He had all sorts of little rules that he followed, about how best to approach a fish and where and when to cast. One of his flies, the orange-hackled Apte Tarpon Fly, appeared on a US Postal Service stamp (like Kreh's). He pioneered a method of fighting big tarpon that is still used by some today, something called "down and dirty," in which he keeps the rod low to the water and uses the butt of it to "program" the fish, as he called it, taking control of the fight with leverage and his strong forearms. He was the master of now legendary spots Coupon Bight and Loggerhead for many years, having had them pretty much to himself. He once poled

onto a flat near Loggerhead to within earshot of another boat, helmed
by someone he didn't know. He staked off and started jawing at the man
in the other boat, telling him how to fish the flat and pointing out all
the things he was doing wrong. The man listened for a while and then
grew impatient and yelled back, "Who do you think you are, Stu Apte?"

"Well . . ."

In May 1961, he was fishing in the Keys with Joe Brooks when Brooks
hooked a big tarpon. As Brooks got the fish close to the boat after a two-
hour fight, Apte gaffed it. The tarpon pulled and Apte went flying into the
water "like a pole-vaulter," he says, still attached to the fish. The tarpon
came loose, and Apte, chest-deep in the water, gaffed it again. The fish
weighed 148 pounds, 8 ounces, the biggest tarpon ever landed on a fly.
That record stood until 1967, when Apte broke it with the 151-pound
tarpon he landed in the Keys while fishing with Valdène. He broke his
own record, again in the Keys, with a 154-pounder in 1971.

When Apte arrived in Homosassa in 1978, he was nearing the age of
fifty but was still very much in his prime as an angler.

∞

Ted Williams, the baseball player and wartime fighter pilot, started
fishing for tarpon in 1947. He would routinely arrive early for the Red Sox
spring training camp in Sarasota so he could get in some fishing. During
camp, he sometimes snuck away and went down to Miami and the Keys
for more fishing. He also fished while doing his fighter pilot training
in Florida. It turned out that his 20/10 vision, incredible quick-twitch
coordination, uncanny patience, and insatiable drive translated very well
to fly fishing on the flats. In his boat, he would stand on his fly box,
rod in hand, eyeing the water and waiting for the fish, just as he had
once stood in the batter's box. *Sports Illustrated* deemed him "an expert
fisherman—maybe the most expert of our time." Even accounting for
some inevitable hyperbole, it's very possible that at different times in his
life, Williams could have been considered the best hitter, fighter pilot,
and saltwater fly fisherman alive.

Williams was deeply loved by his closest friends. But he was also a needler, a perfectionist and competitive to the point of absurdity. He once challenged former guide Hal Chittum to a distance-casting competition. When it appeared that Chittum was about to make the cast that would beat his, Williams tackled him. Like Apte, Williams wasn't shy about letting the world know about his prowess on the water. A clubhouse trainer who overheard him claim to be the best fisherman in the world challenged him on the spot, offering that God was probably better.

"ALL RIGHT," Williams supposedly said. "I'LL GIVE YOU THAT ONE."

He bought a place in Islamorada in 1952 and lived there for the next thirty-six years. Williams liked to fish by himself, but he would occasionally hire Albright, Brothers, or George Hommell to guide him. After he retired from baseball in 1960, his life became subsumed with fishing, mainly for what he deemed the "big three": Atlantic salmon, bonefish, and tarpon. The latter fish, which he called "the silver king," became his greatest fishing obsession. He helped found the Gold Cup tarpon tournament in 1964 and won the event the following year and again in 1967.

He heard of the giant tarpon in Homosassa in the late 1970s and traveled up there with the Islamorada guide Gary Ellis. He was smitten with the place and its fishing at first, getting so into it that he demanded that he and Ellis "ONLY EAT WHAT THE GODDAMN TARPON EAT"—that is, mullet, crabs, and shrimp—so as to get in sync with the species.

In Homosassa, Williams also fished with a guide named "Fearless" Freddie Archibald. On the surface, the two men seemed like a hilariously mismatched pair. Williams was high-strung, impatient, loud, profane, full of kinetic energy, and very confrontational, especially when he drank, which he did with increasing frequency after he retired from baseball. He was conservative of dress and mind.

Archibald lived in the Tampa area. He was of medium height and build, with long, dishwater blonde hair and an unruly mustache that seemed to join an equally unruly set of sideburns on his face. He was a total hippie, a holdover from the McGuane/Harrison era in Key West.

He loved to smoke marijuana and grew some of it in the backseat of a broken-down car with a hole in its roof that sat in his backyard. "You could always tell when you were downwind of Freddie," says Earle Waters, a Homosassa guide. Archibald never wore shoes, not even to funerals. He painted both his push pole and his tarpon boat in psychedelic purple and white. He was a bit of a lazy guide, preferring to stake his boat out, smoke some weed, and wait for the fish to come to him, instead of poling around. Williams adored Archibald, and the feeling was mutual.

One year, Williams went up to Homosassa in late April. The tarpon weren't in yet—they usually didn't start swimming there until May. Williams began to get a little bored. He learned that Evans and Huff were also in Homosassa at the time, also hoping to run into some early fish. Williams asked if he could tag along with them for a few days. They said yes, of course.

When Williams first stepped onto Huff's boat, he immediately started peppering Evans and Huff with questions about tarpon fishing, about their gear, how they cast to fish in a daisy chain, the best way to fight a fish. When he finally paused, Evans asked Williams a question about baseball. "I couldn't help it," says Evans. "I was going fishing with one of my idols."

"YOU DON'T KNOW SHIT ABOUT BASEBALL, BUSH," was William's response.

"Well, it appears you don't know shit about catching big tarpon," Evans replied. Five seconds of uncomfortable silence passed. And then Williams let out a big laugh. "We got along great after that," says Evans. They didn't see any fish, but Williams never stopped pumping Evans and Huff for information, and Evans and Huff marveled at his graceful casts. "One of the prettiest casting strokes I've ever seen, maybe the prettiest," says Evans. "Right up there with Flip."

One evening after they got off the water, Williams told Evans and Huff that he was taking them to dinner in Crystal River. He picked them up later that night at the Riverside in his station wagon. They got in the back. Archibald was riding shotgun. Williams had a big white Styrofoam cup between his legs, filled with some sort of brown liquor on ice. His left elbow was cocked outside the window. His right arm reached across the back of Archibald's headrest. Williams was talkative, happy. When he took a sip of his drink, he held the steering wheel with his knees. On a long, straight stretch of road, a car approached on the other side with its high beams on. Williams flipped his lights from low to high and back again, the universal signal to an oncoming driver to turn off the brights. It had no effect. So Williams began to flick his lights maniacally, but that didn't have any effect, either. Then, much to the surprise and horror of Evans and Huff, Williams flicked his high beams on for good and swerved into the oncoming lane and sped up, heading straight for the other car. The person in the other car finally got the hint and dimmed the lights. Williams then eased back into the proper lane. "TAKE THAT, YOU MOTHERFUCKING SHITBIRD," Williams said as the car passed, then laughed and calmly took a sip of his drink. Archibald never moved a muscle.

Williams would tire of the Homosassa scene rather quickly. He didn't like the crowds that started to build there, so he stopped going. He preferred the Keys and his solitude.

He would, however, come back. In 1988, at the age of seventy, he moved to Crystal River, which was ten miles from the town of Homosassa, living in and becoming the spokesperson for a brand-new housing development—one of many like it that popped up in the area over the years—called the Villages of Citrus Hills. He fished for tarpon occasionally with a man named Ted Johnston, who sold him both of the houses he would live in at Citrus Hills, up until nearly 2000. But by then, the great era in Homosassa had passed. Williams died in Crystal River in 2002, at the age of eighty-three, setting off his bizarre posthumous period, with the very public dispute among his children about his final wishes, which ended up with his head being detached from his body and cryogenically frozen and sent to a facility in Arizona.

Archibald would go on to design a flats skiff, called the "Shipoke," which was ahead of its time in terms of weight and the way it handled. He tied his own flies from his own material, going to cockfights in New Orleans and returning with the capes of the losing birds. One year in

Homosassa, the color black for tarpon flies was all the rage, and everyone had run out of black fly tying material.* Archibald and a friend spotted a hairy black dog in the parking lot of a fast-food restaurant. His friend bought some French fries and fed the dog while Archibald snipped off some of the hair on its tail. Toward the end of his life, Archibald went a little wacky. No one could tell if it was from the drugs or from the paint fumes and glue that he'd inhaled for years in his under-ventilated boatworks shop.

℘

The gentle giant of the Homosassa group was a man named Al Pflueger Jr. He is the son of Al Pflueger Sr., the famous taxidermist. He is not, as is sometimes written, related to the Pflueger family that made the iconic, eponymous fly reel. Pflueger Sr. moved to Florida from New Jersey in 1923 and started his taxidermy business near Miami. It boomed in the mid-20th century, as recreational fishing began to grow in popularity. After college at the University of Miami, Pflueger Jr. got into the business, which worked on commissions. Agents gave fishing captains order forms. Captains encouraged their sports to mount the fish they caught. If the sports obliged, the captains got 20 percent of the price, and the agents got 10 percent. Pflueger Taxidermy initially did skin mounts (that is, used the actual skin of the fish) but later started using sturdier and longer-lasting fiberglass in their taxidermy, which entailed making a mold using the measurements—and no actual part—of the fish.

The Pfluegers made fish mounts for Presidents Kennedy and Nixon. They made a mount of a 1,560-pound black marlin that resides in the Smithsonian. Pflueger Sr. died in 1962 after falling and hitting his head. His son took over the business and grew it into the biggest taxidermist in the world before selling it to the Shakespeare company in the early 1970s.

---

* Anglers and guides during that time in Homosassa routinely snipped off any flies that had worked on the water before they got to the dock, to try to keep them secret. But those secrets were usually uncovered rather swiftly. In his younger years, Al Dopirak would sniff around the boat dock at night to try to see which flies others were using.

From that point on, says Pflueger Jr., "I did a lot of things I wanted to do." Primary among them: fishing for tarpon on the fly, which he calls "the ultimate sport." He first fished in Homosassa with Apte.

Pflueger was six foot six and around 230 pounds, as big as some of the brown bears he used to taxidermy (now eighty-two, he has shrunk a bit). He was, by all accounts, very good at most things he did as an angler. He spent much of the fishing day actually sitting down in the boat, standing only when he sensed fish nearby. By his own admission, he was a good but not great caster, "but it didn't matter because of my height." (Height is a natural advantage in casting a fly because of the clearance it provides.) He was also very adept at hooking fish, at placing the fly securely in the corner of a fish's mouth by simultaneously strip-striking the line and sweeping the rod parallel to the water. What he was not good at, though, was fighting the fish, despite his prodigious size.

He would routinely take at least six to eight hours to reel in a tarpon. Once, in Homosassa, Pflueger hooked a fish at noon. He never really got a good look at the fish, as it made its sole jump only after darkness had descended. At midnight, he finally landed the fish. It weighed just a little more than one hundred pounds, a very small fish by Homosassa standards. Pflueger spent the next two days in bed unable to fish, his right hand frozen in a painful curl.

∞

Carl Navarre Sr. was a gentleman, polite and articulate. He dressed well, traveled well, and ate well. He smoked a corncob pipe while he fished. He first started getting into fly fishing for tarpon in the late 1950s when he traveled to Islamorada and fished with Hommell and Brothers. Navarre was originally from Tennessee, and would become the largest Coca-Cola bottler in South Florida. In 1967, he helped found World Wide Sportsman, the famed Islamorada tackle shop and travel agency, owning it along with Hommell and Pate. In 1976, he bought Cheeca Lodge, also in Islamorada, which was, and still is, one of the premier locations for traveling fishermen in the Keys.

With his wealth, Navarre was able to employ a number of Florida's best flats guides; Eddie Wightman, Billy Knowles, Jim Brewer, and Bill Curtis were all on his payroll at various times. Wightman was ahead of his time in terms of guiding techniques, and was someone a young Steve Huff looked up to. Knowles is a Keys legend, who is still guiding in his late seventies. Brewer died in a plane wreck while searching for tarpon in the Keys. Curtis was a pioneer, the Boss of Biscayne Bay, which he fished in a yellow skiff he called the *Grasshopper*. He had only one good eye, which may be the reason that he was always looking to innovate. In the old days, guides would sometimes stand on their motors to get a little elevation to better see the fish and to get better leverage with the push pole. Curtis wasn't quite athletic enough to do that for a full day, so he came up with a solution: he built a small platform made from plywood that he could stand on to pole and scout for fish (it was originally placed just to the side of the motor, and not on top of it). His fellow guides laughed at him when they saw it, and sarcastically congratulated him for building a fish cleaning station on the back of his skiff. But within six months, they all had poling platforms on the back of their boats, as all flats guides do today.

Navarre, as noted, was one of the first fly fishermen to venture to Homosassa, when he was in his midfifties. On his first trip there, he brought along Wightman and Curtis and his son, Carl Jr., who was then a student at Bennington College in Vermont. They discovered Black Rock with the help of a local redfisherman who had anchored up a sixty-foot boat near the area. The redfisherman complained to them that the thousands of tarpon in the hole woke him up every morning at daylight with their rolling and splashing.

One day, Navarre and his retinue figured out that the fish left Black Rock in the mid-morning and headed down to the big flat to the south. They followed them down there and "jumped fish after fish," says Navarre Jr. At the end of that day, as they were headed home, Wightman said they needed a name for the big flat. Curtis, gruff and forthright, said they'd name it Oklahoma, because "that's where I grew up and this is just like it. A big expanse of nothingness."

"Every day up there was a new discovery, a new adventure," says Navarre Jr. His father enhanced that discovery by using his helicopter, *Yellow Bird*, to scout the area for tarpon, something he also did before tarpon tournaments in the Keys until that practice was outlawed, presumably for being unfair to those competitors who didn't own helicopters. Many of Navarre's fellow anglers in Homosassa believed that the helicopter spooked fish, and Navarre, indeed, did not find as much success with it in Homosassa as he had in the Keys. But he kept at it for a while. The drill went like this: Navarre's pilot would take up one of his guides in the morning. When they found fish, they would drop buoys—sometimes the size of Clorox bottles and sometimes the size of pill bottles—in the area. When they were satisfied with their sightings, they radioed back to the ground to tell Navarre to get ready. The helicopter would land, the guide would get in the boat and launch it with Navarre onboard, and then the helicopter would take off again, leading the boat to the buoys. "We had the life," says Knowles.

Among the most colorful—and most tragic—of the hard-core record-chasers in Homosassa at the time was a man named Jimmy Lopez. His parents were wealthy socialites in Coral Gables. His father studied law but never practiced it. His mother was a champion golfer. At some point when Lopez and his brothers were young, his father found a new woman and divorced his mother, who soon afterward began to drink heavily and died, either of pneumonia or a heart attack. Around that time, Lopez's father went out on his sportfishing boat with his new wife and fell overboard and died. "The rumors were that his new wife ran over him, like a Cuisinart," says Jimmy's nephew, Kiko Lopez. A trust for Jimmy and his two brothers, who were all teenagers, to be vested when each of them reached their thirties, was left in the hands of a family friend, who was a Miami judge and supposedly invested it very well. All of the boys were known as wildmen. "Jimmy was the wildest, though," says Kiko.

Lopez was a champion diver in high school, well built, handsome, and flamboyant. "The girls loved him," says one of his former high school classmates. "They used to line up around the pool to watch him dive." While waiting for his inheritance, Lopez became a pilot for Delta. When he finally got the money, he quit that job. He bought a lime green Lincoln Continental and then a Jaguar and then a Ferrari. He did some work as a contractor in Miami and bought a share of the Seamaster reel company and invested the rest of his money, unwisely, as it turned out. But he spent most of his time fishing.

At one point, Lopez owned sixteen saltwater fly-fishing records, including ones for tuna and bonefish, and a 162-and-a-half-pound tarpon that he caught in 1974 in Islamorada.

By the time Lopez got to Homosassa in 1978, he was well known for his fishing exploits. He had dark, curly hair and a big black mustache. He was still quite the athlete, and did push-ups and sit-ups in the bow of the boat while waiting for the tarpon to show. He once fell from his boat into the water while demonstrating his devastating first serve in tennis. He was intense and competitive as hell, practicing for forty days before tarpon tournaments. He was hell on guides. "He split the sheets with every good guide he had," says Knowles, who guided him for a bit in the late 1970s and early 1980s. Hal Chittum, who also guided him for a while, says, "He was crazy, but he was also the best fly fisherman I've ever seen."

Lopez's intensity and lifestyle and poor investments, along with his obedience to the drug that defined the 1980s, would lead to a wholly spectacular flameout.

∽

And then there was Billy Pate Jr., a somewhat divisive figure who became famous largely through his exploits in Homosassa and, in turn, brought much attention to the area. He was born and raised in Greenville, South Carolina. In the 1930s, his father was a partner in a stock brokerage. During World War II, Pate Sr. worked for a company that made surgical dressings for the military, then he became the owner of the Wunda Weve carpet company, which was the first major producer to use the protectant Scotchgard and to apply antistatic chemicals to its carpets.

In the mid-1950s, Pate Sr. expressed a desire to sell the business. Pate Jr., who had graduated from Davidson College and done a short stint in the Navy, asked him to wait a month. In the interim period, he leveraged everything he had and borrowed money from friends to buy the company from his father. For the next decade, he worked twelve to fifteen hours a day building the business. In 1965, when Pate was thirty-five, he sold the carpet business to textile company Dan River, for a reported $35 million. He would later become a partner in the World Wide Sportsman store in Islamorada, help Ted Juracsik start what would become the Tibor Reel Company, and manage his own money. But really, from the point at which he sold the carpet company on, he pretty much fished for world records on the fly. He loved bonefish and Atlantic salmon. He fished for steelhead in the Pacific Northwest every year. He was the first person ever to record catching a blue marlin on the fly. Above all else, though, he loved the tarpon.

He was not very close to his father, who died in 1979 at the age of seventy-nine. Nor was he close to his sole sibling, Wallace (who was a deep-sea fisherman and an elk hunter). Pate worshipped his mother. At some point around the time his father died, his mother had what appeared to be a series of strokes, and then was diagnosed with Alzheimer's disease. Though she was uncommunicative and bedridden for the last years of her life, Pate continued to visit her with regularity and dote on her and tell her stories from a chair at her bedside, until she died in 1983.

Pate had bright blue eyes and red hair, which turned the color of rust as he aged. The hair on his forearms appeared to be long enough to warrant combing. He always wore nice clothes—collared shirts and pressed shorts—even when tarpon fishing, looking as if he was going to try to get in a quick eighteen after getting off the water. He sometimes added a wide-brimmed straw hat to the ensemble. He spoke in the mellifluous drawl of a Southern gentleman ("consid-uh," "fail-yuh"). At the age of twenty-one, he lost a kneecap in a car accident. His doctors told him that he'd never be able to bend his leg again. But Pate obsessively worked on rehabilitating his knee, which included long waterskiing sessions. One of his best waterskiing buddies was Dick Pope Jr., of Cypress Gardens, who was among the first people to ever waterski barefoot.

Pate was a bit obsessive compulsive. He arranged his clothes in his closet by color. He only ate fried chicken, grapes, and watermelon when fishing. He never ate seafood. He had a special steel gaff made for him in Australia. He almost always fished six straight days and took the seventh day off. He was fanatical about his fitness, and trained constantly for his tarpon trips. He always had a small squeeze ball around, in order to strengthen his hands and forearms. His house in Islamorada was littered with pulleys and contraptions that allowed him to get in a few quick reps, to work on his biceps or his core, as he made his way from the living room to the kitchen. He had a small trampoline on which he jumped while inhaling oxygen from a tank. His mother's decline left him spooked. He did chelation therapy, which entailed intravenously taking drugs that supposedly attached themselves to the heavy metals in the body and then were flushed out in the urine. Pate believed that this therapy could ward off Alzheimer's, though there has never been any solid scientific evidence to back this up. The entire countertop in his bathroom was covered with bottles of vitamins, and he took between twenty-five and forty of them a day.

Pate had a high overhead cast, something he'd developed as a steelheader. His casting accuracy was deadly, and when a tarpon bit, he was very aggressive with the hook-set, rearing back on his rod with five or six strong pulls. When he hooked what he considered to be a small tarpon (one that wasn't a world record, or a "rat," as he called them), he would either fight it and subdue it quickly or break it off. Things changed when he hooked a tarpon he thought might be a record. Like Pflueger, he would get tentative with big fish, thus relinquishing control of the situation. That tarpon of his that I mentioned earlier, the one he fought for twelve hours? He lost it in the middle of the night because his boat ran out of gas.

Equipment was important to Pate, and he was always looking to improve it. When Homosassa guides started using an electric motor or two on the backs of their boats to cover more water on the deep and huge Oklahoma flat, Pate doubled them up by installing four electric motors on the back of his. He tinkered with his lines, using full sinkers and shooting heads, and carrying four differently rigged rods with him on the boat. He built a massive platform near the middle of his boat that he could walk around, which was rimmed with cushioned rails he leaned on when he cast. He had pedals on the platform that allowed him to control his electric motors with his feet. "When you hit the third switch, the boat would just go," says one of his longtime guides, Lee Baker. "It nearly threw you out of the boat." The bow of Pate's boat was surrounded by a makeshift netting, which looked like a table tennis net, to catch his fly line so it wouldn't blow over the side and into the water. His fellow anglers in Homosassa referred to his boat as the "bird's nest" and the "condominium." Evans called it the "African Queen."

There was always a woman, or women, around Pate—girlfriends, wives, or mistresses. "Women were very important to Billy," says Navarre Jr. He would find many of them in the old days via classified ads in local newspapers, and later used the internet. When someone responded to an ad, Pate would bring her in for an initial look-see. If she passed the eye test, he would then put a fly rod in her hand. If she seemed adept at casting, or seemed like she could become adept, she was in. Pate did not like to fish alone in a boat, at least not early on in his career. He preferred an audience. If that audience was a pretty woman, all the better. He frequently encouraged the woman in his boat to sunbathe topless. "We all had binoculars," says Gary Merriman, a fellow Homosassa angler. Pate was married five times. His marriages had trouble for all sorts of reasons. His third wife, Patty, got tired of all the fishing, which left room for nothing else. "All he thought about was fishing. As long as you were happy looking pretty in the back of the boat, you were in heaven," she says. "Otherwise, it got old." His fourth wife, Jodi, wanted to have children. "He thought all kids were nuisances and brats," she says.

Pate was a relentless self-promoter. He used to call the local papers—the *Tampa Tribune* and the *St. Petersburg Times*—when he arrived in Homosassa for his annual five-week stay in the spring, which started in 1978.

He sometimes brought fish back to the dock to be hung and admired that were under world-record weight. He starred in an episode of ABC's *American Sportsman* that was shot in Homosassa, and also did a film with the 3M Company about tarpon fishing there. That promotion—of self and place—angered many of his fellow anglers. The fact that he was an incredible angler who broke many world records added a pinch of jealousy to the beef stew. Evans didn't much like him. He nicknamed him "Willamina Paté."

∞

And so began the golden era, the annual May gathering in Homosassa of the best fly fishermen in the world, the best guides and the most impressive specimens of the most prized gamefish on a fly, all caught up in a fever dream. It seems almost inconceivable now, this time and place and circumstance. There are better anglers around these days, with better tackle and gear and training. There are more exotic places in the world that are loaded with fish and adventure. But what makes this roughly six-year era in Homosassa, which kicked off in 1978, so unusual, if not unique, is that everyone—the anglers, the guides, the fish—was there at the same time.

There were others there, too: Dale Perez, Joe Robinson, Billy Hampton, Ralph Delph, Sandy Moret, Bill Hassett, Tom Richardson, Harry Spear, Dan Malzone, Lenny Berg, Gary Merriman, Nat Ragland, Cecil Keith, Hank Brown, Pierre Affre. There were locals (or those from nearby), like Mike Locklear, Ray DeMarco, Neil Sigvartsen, and Ronnie Richards. And there would be more who dropped in for a visit. Pallot, Fernandez, and Emery fished there a few times. Harrison, Chatham, and Valdène went up one year for a few days to see what all of the commotion was about. "I didn't care for it," says Fernandez. Valdène had almost the exact same reaction. "I didn't like it." Maybe that was because the sport, by this time, had changed. The Homosassa fish were enormous. Records had become a big deal. Competition was now the driving force behind the fishing. The number of "Juniors" in the

Homosassa group—Pflueger, Evans, Pate, Navarre—was a giveaway, a signifier that the generationally wealthy had caught on to the game, had come to play. It was no longer about fishing for fun or for some deeper meaning. The world record was the deepest the meaning got. It was no longer romantic. Or it was, but in a different way.

The place—physically, geographically—certainly had its romance. Onshore, it was still quiet and sparsely populated. There was only a handful of houses on the water, unlike the more developed Keys and Biscayne Bay. There were only a few golf courses around and none of the massive housing communities that would metastasize in the coming decades. The four main spring-fed rivers in the area still pumped hundreds of millions of gallons of freshwater into Homosassa Bay every day. "In those days you could smell the freshwater on the flat," says Dan Malzone, an angler and guide from Tampa. "It was that sweet smell, like just after a rainstorm."

The seemingly endless Oklahoma flat was bordered by the Chassahowitzka National Wildlife Refuge, twenty-five thousand acres of nothing but islands of mangrove, meadows of sawgrass and black needlegrass, and stands of oaks, red cedars, palms, and cypress trees. It gave the entire place a sense of true wilderness. These anglers and guides felt like the explorers of a new territory, and took advantage of naming various spots on the Homosassa flats, either taking cues from the natural environment or coming up with something more whimsical. Along with Oklahoma, Black Rock (or the Cock Hole, if you prefer), Eiger Rocks, Pine Island, and Chassahowitzka Point, there was the Swamp, the Railroad Tracks, Bar and Grill, Who Point, the Dilly Hole, Smith Rock, and the Racks—Bird, High, and Middle—which were remnants of old racks used by commercial fishermen once upon a time to dry their nets.* The Oklahoma flat, despite its depth, was, and remains, a treacherous place to run a boat. At lower tides, the various rock piles eat engines. You do not want a rock named after you on the Homosassa flats—it means you

---

* The U.S. military supposedly collected bird guano below these racks for chemicals used in explosives, but this is likely an apocryphal tale.

either ran into it or you're dead. Guido Rock was named for Malzone, who lost his lower unit on it. Homosassa guide John Bazo also has a rock named after him because he hit it. Pate had a rock pile named for him after he died.

∽

Evans was one of the few regulars at Homosassa who was not from South Florida, and he was the sole Yankee. He was not famous, as Apte, Pflueger, Pate, and Lopez were. He was also one of the few who had an actual nine-to-five job. He felt he was viewed as a latter-day carpetbagger, a bit like an outcast, even though he was allied with the Marathon-based Huff. And yet, early on, he and Huff were the team to beat in Homosassa.

They were on the water, idling out of the Homosassa River, every morning at 5:30. Even when other guides and anglers were up earlier, they'd often wait for Huff to leave and follow him out, because he knew how to navigate the tricky river and its mouth. Evans and Huff were nearly always the last boat in, as well, tying up close to eight at night. "It seemed like we never saw the dock in the light of day," says Evans.

Every day was an endurance test for both angler and guide. "It was an athletic event. We'd kill ourselves, torture ourselves," says Evans. "Steve never wanted to go back in until we were dead. That made him happy." They were both on their feet for around eleven hours a day. Huff learned the flat slowly and painstakingly, one plunk of the push pole at a time, pushing into the fifteen- to twenty-mile-per-hour winds that always seemed to arise in the afternoon off the Gulf. He would never start the engine if fish were around, even if he and Evans were leaving for the day. Instead, he'd pole out of the area, which sometimes added another forty-five minutes to the trip home. "The tarpon were lying around, doing their thing. This was their house. It was disrespectful to blow them out," Huff says.

They stayed out on the water even in the worst of thunderstorms— "some horrible shit," says Huff—dropping a few anchors, hitting the bilge pumps, and lying down in the bottom of the boat like Egyptian mummies as waves crashed over the bow. The lightning and the thunder would "scare the hell out of us," says Evans. But then it would inevitably pass, and the sun would come out and the water would go slick, and the tarpon would start pouring in. Evans always waited for his graphite rod to stop humming from the leftover electricity in the air before he picked it up and started fishing again.

Evans concentrated only on the biggest fish he saw on the flat, the Rocquettas. In a string of tarpon, the largest fish were usually found two to three places behind the lead fish, or maybe two or three spots from the back of the line. If the fish were in a daisy chain, he and Huff observed it for a bit and would "look for the fattest face," says Evans. When that one was identified, Evans cast the fly toward the tail of the fish directly in front of it. When he hooked a fish, he immediately fell into a trance of concentration, getting into the flow of the fish, reading its body language. If the fish was leaping or on a blistering run, he did nothing but hold on to the rod. But as soon as the fish began to slow down, Evans pounced, trying to "own the head," as he called it. He never pulled without purpose. Everything was done to keep the fish off balance. "Every fish is different. But they all tell you what to do if you pay attention. If you don't pay attention, they can easily ruin your day," says Evans.

That's because of the second, third, or fourth wind that a tarpon can get during a fight if an angler relaxes. "If you're resting, you're losing," Evans says. "If you had a fish on for two to three hours, you were wasting the day." He once had a tarpon landed, exhausted by the side of the boat after a thirty-minute fight, when a fellow Homosassa angler motored up and asked if he could use the tarpon for a film he was making. Evans said sure and handed him his rod with the fish still attached. It was 4:30 in the afternoon. At nine that night, the fellow angler showed up at a local restaurant and ran into Evans. The fish had revived and the man had fought it for another three hours and failed to land it.

In the evenings, during the first week of their trips, when they were still fresh, Evans and Huff would go for a four-mile jog after fishing, and then out to dinner. Back at the house, they would make new leaders, using a micrometer to ensure they were legal. One year, they went through six hundred yards of leader material. They tied and re-tied flies, reusing hooks from chewed-up flies.

But as the trips wore on, nerves began to fray, legs and eyelids grew heavy, and things started to go a bit sideways. They skipped the jog. Huff's hands got stuck in a clench and went totally numb from poling all day. He slept with them over the side of the bed to try to get the blood back in them, and it still took forty-five minutes in the morning to get full feeling back. His fingernails grew at an angle toward the pole, and still do to this day. (Perez, his fellow guide, had to get operations on both of his hands after years of gripping the push pole.) One evening, Evans went out to get a pizza. He came back, put the pizza on a table, and began to tie leaders as Huff tied flies on the couch. Suddenly, Evans got a cramp in his leg and pitched forward, falling onto the pizza and breaking the table in two. "Huff just sat there and didn't say a word and kept tying flies," says Evans. "There is no way humans can be civil with each other with no sleep."

Huff was demanding, on himself and on Evans. He's often said that if he ever writes an autobiography, it will be called *Just Shove It*, which works for both the poling he's done for a livelihood and his lack of patience for bullshit. He has never been a yeller, like Apte. But this was a team sport. He'd pole for forty-five minutes to get Evans in a position to cast. If Evans missed, Huff would remain quiet for half an hour, and then utter, out of nowhere, "Well, you fucked that one up." Sometimes when Evans missed badly on a cast, Huff would say, "That fly was closer to the fish *before* you cast." He poled so hard sometimes that Evans fell out of the boat and into the water. They began to call the little casting platform on Huff's boat "the launching pad."

And yet, Evans loved it, even craved it. He had found a guide who was very much like a demanding football coach who brought out the best in him. "We were taking it all to the absolute extreme," says Evans. "I used to get so excited out on the water that I couldn't breathe."

By the late 1970s, "the sky was the limit," says Evans. "We were doing incredible things, hitting our stride, and I was excited because I thought we could do even more incredible things as a team."

That, as it turned out, would not be the case.

7

COLLISION AT HOMOSASSA

Flats guiding in the Keys back in the 1960s was a rather exclusive profession, the province of cranky, tough, hard-driving men who were sizzled by the sun, on the edge of exhaustion (at least some of them) from their freelance careers as late-night dope smugglers, and fiercely protective of their turf and the resource. It was a very difficult club to break into. They had their own set of unwritten rules—about etiquette on the flats, about how and when to fish certain areas. They did not embrace outsiders, but if an angler or fledgling guide demonstrated respect and played by the rules, acceptance would usually come at some point. However, if an angler or guide did *not* play by the rules, bad things happened. Tires were slashed. Boats were sunk. And in extreme cases—for those who openly flaunted the rules over and again—something known as the "sarcophagus" was employed. In this case, the offended guides would wait for the evening until the offender's boat was left unsupervised. Then they would take ten gallons of resin that had been mixed with fiberglass, and cover the entire boat with the concoction, which would harden and make the boat and everything within it inoperable.

Hal Chittum, before he was a storeowner and then a boatbuilder, was a guide in the Keys for sixteen years, starting in the early 1970s. He would have started there even earlier, but the closed group of Keys guides would not allow him in for a few years until he finally demonstrated to them that he could—and would—play by their rules. "It was a culling process and it actually worked pretty well," says Chittum. "I wish we had it these days." He quickly became one of the best in the area at his craft, and he was the preferred guide of the likes of Apte, Pate, and Lopez. At one point, Chittum's clients owned all of the significant world records for tarpon.

As you might suspect, the guides in the Homosassa area did not much like outsiders invading their territory, either. They particularly did not like the interloping guides from the Keys, with their fancy boats and gear, their general disdainful attitudes, and the attention they drew to the area.

One year early on in the great Homosassa run, Chittum decided to go up early, to do some scouting and get prepared for the four weeks he'd be guiding there. He checked in at the Riverside and went to the motel's restaurant to get a late lunch. The place was nearly empty, save for three guys huddled around a corner table. Chittum took a table on the opposite side of the room and ordered a club sandwich.

Within a few minutes, the conversation coming from the other table began to get louder and, it seemed, hostile. "I heard the words 'asshole,' 'Keys guide,' and 'big-mouthed sons of bitches,'" says Chittum. "There was this one guy among them who looked like a pirate, no shoes, sun-bleached blonde hair, big mustache. He looked right at me and said, 'I'm talking about you, asshole.'"

The guy then stood up and rushed at Chittum. "And suddenly we're in this barroom brawl," says Chittum. "We're trying to kill each other."

They knocked down a table. Silverware, plates, and glasses crashed to the floor. The waitress ran to call the cops, who never showed. Neither man got in any killshots, but they were both bleeding. Finally Chittum, who outweighed the man by twenty pounds, wrestled him to the floor, where they both sat, too exhausted to carry on.

"What's your problem, man?" Chittum asked the guy.

"My problem is that you've ruined the greatest fishery in the world by telling people about it. You're the son of a bitch who brought Lefty up here."

"I did not bring Lefty up here," Chittum replied.

"Wait, what?"

"That's not me!" Chittum said.

"It wasn't?"

"No!"

And with that, the man stood up and extended his hand. "I'm Freddie Archibald. Let's have a drink."

"I was like, 'what the fuck?'" says Chittum. "But we had that drink and Freddie and I became great friends."

⁂

Keys anglers and guides also had *their* beefs with the Homosassa locals. They thought the manner in which they fished the place was rather primitive. The locals didn't much like poling. They'd see a school of fish and crank up their engines and run over to them. This angered the Keys guides, with their poling platforms and poles and their insistence on stealth. In truth, though, in those early days, there were so many fish around, it didn't matter all that much.

⁂

In the late 1970s, during the prime month of May, there were, on any given day, maybe ten boats on the water, perhaps a dozen. There was plenty of room. Everyone stayed well spaced out, but close enough to keep tabs on each other. "We were all looking over our shoulders, looking at everybody else," says Evans. Apte was in his boat *Mom's Worry*. Pflueger was over there in *We Should'a*. Curtis was atop the *Grasshopper*. Lopez was doing shirtless push-ups in the bow again. Pate was standing in the condominium. *Wait, did she just take her top off?* The wiry guide in the back, the nose guard in the front—Huff and Evans were easy to make out. Tangy, scented smoke wafted from Archibald's boat. There went Navarre's helicopter, on its way back to land.

They were all after something they now knew existed but had yet to prove: a tarpon that weighed two hundred pounds or more. The Holy Grail of fly angling.

With that much space, those first few years, though full of competitive tension, were well mannered on the water. When someone hooked a big tarpon, the other boats politely moved out of the way, while still paying close attention. (Pate always put a pair of binoculars on a fish hooked by another boat.) The guides were generally friendly with each other, much more than the sports were with their fellow sports. This made practical sense: the guides were the ones who orchestrated the show on the water, and they had to work with each other to make it all flow. They all had CB radios, though some, like Huff, rarely spoke into them. Cliques inevitably formed, and some guides began to pool resources and team up and share information. Some guides spoke in a code they had prearranged with other guides. One guide would tell another on the CB that he was having electrical problems, and that he needed black tape, which meant, in reality, "scoot over near me, there are tons of fish here." Like pitchers and catchers worried about the other team stealing their signals, the guides changed up their code words every once in a while. "I need some black tape" one day might be "Could you bring me a sandwich?" the next.

Everyone knew that if Pflueger or Pate hooked a potential record, they'd likely be dragged off the flat and would not be seen again for a while. Apte commanded respect on the water, but there were several guides who yearned for his humbling. Curtis won no new friends when he adopted the local custom, holstering his pole and cranking up his engine to chase fish. He would run his engine, too, to find the floats that had been dropped by Navarre's helicopter. "There aren't any fish here," Curtis would grumble into the CB for all to hear when he arrived at a float.

"I wonder why," Huff would sardonically ask Evans.

And then the records started to fall.

Joe Robinson was in the insurance business in Miami. He started fly fishing in saltwater, like so many others, on the Tamiami Trail. He'd heard about Homosassa from Norman Duncan. "Norman came knocking on my door one morning at three A.M.," says Robinson. "'Holy shit, you would not believe the size of these tarpon!' he said."

Robinson fished with Dale Perez, who was an ex-baseball player who'd had cups of coffee with the Cardinals, Twins, and White Sox before his career ended when he tore up his knee sliding into second base. Perez nicknamed Robinson "One-Cast" because of his pinpoint accuracy with the fly. Robinson was a serious tarpon angler but not necessarily serious about the record. "My feeling was that I always wanted to let them go," he says. He would make one exception to the rule during his tarpon-fishing career.

One day in May of 1978, Perez was poling Robinson and his wife, Jackie, near Pine Island. Perez spotted a small school of large tarpon. He pointed out the fish that he wanted Robinson to cast to. True to his nickname, Robinson made one cast, and the designated fish sipped in his fly and immediately jumped, something it would do another twenty-three times during the forty-five-minute fight. Perez landed the fish with a lip gaff, and not a kill gaff, knowing Robinson's preference for not killing fish. As the fish lay by the side of the boat, Perez got out his measuring tape and his calculator, using the tried-and-true formula for estimating a tarpon's weight (the girth squared times the length, divided by 800).*

"Joe, shit, this thing is taping out to around 180 pounds," said Perez. "This is probably the record."

Robinson hesitated and then said, without much conviction, that he still wanted to let it go. But Jackie persuaded him to take it in and weigh it. The fish did indeed weigh 180 pounds, and it broke Evans's record of 177 pounds from the year before. Robinson's record did not last long. Almost exactly a year later, Pate topped it with a 182-pounder, caught

---

* Jerald Ault, a marine biologist at the University of Miami, has, in more recent years, developed a chart for the BTT that he says provides a more accurate measurement than the old formula.

with Chittum, which he landed in twenty minutes, an unusually quick fight for him.

These catches were all in the sixteen-pound test tippet category.* Records were also falling in the twelve-pound category. Pate caught a 155-pounder in 1980 on twelve-pound, which finally topped Apte's 1971 fish by a pound.** "It was just impossible to sleep at night then because of what you were expecting might happen on the water the next day," says Robinson.

With the records beginning to fall each season, "the place started cooking," says Evans. Much of that cooking took place off the water.

First of all, there were romantic entanglements. Pate, as stated, always had a woman staying with him while he was in residence at Homosassa. Some of the time, the woman was his wife. Some of the time, the woman (or women, on occasion) were not. Some were flight attendants. Some were women he'd met through the classifieds. Some were brought to Homosassa by a man from New Orleans. Lopez always had a few women hanging around. Others did, too. Even some of the guides got into the action.

Then there were the drugs. The drug of choice was the one that was storming the nation at the time Reagan was about to take office. Blow. Dust. Colombian Marching Powder. Cocaine might have been the only drug that came close to matching the adrenaline spike of hooking a tarpon (it also matched, during the inevitable comedown, the feeling of despair when a tarpon was lost). Some of the anglers and guides obviously sought that high off the water, too. Chief among them was Lopez, but

---

* They were actually on fifteen-pound tippet, but as I explained earlier, that category was replaced by sixteen-pound, and the record was moved up. So we'll stick to calling it sixteen-pound. The same sort of thing applies to the twelve-pound category, which at the time, was ten-pound.

** On the IGFA's website, Pate's 1980 catch is recorded as having broken the record held by Lenny Berg, an ophthalmologist who caught a 128-and-a-half pounder in 1979. Apte's 154-pound tarpon on twelve-pound caught in 1971 was not officially part of the IGFA archives, most likely because it was recorded by the Miami Rod & Reel Club, and not Mark Sosin and the Saltwater Fly Rodders. Nonetheless, it was considered the "true" twelve-pound record, until Pate's 1980 fish. Confusing, eh?

he was far from the only one. All of this, combined with the competitive and strong personalities, began to wreak some havoc.

∽

One early evening on the water, Pflueger's engine broke down on his way back to the Riverside. He dead-drifted for a bit before flagging down two other boats that happened to be going in at the same time, and he asked for a tow. He hooked bowlines to the two boats, tilted up his motor, and off they went. Pflueger, back in his boat, began to notice that the passengers in the other boats seemed to be having a really good time, drinking and periodically leaning over to maybe snort something. They weren't paying a lick of attention to where they were going, or to him back in the towed boat. Pflueger suddenly spotted a huge wooden channel marker. He noticed that the boats towing him were headed for either side of it, and that his boat was headed right for it. He started to yell as loud as he could, but no one heard him. "I thought I was going to die," he says. "I knew I could jump overboard, but then my boat would crash into the marker and possibly kill them." In a last-ditch move, Pflueger put his motor down and turned the wheel so it would drag the other boats. "They turned around and stopped just in time," he says.

∽

Evans and Huff were down near Pine Island, some thirty miles south of Black Rock, fishing the outgoing tide that in those days always encouraged the appearance of massive swimming schools of tarpon, a "poon river," as Evans called it. They were perfectly positioned and had already seen a few fish, the vanguard of the coming wave. Nearby was another boat. On it was a man named Peck Hayne, who was fishing with Chittum. (Evans called Hayne "Peckerhead.") Something seemed amiss on their boat. Hayne was on the bow, casting to fish that were now starting to swim by in masses. But Chittum was not on the platform in the stern, holding the push pole. Instead, he was lying down, crossways, by the back corner of the boat, with his feet over one side and his head over the other. "I said to Steve, 'Look over there. Chittum is blowing bubbles,'" says Evans. "Steve ignored me and kept staring at the water. 'Seriously, Steve, I think Chittum is drowning.'"

Evans says they poled over and asked Hayne what was wrong with Chittum. Hayne just shrugged. "He's fine," he said. But Chittum did not look fine. Far from it. Evans and Huff suspected that he'd ingested something, maybe too much of something. ("I was, um, sick," says Chittum.) Evans jumped into Chittum's boat, and Hayne moved over to Huff's boat, and they motored back thirty miles to the dock. There, Huff walked Chittum back to his rental house like a trainer helping an injured football player off the field. He gave him some cold water and put him in bed and left. When he went back to check on Chittum an hour later, he was gone. Later, Evans and Huff saw him at the Riverside pool, upright, smiling, very much alive, partying with some fellow guests. "We thought he was dying and he was fine an hour later," says Evans. "We ran him back and missed the greatest out-goer in the history of mankind." Huff and Evans began to call Chittum "Shittum."

∽

Jimmy Lopez arrived in Homosassa one year in late April, early for the run. The former Delta pilot took his guide up in his four-seat plane, hoping to spot some fish on the flat. They flew around for an hour and a half without spotting any tarpon.

"I have an idea," Lopez told his guide.

They flew back to the small airport. An attendant began refueling the plane. Lopez disappeared inside the airport. He reappeared with two young women the guide had never seen before. They took off and, again, headed over the flat. But they were no longer looking for tarpon. Lopez leveled off the plane and put it on autopilot.

"Hand me that map bag," he told the guide.

Within were two plastic bags filled with cocaine. Lopez poured some out and began to cut it up. The women giggled.

∽

At the Riverside one evening, Evans spotted an intact toilet behind the building. The motel was undergoing some renovations. He had an idea. Lopez had been driving everyone crazy with his intensity, both on and off the water. That night, Evans brought the toilet down to the docks and placed it on the bow of Lopez's boat, a bright yellow Hewes that had been nicknamed the "yellow banana."

The next morning, as the anglers and guides gathered around the dock to prepare for the day, everyone saw the toilet. Lopez, perhaps a bit tired from the previous evening's activities, hadn't shown up yet. No one knew how he'd react when he did. Would he go nuts?

Lopez appeared. He displayed no reaction when he saw the toilet. He walked onto his boat. His guide started the motor and shoved off. Lopez then stood, dropped his pants and sat on the toilet, and rode in that posture for a few miles down the river.

∽

Many evenings began at the Riverside's Yardarm Lounge or the Monkey Bar. The anglers and the guides (some of whom stayed at the nearby Tradewinds marina) would have a beer and maybe order some food. A large window in the Monkey Bar overlooked a small island, a mostly man-made pile of rocks in the Homosassa River, on top of which stood a small lighthouse. The island was inhabited by a group of spider and squirrel monkeys whose ancestors had been brought to the area to be used for research for the polio vaccine. The monkeys had been put on the island after they'd no longer been needed for the research. They were rowdy and mischievous, and liked to play with themselves in full view of the bar patrons.

Pate didn't stay at the Riverside, renting a house instead. He remained apart from his fellow anglers for most of his time in Homosassa, but he did throw a party every season. The food was always good—Pate usually did some sort of low-country boil—but the affair was always rather sedate. Lopez's parties, which were thrown nearly every night in his room at the Riverside or, really, anywhere he was, were rowdier.

Evans and Huff didn't socialize much. They weren't teetotalers by any means, but they were in Homosassa for a reason. They took it seriously and were usually pretty wiped out by the end of the day anyway. Neither of them liked the party scene. Huff, accompanied by Perez, went to a Lopez party once but left early when the room got eerily quiet and some women started snorting lines on a desk. "I was so naïve then," says Huff. Evans went to an oyster shuck at Archibald's house in the Homosassa River once and got pretty lit up on beer. Lopez gave him a ride home, running the river at full speed outside of the markers, where there were dozens of rock piles. "I thought for sure we were going to hit one of them and die," says Evans.

Evans and Huff were both married, and neither approved much of the womanizing going on during those years at Homosassa. Evans made one exception to that rule, and it would play a role in the dissolution of his partnership with Huff.

∽

The stories from on the water were stupendous, almost too hard to believe, but also, in the aggregate, too hard to ignore. On the Oklahoma flat one day, Perez held the boat steady for Robinson as fish came at the boat from every direction. The tarpon began to form a daisy chain. "And we were somehow in the center of it," says Robinson. "It was thirty feet wide and fifteen feet deep with fish. From the top of the water to the ocean floor, you could see flashes. It was solid tarpon." On the boat, Robinson froze.

"When are you going to cast?" Perez screamed at Robinson.

"I said, 'Cast? Hell, I'm going to sit here and watch this,'" says Robinson. For five minutes, they did just that. "And then the chain finally broke up and they started swimming and I cast and hooked one."

Chittum and Lopez arrived one morning at Black Rock and had it to themselves. Lopez was tying on a fly when Chittum yelled, "Hurry up! There's some fish in front of us." Lopez began to shake. "Hurry up!

There's more fish in front of us," Chittum yelled again. Lopez began to shake harder.

"Hold on," Chittum said a few moments later, his voice calmer now. "Just take your time. There's more fish here than I can count." Chittum and Lopez, too, were in the middle of a daisy chain, it turned out, one comprised of some two thousand fish. Lopez hooked five fish in under two hours. Over the next ten days, he jumped more than two hundred fish. He got sixty-one of those to the boat.

In the afternoons, on the Oklahoma flat, one only had to wait a bit. The show always eventually started. "You'd look to the west when the sea breeze came and see literally thousands of them coming onto the flat," says Malzone. "It was the most amazing thing you've ever seen."

It wasn't just the numbers of fish, though. There were stories every day of massive fish seen but not hooked, or hooked but not landed. Fish of well over two hundred pounds. Everyone had a story. Some of the stories contained some hyperbole. These are, after all, fishermen we're dealing with here. But those fish—those glandular mutants that Huff spoke of—were there.

And those stories of the monsters never to be caught but only seen, or hooked only to be lost, they were told with more relish, more vigor, and more feeling than the stories of the fish that *were* caught, even the ones that became world records. It makes sense. In angling, as in life, it is the ones that get away that haunt our dreams, that push us over the brink into a lustful madness. And Homosassa was the first place in these anglers' lives where, hot damn, those dreams just might come true.

❧

Apte was fishing the flat one day with his guide Ralph Delph when they spotted a giant school of tarpon. Apte was using twelve-pound tippet, just as he had done since he was a young man, eschewing the sixteen-pound class in favor of tradition. He cast into the school. A fish of about 140 pounds took his fly but then immediately spit it out. The school moved by. Delph decided to chase it. He poled like a madman, and soon had Apte in position again. Apte spotted what he thought was the biggest fish in the school and made a cast. The fish took. It was gigantic.

Apte fought the fish for forty-eight minutes (he always kept the exact time of his fights on his watch) and got it to the boat, where it lolled on its side. There was no doubt in either man's mind that this was the biggest tarpon they'd ever seen. Each of the men had a gaff onboard. Delph opted to use his. He extended it over his head and swung down on the broad flank of the fish, as if wielding an ax. The gaff hit home, but the tarpon reacted with a great push of its giant tail. Delph went over the transom and into the water. The gaff pulled out, but Apte still had the fish on.

Nineteen minutes later, Apte again had the fish by the boat, and Delph again grabbed his gaff. "Why don't you use mine, Ralph?" Apte asked. "It's bigger." Delph refused. He swung down on the fish again, and again it pulled him into the water. This time, Delph stayed attached. The tarpon swam to the bottom, some ten feet down. Delph went with it. The tarpon leapt. Delph held onto it like a rodeo cowboy. "Ralph didn't look like he was having much fun," says Apte. "In fact, he looked like he was drowning."

Apte dropped his rod and started the boat. It was Delph's boat, so he was unfamiliar with how the throttle quadrant worked. He put it in forward, and the boat shot toward Delph and the fish. Apte couldn't stop it, and Delph had to let go of the tarpon to avoid getting run over. The fish got away.

Delph climbed in the boat, breathing heavily. He was covered in stinky tarpon slime.

"Why'd you run me over?" he asked Apte.

"I didn't mean to," Apte replied. "You were in trouble."

The duo didn't talk about the fish for the rest of the day. They didn't mention it that night at dinner, or the following day on the water. Finally, two nights after the fish had been hooked, during dinner, Delph asked Apte, "How big was that fish?"

"You were wrapped around it, Ralph. You know better than I do," said Apte.

Apte took a paper napkin and tore it in half. "Let's each write down what we think it weighed," he said.

They did, and then they handed each other the napkin halves.

Delph had written: "230+"

Apte had written: "230-plus"

∾

For two of those great Homosassa years, Huff and Perez partook in something like a busman's holiday, taking a few days off from their respective monthlong-plus guiding days to fish together. Robinson encouraged Perez to take the break. Evans was never happy when Huff did it—especially since it took place during the very prime of the season—but he grudgingly obliged. "The fishing was so good and it was all pretty intense, so it was good to take a few days to just fish," says Perez. One of the reasons Evans didn't like it is that he spent some of those Huff-less days fishing with Pflueger, who says, "I enjoyed fishing with Tom then. He was obsessed with tarpon. I think he loved tarpon fishing more than he loved his first wife. He was great at it. But I think Tom may have only caught one fish with me during that time because I was always fighting them for a long time." Says Evans, "I hated fishing with Pflueger."

Huff and Perez took turns poling each other, switching spots after every hookup. They came up with a novel way to sometimes access the fish, using Perez's past life as a baseball player to get it done. "We'd see a string of fish go by and pole like hell after them, but couldn't catch up," says Huff. "We knew that they sometimes went into a daisy chain if they were spooked. So, if we couldn't catch up, Dale grabbed an apple out of our lunch and launched it at the swimming string. He had a great arm. The apple would splash right on them, they'd chain up, and we'd pole up and start casting." They called it the "Red Delicious method."

One day, when it was Huff's turn to fish, Perez spotted a school of fish from far off (the former baseball player had great eyes, too). Huff began to strip line out, not in any particular hurry. But suddenly Perez shouted, "Right here! Look at the size of that fish!"

A tarpon had snuck up on them. Huff spotted it, threw out seventy feet of line, and let the grizzly-and-purple fly sit until the fish got near it. He stripped the fly and the fish ate it. "Its mouth was so huge," Huff says. "When it took the fly, Dale was right behind me. He said, 'Oh, my God!' I swear that fish was closer to three hundred pounds than two hundred. It looked like a manatee." Huff cleared the line. The fish jumped three times. "Its back was as big as a refrigerator," says Perez. "It was the biggest fucking tarpon I've ever seen in my life." Perez began shedding his clothes because he realized there was no way that fish wasn't going to pull him in. He picked up the gaff. But just ten minutes into the fight, the fish ate through the entire twelve-inch shock leader up to the tippet and swam free.

∽

Pate and Chittum were fishing one day north of Black Rock, near the St. Martins Keys. Back in those days, fish were everywhere, so it was fun and productive, on some days, to go explore. On the boat with them was Patty, Pate's third wife, and Jack Samson, then an editor at *Field & Stream*. The bottom in the St. Martins area was mostly dark grass, so it was harder to spot fish there than it was on the white sand of the Oklahoma flat. But the fish that day were in daisy chains near the top, making themselves easily visible.

Chittum spotted a particularly large fish swimming in one of those daisy chains. Pate was using a shooting head that he'd patched together the night before. He cast the fly and hooked the fish. "It was absolutely immense," says Chittum.

Pate, as he pretty much always did with potential record tarpon, applied very little pressure to the fish. Chittum used the trolling motors to follow the tarpon. Two hours and many miles later, Chittum was still after the fish, but the batteries on the trolling motors were dying. When they finally failed, Chittum began to pole after the fish but lost ground. The St. Martins area was littered with small islands, which had deep cuts next to them, under the overhang of mangroves. The tarpon seemed to like to swim close to these parts of the islands, and Chittum and Pate grew worried that the fish was going to get hung up in the mangroves. Chittum poled as hard as he could but could not catch up. And then, distressingly for both angler and guide, the tarpon began to head for a point on an island. It was pretty clear that if the fish went around the point, it would break Pate off.

Samson had been a competitive swimmer in college. He stood up in the boat and declared that he was going to jump in and scare the fish away from the point. Samson also happened to be a very accomplished drinker of beer. "I think he was already into his ninth beer of the day, but before I could tell him to not jump in, *splash*. And he thrashed around but couldn't keep up. We passed him like he was standing still," says Chittum.

Patty, without saying a word, went immediately to the ice chest, grabbed a six-pack of beer, and tossed it to Samson. "We'll come get you later!" she yelled.

"It was one of the coolest moves I've ever seen," says Chittum. "But I had no idea how we were going to find him later. All of those islands looked the same."

The tarpon avoided the point, and the fight went on for another couple of hours before the fish appeared to be ready to quit. Chittum got out the gaff. He needed to be about two feet closer to the fish to reach it. And then Pate's homemade shooting head popped. "I looked at that fish for hours," says Chittum. "It was 240 pounds, easy."

When they eventually found Samson, the six cans of beer were empty, and he was all smiles.

One spring in Homosassa in the late 1970s, Evans was going through a divorce from his first wife, a woman he'd begun dating in high school and had married after college. A cold front that year in Homosassa lasted for nearly two weeks, scotching the fishing. Evans decided then, finally, to say yes when a man from New Orleans offered him the company of two women. Huff, now in another room at the Riverside, still didn't like the womanizing from a moral standpoint, but he didn't like it from a practical one, either. It was a distraction. There were no fish around, but still.

When the front finally lifted, the fish showed up. Evans sent his company away and told Huff that he was ready to fish. By now it was June—the prime season had been pushed back a few weeks because of the weather. There were thousands of fish, and they caught a bunch of them.

But something now was clearly amiss, something that had been brewing between the men for a while. They were both high-strung, type A personalities. It's possible that there was something never really resolved about Huff's 186-pound tarpon, or about Huff and Perez taking time off to fish together. Or maybe that tension, that fine line between the wealthy sport and the unwealthy guide, that less-than-clear division of labor and management—maybe that line was no longer walked, but crossed? It could be, too, that the time had just come after so many days spent together on the water, under pressure, trying to do what seemed like the impossible. The skiff, as Pallot said, is a very small space and can feel truly confined if the guide and the sport get out of rhythm.

And this is when their partnership ended. They each have differing versions of how it happened, of what was said and when it was said. The one thing they agree on: Huff told Evans that he was the most selfish person he'd ever met and fired him.

Though their versions of the story may differ, both of them get us to the same place: after more than a decade of fishing together, Evans and Huff were done. "That was that," says Evans. "I'm not sure who was the selfish one in this case, but when Huff says something, that's it."

To this day, it seems, Evans can't quite shake the hurt of Huff leaving him. "It broke me for a good while," Evans says. "I really thought we were building this thing together. Honestly, from my point of view, it felt like a divorce." He gets reflective about it, something he's not usually prone to doing. "I'm sure I'm self-centered," he says. "Tania would probably tell you the same thing, but she's been married to me for forty years."

Evans and Huff have maintained a mutual respect. They've talked on the phone, and they have seen each other a handful of times in the past four decades. The encounters have mostly been brief and cordial, the past either behind them or buried too deep to access in such a short time. There would be one meeting decades later, however, when the unresolved past would come roaring back and clashed over memorably, not by them, but by their children.

Huff continued to fish Homosassa for a few seasons, with anglers like Sandy Moret, Tom Richardson, and Bill Hassett. It would never really feel the same to him, though, and he would leave for good in the early 1980s, just as the crowds began to show up.

Evans became a bit unmoored after Huff left. The first thing he needed was a new guide in Homosassa. He knew that Robinson, at that time, was paring back his fishing days. So he called Perez.

∾

On May 21, 1981, Evans and Perez were stuck on land in the morning because of a sustained thunderstorm. In Perez, Evans had landed a guide who was very similar to Huff. Both were excellent at poling and had good eyes and instincts. Both had that same soothing South Florida accent and, in fact, their voices were eerily similar in sound. There were differences, though. Perez was darker, both in appearance— with his black hair and deep, mournful eyes—and in demeanor. He was prone to sustained brooding silences that left Evans wondering what was bothering him. His boat wasn't quite as squared away as Huff's. Evans called it the "snagcraft," and Perez sometimes had to lift the top of the motor and hit it with a wrench to get the engine started. And, unlike Huff, he did not like to be on the water during thunderstorms.

At around 3:00 P.M. that day, the sky started to clear, though the wind still blew at twenty miles per hour. Evans and Perez went out. They ran down to a place on the Oklahoma flat that Huff had nick-named Fetlock, where the sandy bottom was dotted with some swaying, spongy grasses. There, Perez spotted the roll of a large tarpon. He jumped down from the poling platform into the gunwale, and drove his pole into the ocean floor to keep the windblown boat off the fish. Evans made a cast, and the fish flashed at the fly but missed. He kept stripping, and the fish came back, and this time, Evans hooked it. Just a few seconds after the bite, a big wave smacked the side of the boat. It knocked Perez into the water and tossed Evans into the stern. The fish jumped at that very moment, and neither man saw it. "We had no idea how big it was," says Perez.

Evans stayed attached and got the fish in quickly, as was his custom. Perez, back in the boat, lip-gaffed it and dragged it into the bow and measured it.

"You did it," he said.

The 186-pound, 8-ounce tarpon topped Pate's 182-pounder from two years before, becoming the biggest tarpon ever caught on a fly in recorded history (it was on sixteen-pound tippet). More important to Evans, it exorcised a demon that had been hot on his tail for four years. He'd finally topped Huff's unofficial 186-pounder from 1977.

That evening, Perez suggested that since they had the sixteen-pound record, they should give the twelve-pound one a try. The twelve-pound record at the time—155 pounds—was held by Pate, which added some incentive for Evans.

The next day, Evans cast into an oncoming school of tarpon and hooked one. Ten minutes later, he had the fish beside the boat. Perez hit it with the kill gaff, and was—yes—launched into the water. Perez was quickly pulled three hundred feet from the boat. Huff and Moret, who were fishing nearby, poled over. Huff handed Perez his lip gaff. With two gaffs now in the fish, Perez was finally able to subdue it. But just then, Evans came roaring over in Perez's boat. He tried to slow it down by putting it in neutral, but the boat didn't really have a neutral, and he slammed into Perez, who somehow managed to hold onto the fish.

That fish officially weighed 155 pounds, 7 ounces. Because it was within eight ounces of Pate's record, it technically qualified as a tie with

Pate's fish according to IGFA rules.* The two rivals would begrudgingly have to share the title. But not for long.

∾

More records fell the following year. Apte and Delph were at Black Rock one day at dawn. Apte, still fishing twelve-pound, says he could just barely make out some fish gurgling seventy-five feet away in the dim light. He cast his fly in that direction and hooked a tarpon. Exactly twenty-two minutes later (remember: the watch), he landed the fish. They took the tarpon in, passing some boats that were just coming out for the day. The fish weighed 164 pounds, 12 ounces, beating Pate and Evans's shared record by more than nine pounds.

Apte and Delph went back out in the afternoon. Apte hooked another fish, which took twenty-eight minutes to land. When they got back to the dock, the scale read 166 pounds. Apte, in what was a fitting capstone to his tarpon-fishing career, had broken the twelve-pound record twice in one day.

∾

We've had a lot of fish-catching stories in this chapter, haven't we? There is one more that we have to talk about.

On May 13, 1982, Evans and Perez were on the Oklahoma flat when they saw Pate, who was fishing that day with a Riverside bookkeeper and part-time guide named Rick Doyle, hook into a fish.

"Fuck," Evans said.

"What?" asked Perez.

"Pate's got a poon on. It might be *the* poon."

Pate and his poon soon disappeared into the Gulf. Evans and Perez fished the rest of the day. As they idled up to the docks at the Riverside

---

* According to the IGFA rules, for fish of over one hundred pounds, any new world record must clear the old one by eight ounces or more.

that evening, they saw a giant tarpon hanging by a hook. Pate was standing next to it, smiling, surrounded by onlookers, some of whom were taking photographs. Perez, distracted, ran his boat into the dock.

That 188-pound tarpon caught by Pate on sixteen-pound tippet beat Evans's record by a pound and change. It would remain the world record for the next twenty-one years, an almost unimaginable run. It was considered by many during that time to be the best fly-rod catch ever, and it solidified Pate's position as one of the greatest fly anglers who ever lived. And it would drive Evans crazy for each and every one of those years it existed.

This would drive him crazy, too: a few months after Pate's catch, Evans received a letter at his Vermont home. Evans says it was from Pate. The letter began:

> Dear Tom,
> I am writing to inform you that the 188-pound tarpon I caught in Homosassa in May of this year has been officially accepted by the IGFA as the new world record, replacing yours.

Evans crumpled up the letter and threw it into a wastebasket. He now wishes he had saved it.

In 1983, Evans did not go to Homosassa, one of only two seasons he would miss in forty-three years. Work got in the way. His firm had taken a big position in the stock of an American oil company, and that stock was going south, and he needed to figure his way out of it.

The following year, in 1984, Evans booked a guide named Mike Souchak. Souchak's father had been a professional golfer who had won fifteen times on the PGA Tour, which included one-stroke victories in separate tournaments over Arnold Palmer and Jack Nicklaus. Souchak had graduated from Duke before becoming a fishing guide. He wasn't as fish-savvy as Huff or Perez, but he was book-smart, sometimes annoyingly so to Evans. "We'd be at breakfast at the local spot, Becky's, and Mike would read the weather report in the newspaper and would tell me that it wasn't going to rain," says Evans. "I'd look outside and it was raining. 'Mike, it's raining right now.' And he would say, 'No, the paper says it's not.'"

Evans fished with Souchak that season with the growing realization that he'd need to find another guide soon. "It just didn't feel right," says Evans, who still had a Huff hangover. One day during the last week of the season, Evans slipped on some grease in Souchak's boat and fell and landed on the boat's battery. "I was all purple and green," he says. At this point, both men realized that their partnership was over. Guiding wasn't Souchak's calling, and he knew it.* Evans needed someone who was as into it as he was.

On the last day of the season, Souchak suggested that Evans fish with a young guide he knew who seemed to be quickly figuring out Homosassa. The guide's name was Al Dopirak. Evans went out with Dopirak that day, and they boated seven tarpon, all of them over 140 pounds.

That evening, Evans and Tania—who were married by then—drove to Tampa to stay in an airport hotel before their flight home the next day. Evans couldn't sleep at all that night because of the spasms in his back from fighting all of those fish. He was ecstatic. He rolled over in the bed in the morning and told Tania, "I found him. I'm back in the game."

---

* Souchak would quit guiding a little while later and head out to Las Vegas to play in poker tournaments and cash games, which he still does to this day.

INTERLUDE 2
THE GLOSSARY

Yes, it's true, most glossaries are found at either the very beginning or the very end of a book. For most books, this placement represents the utmost in sensibility. But not for this one. We feel strongly that a word list at this particular juncture, this period of slack tide, so to speak, will help us all get through the rest of this book intact.

There are a couple of things going on here with this glossary. Tom Evans speaks in what is basically his own language, comprised of nicknames and acronyms, some ribald, some not. Evans-speak can take weeks, if not months, to decipher. Much of it is, of course, related to tarpon fishing, which is fitting, because tarpon anglers, as a whole, *also* speak a language of their own, one that, without intimate knowledge, can seem, frankly, quite foreign. (Tarpon anglers were, I think, the people who made a beeline from the Tower of Babel right to the sea.) And then within *that* tarpon language, Al Dopirak has his own local dialect and words and phrases. Confused yet? We hope you won't be after perusing the glossary below.

AP

An Evans-ism for "Advantage Poon" (see: *poon*). When a casted fly ends up barb-deep in your neck (or, as in Pierre Affre's case, someplace lower on your body), or when a hooked tarpon breaks off because you're standing on the line, or when the weather is unfishable, or, really, when any type of man-made or natural disaster allows a tarpon to evade an angler, that's AP.

Bean-picker

A newbie or beginner to the sport of fly fishing for tarpon. Also known in some other fishing circles as a "googan."

Bow-mounter

An angler or guide who has put a trolling motor on the front of his or her boat, which, according to Evans, is an easy way to identify a bean-picker (see above) or an unskilled angler or a guide; a trolling motor in that spot on the boat can easily entangle an angler's fly line. Bow-mounters oftentimes also use white push poles, a double-whammy that takes the whole thing to another level (most push poles are a black matte color; white reflects sunlight, which supposedly can scare fish).

BS

An Evans-ism for "bottom shit," as in something on the ocean's floor that, at quick glance, might be mistaken for a tarpon, like a rock or a patch of sea grass.

Chanel No. 5

Dean Butler's name for Black Rock, aka the Cock Hole, which is located near the Chassahowitzka River's channel marker number five. This is perhaps the only frequently used phrase of Butler's that's fit for a family publication, such as this.

Dilly Hole

A spot on the Oklahoma flat. A phrase also used for any type of honey hole, or productive tarpon spot. A Dopirak-ism.

Dogging It

A Dopirak-ism for when a tarpon slowly follows a fly for an excruciatingly long time. Such fish rarely bite. They are merely curious.

Farmered It

To screw up a cast to, or a hook-set on, a tarpon.

FFC

Flat-fucking-calm. Not an ideal weather condition for tarpon fishing. A light ripple, which slightly obscures the fish's view of what's going on above the water, is a better condition. An Evans-ism.

Fuck Santa Claus

A Dopirak-ism, said softly and quietly, when his sport misses a bite or a tarpon swims away from a well-presented fly.

Garbaged It

When a tarpon absolutely crushes a fly.

A Good PM

A good "poon movement," i.e., when the tarpon begin to move, en masse, from Black Rock to the Oklahoma flat in the mid-morning. An Evans-ism.

Greenie

A Dopirak-ism for a liberal environmentalist.

Guru Shit

A Dopirak-ism for things that famous guides or anglers, like Huff or Andy Mill, do that are quickly imitated by others. An example would be the bandana that Huff has worn over his face for much of his guiding career, for sun protection. A company called Buff has commercialized this simple article of clothing, selling a tubelike cloth mask, open at both ends, which covers the neck and face of the angler and comes in all sorts of colorful varieties. It's highly unusual these days to see anyone on the water who is *not* wearing a Buff or something similar.

High Voltage

When you're in an area of the flats where many boats are using trolling motors to move around and are, most likely, spooking the tarpon by doing so. An Evans-ism.

Homo Sapiens

An Evans-ism for the guides and anglers who live or launch out of Homosassa. (Evans and most serious record hunters have launched farther south, from Bayport, since the 1990s.) Evans often utters this phrase when he sees said guides and anglers chucking flies and lures into the mass of rolling tarpon at Black Rock in the early mornings.

Icicled

When a fish is totally spent from a fight and is motionless in the water, its tail suspended over its head.

Lasered

When a slowly approaching tarpon suddenly kicks into high gear and whizzes by the boat in a flash of silver.

Low-cost Valley

An Evans-ism for Locust Valley, New York.

Molding Around

A Dopirak-ism for tarpon that are moving around a certain area, as in: "Those fish are just molding around out there, dawg."

Nipper

A fish that cautiously bites at the butt of the fly but never commits with a full, hearty chomp.

Nut

A word for the formation made by daisy-chaining tarpon.

Oiled to the Bottom

A Dopirak-ism for tarpon that are swimming near the ocean floor. Fish that do this are usually reluctant to take a fly.

Ping-ponging

When the flat is crowded and tarpon appear to bounce from boat to boat. Also known as "pin-balling."

Poon

As mentioned previously, this is shorthand for "tarpon." Evans claims to have come up with the word, a vulgar retort to what he perceived as Pate's hoity-toity pronunciation of the fish as "taw-puhn." The word "poon" is now pretty much universally used by tarpon anglers. A handful of people doubt Evans's claim of coining the term. But it certainly fits into his proclivity for nicknames, and one guesses that if Sotheby's were to ever auction the word off, Evans would be its provenance. That it conjures the word "poontang" (once commonly used slang for female genitalia) is no accident.

Poon-fucker

A person who runs a boat, in full motor, right across a tarpon flat. Said person is usually a red or trout fisherman, or an oblivious weekender out for a cruise.

Poon shack

A house rented for a tarpon trip.

Poon-tamer

An Evans-ism for someone who does not know how to properly fight a big tarpon. Pate and Pflueger were both poon-tamers in their respective heydays.

Porpussy

An Evans-ism for a porpoise.

SFO

An Evans-ism for "solid fucking overcast," not ideal weather for tarpon fishing.

Taking a Shit

A description of the crouch most sports automatically go into when they spot a tarpon from the bow of a skiff. It's a completely natural, ready-for-action reaction to the excitement of that moment. When a sport is spotted doing this on another boat, it can be useful information to others around him or her, as in: "Look, Rob's taking a shit. Those fish might be coming this way."

Toad

A very big tarpon.

A Treatment

An Evans-ism for a slow, tough day on the water. After a cloudy, rainy, windy, and/or fishless day, Evans will inevitably get into Dopirak's truck at the boat ramp and declare, with a tired sigh, "That was a treatment."

Turdholes

An Evans-ism for sea turtles, which can be numerous on the Homosassa flats and, when spooked by a boat, make a splashing sound that's eerily similar to the sound of a rolling tarpon.

Sea Turds

An Evans-ism for sailfish, which are the least of the great billfish.

Sliding

The motion of tarpon that seem to casually ease their way past the boat, spooked and unwilling to take a fly.

Wally

An Evans-ism for a manatee.

8

HOMOSMASHA

Al Dopirak remembers the first time he laid eyes on Tom Evans. It was on a dock after a day of fishing, still a few years before they would team up at the suggestion of Mike Souchak. Dopirak had just started guiding in Homosassa at the time, but he was well aware of Evans's reputation. "I saw that big dude and thought to myself, 'Man, if I could get that fucker on my boat, we'd fuck 'em up good.'"

Dopirak was born at Fort Bragg, in North Carolina, where his father was stationed in the army. When Dopirak was three years old, his family moved to the town of Dunedin, Florida, outside of Clearwater. As a kid, Dopirak excelled as an athlete, playing baseball and tennis. He became a firefighter at the age of twenty, and did some tennis instructing on the side. But his true passion was fishing.

He started hanging around the tackle shops near Dunedin and eventually met a man named Neil Sigvartsen. Sigvartsen was a true complete angler. He was an excellent poler of the boat. He could fix any engine. He had mastered spin, plug, and fly fishing for redfish, sharks, trout, grouper, and tarpon. The young and hungry Dopirak had found the right man to follow around. He asked Sigvartsen to teach him to fly cast. Sigvartsen took him to his lawn, and they threw hookless flies at Sigvartsen's muscly pit bull. Soon, Dopirak became something of a mirror image of his mentor. He had the eyes, the coordination, the instincts, and the drive. "You could put Al on a mud puddle and he'd find fish in it," says Sigvartsen.

It was Sigvartsen who first took Dopirak to Homosassa. Dopirak was awestruck. "It was just crazy seeing all of those giant fish," he says. "You'd look out across the place and your eyes would get huge and your heart would start thumping. It was ridiculous."

After a few trips there, Dopirak decided he wanted to become a guide. He befriended Freddie Archibald, who, in his own laid-back way, taught him some of the ins and outs of the profession, as well as some of the quirks of the Homosassa fishery. And, eventually, Archibald started giving Dopirak some of his client overflow. In order to clear up enough time to guide during the tarpon season in Homosassa, Dopirak paid some of his fellow firefighters to pick up his shifts.

His clients early on, he says, "were just terrible fishermen." Dopirak remembers one client who could not cast at all. The man spent the entire morning making casts that were coming up twenty feet short of the targeted fish. During a lull in the action, Dopirak finally told the man to just cast his fly and pull some line out of his reel and shake it out of his rod tip and leave it there in the water. Dopirak waited. When he spotted a string of fish coming for the boat, he started poling the boat backward to straighten the line and give the fly some movement. "That was the only fish that guy hooked that day," says Dopirak.

After a few seasons, Dopirak began to grow frustrated. He had learned the Homosassa fishery well. He could find the fish and position the boat. But his inept clients were dragging him down. "I knew I could do it," he says. "I just needed someone good in my boat."

He found that person during the 1984 season. And with that "big dude," they indeed started to "fuck 'em up."

Dopirak retired from his job as a firefighter and started guiding full-time at the age of thirty-five.* By then, he had earned the respect of the other guides. He was neither from the Keys nor from Homosassa, so

---

* One can retire from firefighting in Florida with full benefits after ten years of service if one works in high-risk situations, like on-scene firefighting, as Dopirak did.

he was friendly with both sets of guides, who were increasingly at each other's throats. On the water, Dopirak earned the nickname Wormy, for his uncanny ability to "worm" his way through and around a line of boats to get to the prime spot on the flat, a sleight of hand that never quite breached the unwritten code of etiquette.

The ultimate sign of respect came from Huff, who by then was already considered by most in the saltwater-flats fishing world to be, perhaps, the best guide ever. He and Dopirak overlapped in Homosassa for just a season or two, but Huff was impressed. "I felt like every time I looked up, Al was hooked up," he says. "We were all just playing catch-up."

∽

By the mid-1980s, Homosassa was changing. The word was fully out and had spread across the country. The big newswires published stories about the world-record chase, as had all of the major newspapers in Florida. The *New York Times* and *Toronto Globe & Mail* ran pieces. *Sports Illustrated* sent a writer down to spend a week chronicling the record-chasers, which resulted in a lengthy feature.

The regulars and diehards were now joined by those who had heard about the records and the chance, maybe, at a tarpon of two hundred pounds or more. Some were weekend-warrior types, like Jack Nicklaus and the hockey great Bobby Orr, who both came down for a spell. Some were more serious. Christopher Parkening is a classical guitarist whom the *Washington Post*, in 1990, described as "one of the most respected guitarists alive." He traveled from California to fish Homosassa, first with Harry Spear and then with Dopirak. Parkening, a born-again Christian who had studied guitar under the Spanish virtuoso Andrés Segovia, once hooked thirty-five tarpon in a day with Dopirak. (The musician taped up his fingers as a precaution when fishing for tarpon.) On one of those fish, Parkening's line wrapped around the butt of his rod. Without a word, he jumped off the boat to give himself some slack and cleared the line in midair before hitting the water. He landed the fish. "Chris was the best caster and best feeder of fish I'd ever seen," says Dopirak. "He was intense and super religious, but not a fake."

The new boats and people on the water started to drive the regulars a bit mad. Archibald couldn't stand seeing some of the less experienced anglers hook tarpon and then incompetently fight them for hours. When he spotted someone hooked up to a fish, he'd get on his CB and tell the angler's guide to break the fish off after thirty minutes. Not many guides listened to him, but he persisted. If he saw a hooked fish get away, Archibald would again get on the CB and yell, "Yay for the tarpon!" for all to hear, a man ahead of his time when it came to tarpon conservation.

Archibald also put a stop sign on the ocean floor at Chassahowitzka Point, his favorite spot, in an attempt to keep newcomers away. One morning, he arrived to find another boat there. He started shouting at the man in the other boat. "And then they both took up their push poles and went after each other, like a jousting match," says Dan Malzone, who watched the episode unfold.

Tensions boiled over in other ways, too. Two new guides, in front of their respective clients, beat the shit out of each other on the water until both collapsed. Two anglers in separate boats once cast for the same fish and ended up hooking each other. One didn't realize what had happened, though, and he pulled hard on his line and yanked the other man into the water. Yet another toilet ended up out on the water, this time atop Guido Rock in the middle of the flat. An angler named Bill Bishop got angry about a boat that had pulled up too close to his, so he took off all of his clothes and started swimming for it. "The guy quickly pulled up his anchor and took off," says Bishop. By the time Bishop got back to the dock, word had spread of his naked exploits. "So, you took off your clothes and attacked a boat, huh?" his wife said. Poon-fuckers ran across the flats daily. Training flights from MacDill Air Force base, located near Tampa, started running over the Homosassa flats. "You could see the sunglasses on the pilots," says Dopirak. "The place was kind of a zoo."

The actions of one of the most well-known world-record chasers also played a big role in the explosion of popularity—and the ire that came with it.

It annoyed some Homosassa anglers when Billy Pate called the news-papers to announce his arrival in Homosassa, or when he sometimes killed and hung up tarpon that were well under world-record weight. But it was the films he did about the tarpon fishing in Homosassa that brought the rage.

The American Sportsman, which aired on ABC during a prime Sunday afternoon slot from 1965 until 1986, was the preeminent outdoor televi-sion show of its time and, likely, ever, with millions of weekly viewers. It had a reach that's unimaginable today, when major sports leagues dominate the networks and outdoor shows are found somewhere in the ether of cable television's hundreds of options. The show was hosted, at its height, by Curt Gowdy, and it featured the reigning celebrities of the time—including Bing Crosby, Jimmy Carter, Burt Reynolds, Cheryl Tiegs, and William Shatner—who would join Gowdy on hunting and fishing expeditions.

Pate was friendly with Gowdy, and he convinced him to do an episode of the show with him in Homosassa in 1980. Joining them was Paul Michael Glaser, better known then as the actor who played Detective David Starsky on the 1970s cop show *Starsky & Hutch*.

A few years later, Pate began working on a film for the company 3M (which, at the time, owned Scientific Anglers, a maker of fly lines, leaders, and tippet). News reports from that time claimed that 3M and its partner, Leisure Time Products, spent $400,000 making the film. Its official title was *The Challenge of Big Tarpon with Billy Pate*, but it was known more colloquially around Homosassa as "that fucking movie."

The news that a big movie was being filmed at Homosassa brought even more attention to the area. The camera boats and airplanes and helicopters (which 3M flew to scout for tarpon) became a nuisance to those on the flats. "A lot of anglers took issue with it," says Nat Ragland, one of Pate's guides, who was on a camera boat during the shoots. That Pate was somewhat aloof off the water and never warned anyone about the film before it happened didn't help soothe those issues. Most of the anglers steered clear of the camera crews on the water, but they groused about the space they took up and the commotion they caused. Some anglers and guides chose to express that anger through acts of civil disobedience. "Freddie [Archibald] would pole up close by as they were shooting and he'd start firing off bottle rockets at them," says Mike Locklear, a longtime guide in the area.

That the film took three seasons to shoot caused even greater frustration on the flat. The shoot in the first season was a disaster, according to Lee Baker, who guided Pate in the movie. "They were shooting with expensive 8mm film, and the number-one cameraman was always trying to save film," says Baker. "We'd hook a fish and the guy would say, 'Let me know when the fish is going to jump,' which is almost impossible to do. So he missed the shots. He should have been shooting the entire time."

Though the movie was shot for three seasons in the mid-1980s, it wasn't released until 1989. Pate is the star of the film, and in it, he wears his signature straw hat and a guayabera shirt. His back cast is high, like the steelheader he was. When he hooks a fish, he strikes it with great force, five or six times, to cinch the hook. He calls tarpon that are under world-record weight "rats" and quickly breaks them off. In the film, he kills two tarpon, neither of which is a world record. He fights the second of those fish for nine and a half hours, and it drags Pate and Baker for fifteen miles into the night. The film succeeds with its intended effect. The viewer comes out of it believing that Pate was a great angler, which he was.

When asked what motivated Pate to do the film and the *American Sportsman* show, Baker replies, simply, "Ego."

To some, the filming of the movie, and its subsequent release, forever changed the fishery. "After that, it was 'Katie, bar the door' in Homosassa," says Ragland. "It was already getting more popular, but that really got it going."

∽

A brief digression, re: obsession:

"Chasing that fish was so mentally, physically, and financially painful," Evans says. "The easiest part for me was the financial. The physical part was tough, but I could handle it. The mental part was the worst. The mental stamina you needed to keep going after it, year after year, when nothing happened, the concentration, the pressure, the fear. It's not really fear of failure that gets people. It's easy to make excuses if you have that fear. It's the fear of greatness, that point you reach where you can no longer rely on any excuses for failure.

"The thing is, I never really thought about any of that back then. I would put it out of my mind, because if I'd thought about the physical and mental toll, I would have never set foot in Homosassa. The problem was, once I saw those fish, those toads coming from four hundred yards away, I was fucked all over. I'd see one jump and put a hole in the water and it was like I stuck my finger in a light socket. These tarpon were a giant step up the ladder from everything else. You can admire a good painting and then see a Van Gogh. There are degrees in everything. This was the biggest challenge in the fishing world, these giant fish in clear water and on white sand. There's never been anything else like it. I wanted it more than anything else. I couldn't think of anything else, ever, other than tarpon back then. Even when I wasn't there, I was there."

∽

This whole thing is totally silly, isn't it? Think about the sheer amount of time these men spent trying to catch the world-record tarpon. Remember, Evans has spent three and a half years of his life in Homosassa. These were all accomplished, otherwise successful people who could have spent that considerable amount of time—and money—doing almost literally anything else. Instead, they spent their time and money and effort in the pursuit of something that most people outside their small, hermetic world would certainly view as astoundingly trivial.

Think of the failure rate. Evans has caught a world record once every seven years or so during his fifty-one years of tarpon fishing. Most others have, or had, worse batting averages than that. Some never made contact with the ball. Think of the bickering and backstabbing, of the angst surrounding Pate's movie, or the bitterness Evans felt toward Pate, or the jousting on the water. Sayre's Law is very much in effect here: "In any dispute, the intensity of feeling is inversely proportional to the value of the issues at stake."

∽

And yet.

It is not totally silly.

I've mentioned Susan Orlean and Robert Frost when I've written about obsession in the past. I can't help but return to them now. In her book *The Orchid Thief*—which can really be read as an extended meditation on obsession—Orlean writes that once people become adults, they tend to view obsessions over seemingly frivolous things, like chasing rare flowers (as her main character does) or an even rarer fish, as a bit naïve and embarrassing. This is very true. And yet, the world is full of these tiny, niche obsessions, and there can be some enlightenment gained from them, some focus and refined ability to perceive. In fact, these tiny obsessions, all taken together, are arguably what makes the world go round. Chasing world-record tarpon, in a sense, is not too different from trying to summit Mount Everest, or attempting a long-distance swim, or collecting rare books, or trying to win the World Series of Poker. People become obsessed because of a desire to subject themselves to tests of character, to seek answers about who they are. Obsessions are, essentially, stories that we—the most and least successful among us—invent about ourselves to get through the day, the week, the decades. The stories are about our lives and the meaning that we, and others, bestow upon them. They give people a sense of purpose in a world that seems ever more chaotic, where, as Thoreau once famously said, most of us "lead lives of quiet desperation." An obsession can be, as Frost once described the form of a poem, a "momentary stay against confusion."

Or, as Evans puts it, "The poon can get rid of everything that gives you a problem."

∽

Alas, the poon also creates some problems, as many obsessions can do if they're taken too far. "I desire the things which will destroy me in the end," Sylvia Plath once wrote in her journal.

The volatile mix of competitive tension, ego, pressure, drugs, women, and the growing crowds eventually took its toll in Homosassa. It couldn't last, couldn't go on like this without repercussions. People began to call the place "Homosmasha." "I've never seen a group of people fall faster," says Evans. "If you let the poon totally grab hold of your life, it shattered it."

Many of the serious record hunters, and some of the guides—Evans, Huff, Pflueger, Apte, Robinson, Perez, Pate, Lopez—went through divorces around that time. Pflueger left Homosassa and never returned, frustrated by the fish and the scene. "The quest was all about ego," he says. He threw himself into the solitary sport of turkey hunting, sitting silently and motionless in the spring woods for hours on end. Perez went back to the Keys, teetered for a bit, then burned himself out. One year, he guided for 127 days in a row. "On the 127th day, I ran the boat out and got somewhere and looked around and had no idea where I was for a full five minutes," he says. He's righted himself since then, but things have never been the same on the water since Homosassa, everything since one long, slow comedown from that once-in-a-lifetime high. He lives in Islamorada and continues to guide a few days of the week during tarpon season. He hasn't been back to Homosassa in three decades. Huff, too, went home, to Marathon, and never fished Homosassa again. He lasted another decade or so in the Keys until the impatient and boorish hordes invaded those flats, too. He moved to the Everglades in 1996, the more remote western part, where he could get lost in the inscrutable tangle of mangroves and water, and find something pure and untouched, at least as pure and untouched as it gets in the continental United States.

In his last spring of serious tarpon angling, Lopez booked Chittum from April through part of August. The plan was to start in Islamorada and, with some zigzagging, fish for tarpon up and across the Gulf of Mexico to perhaps Texas, a moveable feast of pleasure, on and off the water. In April, they fished the Keys. Then Chittum trailered the boat and Lopez hopped in his plane, and they met in Homosassa, where they stayed for the month of May. They returned to the Keys for the tarpon tournament season, and then headed back north to the Panhandle. Sometime in mid-July—Chittum doesn't remember where they were at the time, it all became a blur—they tapped out, physically and mentally done. "That did him in," says Chittum. "It nearly did me in, too."

Lopez's life fell apart after that. He had invested much of his inheritance in oil fields in Texas, and those fields had gone fallow. He left Florida for a while and spent some time in prison. When he came back to Islamorada, "he was a completely different person," says Navarre Jr. "He was crazy and violently erratic." Lopez started guiding, moving from the front of the boat to the back of it. He made many enemies on the water. He lived for a time in a truck parked near his ex-wife's house. He punched his parole officer. He was involved in a road rage incident on US 1. When the cops arrived on the scene, he pulled a knife on them and they beat the crap out of him. One person says that the last time he saw Lopez, he was sitting on the porch of his ex-wife's house holding a loaded revolver. "I'm waiting for the neighbor's dog to come into the yard again," he said, by way of explanation. Despite everything, he somehow managed to be a different person around his two daughters, doting on them throughout it all.

He left the Keys again after five unhappy years, disappeared, and died sometime in the late 2000s.

In 1981, Carl Navarre Jr. and his guide Eddie Wightman stood on the tarmac of the small airport in Crystal River. Navarre Sr.'s plane had just arrived, and his son and Wightman were there to pick him up to start their fishing trip. But Navarre Sr. emerged from the plane wearing a suit. He was also followed by his wife. "I knew something was wrong," says Navarre Jr. His father had found out the night before that he had an advanced stage of cancer, and rather than fishing, he had come to pick up his son to fly with him to New York for immediate surgery. They ended up staying in New York for three months. Navarre Sr. continued to hunt and fish for a few more years before succumbing to the cancer in 1985, at the age of sixty-five.

Navarre Jr. was one of the few who escaped Homosassa relatively unscathed. He became a journalist, then used part of his inheritance to buy the Atlantic Monthly Press in 1986, where he published books by Richard Ford, Ron Chernow, and P. J. O'Rourke, among others. He sold the publishing house five years later and invented a color printing and manufacturing system known as MyPublisher, which produced high-quality, single-copy books. Apple, Adobe, and Microsoft hired his company to provide exclusive digital print services. In 2012, Navarre Jr. sold MyPublisher to Shutterfly for tens of millions of dollars. He remains an avid tarpon fisherman, but, like Perez and Huff and Pflueger, he never returned to fish Homosassa.

∽

Sometime in the late 1980s, Pate started to lobby the IGFA to make two rule changes. He wanted to include a twenty-pound tippet class for fly fishing, and he wanted a longer legal bite tippet (twelve inches was the longest it could be). He desired these changes, ostensibly, for billfish. But he also wanted them for tarpon. "Billy was always trying to change the rules so he could catch more records," says Billy Knowles.

To many of his fellow anglers, twenty-pound tippet, because of its added strength, was sacrilege, going against the very principle that made fly fishing for tarpon a sport—that is, the testing of oneself against the greatest of fly fishing's limitations, with giant fish and small tippets, that net in tennis that McGuane wrote about. The thought was that twenty-pound would be lowering that net nearly to the ground. Huff hated it. So did Pate's guide, Lee Baker. "I was disappointed. Everybody was ticked off," he says. Perez says twenty-pound "isn't fly fishing." Apte thought it was less sporting. "Big tarpon were caught without it," he says. "It took skill, but it was done." Pallot says he's "never been a fan" of it.

Despite the significant opposition, Pate prevailed, and the IGFA introduced a twenty-pound tippet class category in 1991. (They did not introduce a longer bite tippet, however.)

When he heard that the new rule had been passed, Evans, who still seethes about it to this day, decided to go out and establish a high bar in the new category so the record wouldn't start out at, say, ninety pounds and move up incrementally. In successive days in 1991 with Dopirak, he landed a 176-pound tarpon and then a 180-pound tarpon on sixteen-pound test (stubbornly refusing to use the newly approved tippet) and entered them in the twenty-pound category to set the mark. Pate, by that time, was looking farther afield for new record opportunities.

∽

In April 1992, Pate was part of a group of tarpon anglers who traveled to Sierra Leone, located on the southwest coast of Africa. Among the others on the trip were Tom Gibson, a Houstonian who fished for tarpon mainly on conventional tackle, Brian O'Keefe, a photographer who was there to document the trip for a fishing magazine, and Pierre Affre. The trip had been arranged with the help of Affre and a French travel outfit. The idea was to develop the coast of Sierra Leone as a tarpon-fishing destination. Pate had heard that the tarpon in Africa grew to immense sizes, perhaps even bigger than the ones in Homosassa. Armed with his twenty-pound tippet, he believed he could set the new world record there.

Pate, Gibson, and O'Keefe flew to Paris to meet up with Affre and stayed a night. The group then flew down to Freetown, the capital of Sierra Leone. They had with them rods, reels, lines, tippet material, and gaffs. They also carried several canisters of liquid nitrogen. Some fisheries biologists had asked them to keep samples of the tarpon they caught—the heads and the otoliths, which are bones in the inner ear that help determine the fish's age. The liquid nitrogen would act as a preservative.

In Freetown, the group was greeted by menacing, shirtless men brandishing machetes. On the drive south to their destination—Sherbro Island—they were stopped periodically at makeshift roadblocks and not allowed to pass until they paid a desired sum of money. The sound of sporadic gunfire echoed in the hills around them. On a boat on the way out to the mothership that would act as their base for their trip, the men saw a stick in the water, which was topped with a severed human head. "We didn't realize until we got there that Sierra Leone was in the middle of a friggin' civil war," says O'Keefe.

They fished anyway, going out every day in Boston Whalers. The guides led them to a seam, where dark, muddy water from a river hits the clear ocean water. The tarpon showed themselves there with rolls and then descended directly twenty to thirty feet down to the bottom. It was not the type of flats fishing that the anglers were used to back in the United States.

Pate and O'Keefe hit it off at the beginning of the trip, and Pate even gave O'Keefe a custom-made fly reel. But the friendliness didn't last long.

O'Keefe had paid his own way for the trip (the magazine didn't have the budget), and thus he believed it was perfectly okay to fish a bit while there. Out of respect for Pate and his attempt at a world record, O'Keefe says he didn't make any casts for the first few days, and instead took photos. He followed Pate around for a bit and noticed that he wasn't taking the advice from the guides about where to fish. Pate used a floating line and tried to find fish on the clear sandy spots in the area, which were few and far between. "It was almost like he felt some sort of pressure from back home in Florida to fish in a way that would be suitable to his friends there, like he didn't want the bad optics," says O'Keefe. Pate landed a few fish, from eighty to one hundred pounds or so, well under the weight he desired.

After four days of taking photos, O'Keefe decided it was time to fish. Unlike Pate, he fished where the guides wanted him to, and he went full in on the gear he believed best matched the conditions and the quarry. He used a thirteen-weight rod, a Jim Teeny running line, the heaviest sink tip he could find, and twenty-pound tippet. He fished a ten-inch fly and threw it far up-current, mending his line several times to get it as deep in the water as possible, before stripping it back. And he wrecked the fish. "Most of them broke off," he says. "They were just impossibly large." There were, indeed, some true monsters around. One of the spin fishermen on the trip landed a 240-pounder, and the all-tackle record—286 pounds, 9 ounces—would be caught by a Frenchman on live mullet eleven years later up the coast near Guinea-Bissau.

On April 9, one of the last days of the trip, O'Keefe landed a massive tarpon. Affre believed it could be the new record. "I can't stand records," says O'Keefe. "I just wanted to throw the leader away and keep fishing." But Affre, envisioning the possible marketing opportunities that a world-record tarpon could bring to the area, insisted that he enter the fish. O'Keefe's tarpon, 187 pounds, 6 ounces, would indeed turn out to be the new world record in the twenty-pound class. "Billy stopped talking to me after I caught that fish," says O'Keefe.

According to Jodi Pate Ahearn, who was married to Pate at the time, Pate "felt defeated by that fish and walked all over by O'Keefe." Pate told friends that O'Keefe wasn't even supposed to fish. "Billy thought that Brian kind of wiggled his way onto the trip," says Tom Gibson. ("Despite the reel he brought me, I guess," says O'Keefe.)

When O'Keefe got home to Oregon, he says, he began getting calls from some of Pate's friends, who questioned him about the fish in somewhat threatening tones. "I began to realize that this was the dumbest thing I'd ever done," says O'Keefe. "I didn't care about the record at all, and now I was suddenly getting heat from Pate and his buddies. I learned a lot about fishing with a really rich person who had an ego. Billy was the consummate Southern gentleman when he needed to be. But if you ever caught a bigger fish than he did, you became a serious enemy. It was sad, in a way. I almost felt sorry for him."[*]

It wouldn't be the last time Pate was haunted by the twenty-pound tippet class that he'd made happen.

Smashed lives. Smashed families. Smashed egos. But for all the destruction that took place during that time in Homosassa, one thing was hit harder than anything else—the fishery, which proved once again that the

[*] O'Keefe's story and photos of that Africa trip never made it into the public domain. The magazine that had commissioned the piece went out of business before it could be published.

single abiding trait of mankind, going all the way back to Adam and Eve if you believe that sort of stuff, is our unerring ability to fuck up paradise.

"I don't think that any one of us who fished Homosassa back then thought that it would ever end," says Evans. And why would they? There were thousands and thousands of fish, maybe ten thousand, so many that they couldn't even begin to fish them all, and they came in year after year after year.

Evans says that only now, in retrospect, does he remember having the smallest inkling of something happening in Homosassa at that time, some change taking place off the water. One year in the late 1970s, Evans took off in his Piper Aztec from the airport in Crystal River. He was heading home after his month of fishing in Homosassa. As was his custom, he flew around the area for one last look, to soak it all in—the miles of uninterrupted woodlands, the four limpid, winding rivers, that huge, expansive flat in the bay.

Near the headwaters of one of the rivers, Evans noticed that a large area had been cleared. Felled trees lay on their sides. Bulldozers had worked over the dirt. He remembers turning his plane around and flying over it for one more look. "I thought it was interesting, but I didn't pay it much mind at the time," says Evans.

He then forgot about it, wholly engrossed with thoughts of tarpon, and headed north, for home.

INTERLEWD

The Scene: A Gulf-side bar somewhere in the Keys that's frequented by anglers, guides, and a healthy dose of your run-of-the-mill barflies. The angle of the post-fishing, late afternoon sun has conveyed some unspoken signal to everyone in the bar, almost like the turning of the tide, that the hour is now officially happy. The volume of the classic rock music goes up a few notches. The sunburned patrons, hands clamped to their drinks, talk loudly, smiling and ebullient as they bid *adios* to the sunlight and some of their brain cells. I am sitting at a table in the middle of it all, wrapping up an interview. Later, when listening to the last bits of my interview tape, the lyrics of Lynyrd Skynyrd's "Gimme Three Steps" will come through clearer than the words of my interviewee.

Me: I gotta ask you one more thing. It's about a fly someone told me you once tied.

Prominent Keys Tarpon Guide (PKTG): Okay. Shoot.

Me: This someone told me that you once tied a tarpon fly out of pubic hair.

PKTG: . . .

Me: So?

PKTG: [Sighs] I did.

Me: Was it your own pubic hair?

PKTG: [Raises voice] Hell no, man! It was my girlfriend's. It was just something I tried, man. I got a lot of different stuff around my fly-tying desk.

Me: So she knew you were cutting it to create a fly?

PKTG: Well, she was shaving it off anyway, and I just asked if I could use some.

Me: Did the fly have a name?

PKTG: Hell, no.

Me: Did the fly work?

PKTG: Nah. Not too well. Didn't swim right. The hair's too thin. I would have needed to get a lot more of it. Which would have, you know, entailed me asking my girlfriend to ask her girlfriends for some, which wouldn't have gone over too well . . . Hey, you're not going to put my damn name in your book with this pubic hair fly business, are you?

Me: It's just a fly. And it's kinda funny.

PKTG: I know, man. But I don't want to be known as the "pubic hair fly tarpon guide." I'm already known as the "dope-smoking tarpon guide."

Me: I think it's kind of interesting. It adds nuance to your personality, your character.

PKTG: Please, man?

Me: Okay. I guess if it bothers you enough, you can remain anonymous.

PKTG: Thank you. And anyway, that fly was nothing. If you think that's crazy, you should see some of the shit I've done with permit flies.

9

LOOK AT MOTHER NATURE
ON THE RUN

B y Tom Evans's estimation, there were, at most, twenty-five boats on the water on any given day during the 1981 Homosassa tarpon season. The fishery wasn't the nearly empty space it was back in 1977, but it was all manageable. That didn't last long. What started as a snowball (Lefty's leak, Huff's unofficial record, Evans's official one) became an avalanche (the subsequent year-after-year records, the newspaper and magazine stories, Pate's movie). In retrospect, the unsustainable popularity of the Homosassa fishery, the tragedy of its commons, seems like it was inevitable.

By the mid-1980s, according to Billy Knowles, Lee Baker, and Dale Perez, there were usually sixty boats on the water during the height of the season. By the end of that decade, says Gary Merriman, that number rose to seventy or eighty. Kent Davenport claims that by the time he started fishing Homosassa in the early 1990s—just after Pate's movie came out—the number of boats on the water at the height of the season approached one hundred. "You could walk the flat across the gunwales," he says.

It became, quite obviously, a problem. Boats spook fish. Tarpon ping-ponged from one boat to another, getting warier—and less likely to take a fly—with each new encounter. The fish started acting oddly, racing through the flat and forming daisy chains close to the ocean floor, as opposed to the water's surface. They completely ignored flies that were placed right in front of them.

The boat launches were choked with traffic in the morning. Many of the new boats were helmed inexpertly. Almost all of the newcomers had at least two trolling motors on their boats and used them, instead of push poles, to move about the flat. Though the hum of a trolling motor is somewhat discreet, it still spooks fish. There was also still some running-and-gunning with the big engines to track down swimming fish, only now the fish no longer took flies as they did in the late 1970s. One new guide did try to learn how to pole the flat, bless his heart. His boat, however, earned the nickname "Circles," because that was the motion it described whenever the guide started to pole.

The flat had turned into a circus, and the stars of the show were not happy. "You'd see the tarpon come in and start to bounce from boat to boat, all with their trolling motors going, and then the fish would suddenly turn and start flying out into the Gulf," says Rufus Wakeman, who started fishing Homosassa in the late 1980s. "It was so depressing to see a big string of big fish move west in a hurry like that."

And—again, inevitably, in retrospect—the tarpon fishing in Homosassa fell off a cliff. By the early to mid-1990s, "You could go out for seven straight days and not even make a cast," says Bill Bishop. "Because there weren't any fish to cast to." Whenever fish did show up, they got mobbed and horribly hassled. "There'd be fifteen to twenty boats fishing a single string of fish," says Jimmy Long, a Homosassa-based guide. In 1995, a massive red tide in May and June wiped out some of the fishing season. Evans spent forty days fishing Homosassa in 1996. He did not catch one fish. The record chasers at Homosassa were like the main character in John Cheever's "The Swimmer." When they started their quest, everything was bright and beautiful, robust and vigorous. But as the journey progressed, it got darker and darker, and by the end, everything was exhausted and tattered, and the home they thought was theirs was no longer.

Tarpon are an ancient species—fifty million years old, if you remember. During their time on Earth, they have survived the extreme heat of the early Eocene epoch, the extreme cold of the Pleistocene Ice Age, and the massive die-off of large animals that happened thirteen thousand years ago. They also, as individuals, can live to an old age. They have proven to be highly adaptable.

They certainly can become habituated to human behavior. A healthy population of tarpon frequent the docks at Robbie's Restaurant in Islamorada, where they are fed daily by tourists. There is a group of tarpon that tend to stay near the docks and boat slips of Bud & Mary's Marina in Islamorada, a no-fishing zone, and thus a safe haven. It makes sense that if tarpon can become conditioned to the food and safety that humans provide them, they can also become conditioned to any human-caused signs of potential danger or discomfort.

It is believed by scientists that the tarpon that come to Homosassa in May are a specific subgroup of the greater tarpon population. They have dark black backs, perhaps, it's theorized, because they are reared and live much of their lives in the muddy waters of the Mississippi River Delta. They are shorter and fatter than the tarpon in the Keys, and they weigh more. This Homosassa subgroup likely returned to the area every spring, en masse, as part of their pre-spawning ritual because that's what their forebearers did for eons—until something happened that changed their habits, or at least the habits of most of them.

Tarpon have been known to disappear from some spots in the world. Port Aransas, Texas, near Corpus Christi, was a famous tarpon-fishing destination in the 1930s and 1940s. At the height of its popularity, hundreds of tarpon were caught a day during the season there, and all of them were killed (these were the days when it was believed that our oceans contained a limitless bounty). The dead tarpon were displayed back at the docks as proof of a successful day of angling, then their carcasses were thrown back in the water or used as garden fertilizer. By the 1950s, the Port Aransas tarpon fishery was no more.

Homosassa's tarpon were not eliminated in this way, of course. Even during the height of the world-record madness, maybe five fish a year were purposely killed, and even if five or ten times that number died after being released (from sharks or stress), overkilling wasn't the reason Homosassa's tarpon didn't return.

The boats and the increased pressure surely played a role—and perhaps a significant one—in the destruction of the fishery, with tarpon adapting to that discomfort. There were other factors, though, that likely contributed in a much more significant way. After all, the tarpon in the Keys are subjected to a great number of boats all year long. And while they are much harder to fool with a fly these days than they were decades ago when they were less pressured, they continue to show up there in robust numbers. The tarpon in Homosassa, on the other hand, have not.

∽

Artifacts from the Homosassa area indicate that Native American tribes first settled or visited there some ten thousand years ago, likely attracted to the numerous and bountiful springs. The largest of those springs culminate in the region's four major rivers—the Crystal, Chassahowitzka, Weeki Wachee, and Homosassa (which in the Seminole language supposedly means "river of fishes"). The Spanish explorer Hernando de Soto marched through the area with his army in 1539, searching for gold. One of the first permanent white settlements in Homosassa was built by a man named David Levy Yulee, whose family had immigrated to Florida from St. Thomas in the 1820s (Yulee's father purchased fifty thousand acres near Jacksonville with the idea of creating a Jewish agrarian utopia, which never quite got off the ground).

Yulee studied law in St. Augustine and set up a practice there in 1832. In 1845, when Florida officially became a state, he was elected as a US senator, the first Jewish person to ever hold that position. Yulee became known on Capitol Hill as the "Florida Fire Eater" for the vehement pro-slavery rants he delivered on the Senate floor. In 1851, he built a five-thousand-acre plantation, called "Margarita," on the Homosassa

River. There, his 150 slaves grew sugar cane, cotton, and oranges. Yulee was also president of the Florida Railroad Company, which constructed some of the railroad lines that Henry B. Plant would consolidate after the Civil War. In 1864, Yulee's plantation house on the Homosassa River was destroyed by Union gunboats (the ruins of his sugar mill are now a state park). After the Civil War, Yulee spent nine months in prison for his role in helping Jefferson Davis briefly escape Union forces. Yulee never rebuilt his Homosassa home, and the area would remain relatively sleepy in terms of development for the next century.

∾

The painter Winslow Homer began visiting Florida and the Caribbean in 1884, a ritual he would undertake in the late winter and spring for the next twenty-four years to get away from the lingering cold grip of the Northeast (he was living in Maine at the time). One of his favorite spots in the south was Homosassa, where he spent three full seasons.

Homer visited Homosassa primarily to fish, and he once told his brother in a letter that the angling there was "the best in America as far as I can find." Homer was, by most accounts, a competent fly fisherman. He mostly targeted largemouth bass, which were plentiful in those days in the Homosassa River. Though his trips to Homosassa were more restorative than anything else, Homer did paint eleven watercolors depicting the area, with a few of them featuring fishermen holding bent rods high in the air.

Homer's Homosassa paintings have a bit of a rough, unfinished feel to them, almost impressionistic. But Stephanie Herdrich, a curator of late-19th-century American paintings at the Metropolitan Museum of Art, cautions against dismissing them as merely vacation watercolors. "They are a larger meditation on man and nature and the fragility of the two," she says. And indeed in two of his most famous Homosassa watercolors—*Red Shirt, Homosassa, Florida* and *Homosassa River* (both done in 1904)—the jungle, with its towering palm trees and swaying bankside grasses, dwarfs the tiny fishermen found tucked into the corners of their respective paintings. What's striking about all eleven of Homer's Homosassa watercolors is how serene and sensuous they are, a marked contrast from his paintings set in the Northeast, where nature—mainly the sea—is depicted as menacing and disturbing, something to struggle against, not peaceably coexist with. Herdrich thinks it may be the case that the Homosassa paintings reflect Homer's relaxed state of mind while there.

By Homer's last visit to Homosassa in February 1908, the area appeared to be on the verge of discovery (Homer died two years later). John Jacob Astor, Grover Cleveland, and Thomas Edison had stayed in the area as well by that time. Dimock was there, too, reporting *The Book Of The Tarpon*, which would be published in 1911. But the Great Depression in the 1930s brought development and tourism to a halt. When Huff and Evans first arrived there in the late 1970s, they saw basically what Homer had seen.

∽

The clear-cutting and bulldozing that Evans spotted from his plane while leaving Homosassa that spring in the late 1970s? It was likely the Villages of Citrus Hills, located near the Crystal River, which was built around that time, and now has four golf courses and around three thousand houses. (This is the community where Ted Williams spent his final years.) That planned community was joined by Sugarmill Woods, located near the headwaters of the Chassahowitzka River, which was also built and began to flourish around that time in the 1970s. It now has some four thousand houses and two golf courses, with forty-five total holes.

These two master-planned communities were on the vanguard of a major change for the area. Citrus County (where Homosassa is located) and Hernando County (which borders much of the Oklahoma flat south of Citrus County) were, for a few decades following the 1970s, two of the fastest-growing counties in the United States. In 1970, Citrus County had 19,000 inhabitants. By 1990, it had 93,500, and in 2020 it has 150,000. Hernando County had 17,000 residents in 1970. By 1990, that number had risen to 101,000, and in 2020, now stands at 194,000. Retirees fueled most of the growth, and dozens of planned communities were built to accommodate them. In the late 1960s, Citrus and Hernando Counties had only a handful of golf courses. By 2000, Hernando County had nineteen courses, which was three times as many, per capita, than the national average. The two counties have close to thirty-five combined as of 2020.

The one thing all of those new developments and golf courses have in common is the need for significant amounts of freshwater. That freshwater comes from a portion of the upper Floridan aquifer, which lies beneath Citrus and Hernando Counties and feeds the area's springs. By the early 2000s, Hernando County alone was using fifty million gallons of water a day.* Home sites, agriculture, and some residual mining pumped out a lot of that water. So did the golf courses, which used something like 370,000 gallons per course every day of the year. (In 2001, six Hernando County golf courses were caught pumping more than their prescribed limit.) That water usage, coupled with severe droughts in Florida in 1980 and 1984, served to draw down the aquifer and reduce the flow of the local springs. Adding insult to that injury, much of the groundwater became polluted with pesticides and other lawn-maintenance chemicals, as well as nitrates from fertilizer, cow dung, and leaky septic tanks. Nitrate levels in the region's four main rivers increased by a factor of five between the 1960s and 1990s. Eighty-five percent of the pollution in the Homosassa River is caused by humans (from fertilizer, livestock waste, etc.). In the Chassahowitzka River, humans account for 81 percent of the pollution.**

Historically, the area's four main rivers, along with the many adjacent smaller springs—all of which collectively make up what's known as the "Springs Coast"—pumped around a billion gallons of freshwater into the Homosassa Bay every day. This was the reason for that

---

* According to USGS data, 1.3 billion gallons of water were withdrawn from the upper Floridan aquifer—which ranges from South Carolina to Florida—in 1960. By 2005, the withdrawals had reached 3.2 billion gallons. The state of Florida accounts for 80 percent of withdrawn water from the aquifer.

** Forest fires and biological decay are two types of nonhuman pollution, just FYI.

just-after-a-thunderstorm smell that was once omnipresent on the Homosassa flats that Dan Malzone talked about. But since 1980, there has
been a drastic decline in the amount of freshwater entering the bay. The
flow in the Crystal River has been reduced by 58 percent, and the flow of
the Chassahowitzka River has been reduced by 55 percent. The Florida
Springs Institute, a science-based nonprofit, recently released a report
that assigned grades for Florida's major spring-fed rivers, based on their
flow. The Homosassa-area rivers did not fare well. The Crystal, Chassahowitzka, and Homosassa Rivers all received Fs. The Weeki Wachee
River, star student of the bunch, got a D. Less freshwater means more
salinity in the bay and in the springs, a problem that's been exacerbated, as
noted earlier, by rising sea levels in recent years. Ryan Gandy, a research
scientist for Florida Fish and Wildlife Conservation Commission, grew
up on the Springs Coast. He says he used to fish for largemouth bass (a
freshwater fish that can tolerate a bit of brackish water) in the Chassahowitzka River, as Homer had done in the Homosassa River. "But those
fish haven't been there for a while now," he says.

This lack of freshwater has had consequences.

∞

In the 1960s, commercial crabbing was the biggest industry in Homosassa. Blue crabs were everywhere—mating in rivers and floating the
ocean currents in Homosassa Bay, plentiful to the point of absurdity.
The crabs attached themselves to the trim tabs on the backs of flats
skiffs. They tried to grab hold of push poles, their pincers futilely clacking
against the graphite.

The tarpon that came to Homosassa feasted on those crabs. "Every
day you'd see the crabs swimming all over the surface of the water and
the tarpon busting on them," says Ronnie Richards, a longtime local
guide. Huff says that nearly every tarpon landed back in the late 1970s
and early 1980s "had crabs coming out of it, from both ends." It was the
sheer abundance of the nutrient- and oil-rich crabs that likely attracted
those Homosassa tarpon to the area in the first place, and also helped

them attain their stupendous size. And it may be that the sudden disap-
pearance of those blue crabs drove the tarpon away.[*]

The blue crabs of Homosassa Bay, as it turns out, needed freshwater,
too. They mate in freshwater and, because the spring-fed rivers that
empty into Homosassa Bay are not rich in organic nutrients, they relied
on the plentiful brackish areas—which *are* rich in nutrients—to feed.
The abundance or scarcity of blue crabs is "directly tied to freshwater
flow," says Gandy. The higher salinity levels that result from reduced
freshwater flow are associated with lower survival rates, slower molting,
and higher predation mortality for blue crabs, according to a study done
by the University of North Carolina–Wilmington. As the freshwater
flow into Homosassa Bay dissipated, so did the number of blue crabs. By
2000, Gandy says, the biomass of blue crabs in the area had dropped to
half of what it was in the 1970s. (There are only a handful of commercial
crabbers left in the area.) Thus, the Homosassa tarpon no longer had
quite the impressive buffet spread they'd become accustomed to. And it
is likely no coincidence that when the blue crabs no longer appeared in
great numbers, neither did the tarpon. The equation is rather simple: less
freshwater means fewer crabs, fewer crabs means fewer tarpon.

⚬⚬

Alas, the state of Florida, that beautiful, fucked-up wonder world, seems
to always do its best—at least when it comes to the work of its state
officials—to remain beautifully fucked up . . .

The exhaustion of aquifers is a problem for more than just tarpon
anglers, of course. Without proper management, entire ecosystems—and
the state's water supply—are in peril (80 to 90 percent of the freshwater
used in Florida is groundwater). The Southwest Florida Water Management District (SWFWMD) is the state agency in charge of monitoring
the health of the area's aquifers and water supply. And it is their official

---

[*] Scientists believe one of the reasons that so many tarpon congregate in the Boca
Grande Pass is its abundance of blue and pass crabs.

position that a lack of rainfall, and not groundwater pumping, is the main cause of the depletion of the aquifer on the Springs Coast. "Rainfall in that area was a lot higher in the sixties and seventies," says Kym Rouse Holzwart, a senior environmental scientist for the SWFWMD. "Then it went down."

Scientific and environmental groups disagree with this assessment. "That's a lie. It's a political answer," says Robert Knight, an environmental scientist who runs the Florida Springs Institute. "The SWFWMD toes this line because if they told people that they couldn't take any more groundwater, every developer in the state would get a new legislature elected. The government and the water management districts are just doing the bidding of the developers."

I suppose people will believe whichever side of this argument they want to believe, as is the standard operating procedure these days. But there are facts involved here, and let's *let* them get in the way, shall we? Yes, rainfall is the way the aquifer is replenished. But the SWFWMD's claim that there has been much less rain since the 1960s and 1970s? The data on the SWFWMD's own website reflect that the 1980s were pretty wet, and that the 1990s were a bit drier, and that the first two decades of the new millennium have been mixed when it comes to rainfall, with one decade being dry and another being wet. In other words, the data demonstrate fluctuations in annual rainfall by decades. These fluctuations in rainfall have been the norm, and not the exception, forever.

So, the claim that there has been some drastic difference in rainfall by the decades is overstated, at the very least. But this is beside the point, and focusing on rainfall is a misdirection, and perhaps a deliberate one. What matters here is that, historically, throughout all of those drought years and all of those wet years—all of those fluctuations—the springs *always* maintained their sustained, normal flow, according to Todd Kincaid, a geohydrologist who has extensively studied the Homosassa area's springs. The difference between now and 1910, or now and even 1960? The springs no longer sustain their normal flow, even in non-drought years. And that's because of one thing: groundwater withdrawal. "People just want to believe in magic, that you can just take as much water as you like for as long as you like from the aquifer and have no deleterious effect," says Kincaid. "That's just ludicrous."

Indeed, government agencies in Florida do not have a stellar track record when it comes to protecting and conserving the state's water, in specific, and its environment, in general. Former Florida governor Jeb Bush did once try to help the springs, signing a springs restoration initiative into law. But four years after he left office, Rick Scott, a governor notorious for his pro-development and anti-environment stances, undid the law. In fact, Scott's SWFWMD board was so egregiously anti-environment and so obviously in the pocket of one of the state's biggest polluters (the sugar industry) that every single member was forced to resign after Scott left office in 2019. "We do the science and we publish reports," says Knight. "And then the government changes laws to reflect that. But the SWFWMD doesn't enforce existing laws. The pumping is the problem, and they're still issuing permits every day."

The problem isn't really a technical one. It's a political one.

It's also a solvable one, which makes it all the more frustrating. It's hard for us, as individuals, to truly believe that we have any control over some of our bigger environmental challenges, like global warming, which is almost so large a problem that it's ungraspable. It is more within our purview to be able to exert some control, and have some influence, over smaller things that happen more locally, like the polluting of estuaries and the depletion of aquifers. But when that available control is left unexecuted, it makes these minor tragedies—which, all linked together, create the big, ungraspable one—more frustrating and, well, sadder. They are more tangible and they are preventable, and when they occur, the loss is felt more deeply.

What's happened in Homosassa serves as a microcosm for what's happened all over Florida, inland and on the coasts, from the nitrate-based toxic algae in Lake Okeechobee, which is periodically and disastrously flushed out to both coasts, to the freshwater-starved Everglades and Florida Bay, which are dying right in front of our eyes. Ill-thought-out development, bought-and-paid-for politicians, the drying up of aquifers, the unsustainable development of coastal lands, the intentional misinformation, the worshipping of economic progress above all other types of progress . . . all of this has led to an ecological catastrophe that's yet to be fully acknowledged. The loss of the tarpon in Homosassa is just a harbinger of worse things to come.

∽

In Homosassa, the crowds showed up. The freshwater flow decreased. The crab population crashed. The tarpon left. And, eventually, so did the anglers.

By the mid-1990s, most of the record-hunting regulars had departed Homosassa for good. The exceptions were Evans and Pate, the two men most dedicated to the pursuit. But even they showed signs of restlessness and frustration. Pate's 1992 trip to Africa was an indication of a wandering eye (he would go to Sierra Leone a few more times and even ventured to Guinea-Bissau and Gambia in search of tarpon). Evans, though he continued to show up in Homosassa every year, started spending some serious time fly fishing for billfish, first in Central America and then mainly in Oceania. He broke some records for billfish, many in fact, and the billfishing in Australia and New Zealand led him to Dean Butler, who would become an important figure in Evans's later years. But Evans and Pate were never completely out of Homosassa's grasp. Neither could ever shake the place, unable to completely free their minds of what they'd seen during its heyday.

That heyday was over, though. The era from roughly the mid- to late-1980s until 2000 represented Homosassa's dark ages. There were a few significant catches during those years, however. In 1986, Dan Malzone, fishing on the first of June, caught a 167-pound tarpon on twelve-pound tippet, which broke Apte's 1982 world record by three pounds. And Evans registered his two records, caught on sixteen-pound, in the then brand-new twenty-pound class in 1991.

That year, Rufus Wakeman, a Falstaffian descendent of John Deere, hooked and landed a tarpon on sixteen-pound tippet that taped out bigger than Pate's 188-pound tarpon, even though Wakeman's fish was missing part of its tail from an old wound. Pate watched Wakeman fight the fish, only putting down his binoculars when Wakeman started up his motor and took the fish to shore to be weighed. "The scale jumped up above 190 initially," says Wakeman. "My heart just stopped." But it eventually settled on 186 pounds. "That missing tail, man," he says. "That's probably the only piece of tail I've ever been bummed about."

Wakeman left Homosassa in 1995 after a few years of extremely poor fishing. "I wish it was thirty years ago," he says now, recalling a song he used to belt out on the Homosassa flats, sung to the tune of "Loch Lomond":

> You take the High Rack
> and I'll take the Low Rack,
> And I'll catch a tarpon before ye.
> And we'll meet again
> To try to catch ol' Gunga Din
> On the bonnie, bonnie flats of Oklahomie.

And then there was Clyde Balch, the plastic surgeon who began his professional life treating trauma patients but ended up as a cosmetic specialist. He started his surgery career in Miami, where he fished with Bill Curtis in Biscayne Bay, and later moved to Naples on the West Coast. It was Curtis who first brought him to Homosassa, where he would later fish with Malzone and, occasionally, Dopirak.

On May 15, 1994, Balch was fishing with Malzone when, he says, he saw a "big dark wad of fish on the bottom" and cast his fly, a Malzone creation called the "Guido's Blonde Bomber," into the middle of it. A fish took the fly, and nearly two hours later, Balch had a six-foot, five-inch-tall tarpon with a forty-one-inch girth lying in the boat. The fish weighed 177 pounds, the new world record for twelve-pound tippet, a full ten pounds heavier than . . . Malzone's now former world record. Asked if Malzone ever seemed peeved about his record being broken, Balch says, "Nah. I guess if he had been he could have intentionally screwed up the gaffing."

"I was happy for Clyde," says Malzone. "But he acted weird about it. Not because of me. But because he always worried about Evans." Balch knew that Evans was intense and insatiable, and that he had the time and money and desire to keep pursuing records. Balch also didn't like Evans very much. "I always thought he was a bit arrogant," Balch says. His anxiety was not misplaced.

Balch fished Homosassa for another decade or so. But, because of back problems, the now eighty-two-year-old hasn't done any tarpon fishing at all in the last few years. He now spends his spring seasons in another pursuit. "I chase Ukrainian women. I go over to Ukraine every year alone," he says, with a rather yucky grin. "But I have company once I get there."

⁂

Pate's 188-pound world-record tarpon, caught on sixteen-pound tippet in 1982, now seemed like it would never be topped. Balch's 177-pounder on twelve-pound tippet looked that way, too. Homosassa appeared to be done for good, a fishing paradise lost, a piece of fishing lore, a story that old-timers would talk about constantly, boring the hell out of their younger acquaintances. This was a miserable period for the Homosassa fishery, especially for those who had seen it in its more bountiful state. And it was made all the more miserable by the dominating personality of a man who would first show up in Homosassa around that time. A man named Bobby Erra.

10
THE ERRA ERA

One evening in the mid-1980s, Bobby Erra, a Miami gangster, took his married girlfriend, beautiful, former Orange Bowl queen Marcia Valibus Ludwig, to the Jockey Club for dinner. The club, at the time, was just on the tail end of its heyday as one of Miami's trendiest hot spots, the haunt of the rich and glamorous, of stars like Jerry Lewis and Charlton Heston. When Erra and Ludwig arrived, the maître d' informed them that their table wasn't quite ready. Erra became incensed. His face reddened. "Do you know who the fuck I am?" he screamed. The maître d' apologized profusely and led the pair into the restaurant's bar area, seating them at a table and telling them that while they waited, drinks were on the house. He summoned a waiter, who immediately placed a glass pitcher of sparkling water on their table, nervously took their drink orders, and hurried off to the bar. Erra was still seething, grumbling about the show of disrespect and how he should do something about it. Ludwig, as she always did, calmed him down with a smile.

Moments later, another patron of the bar, a chubby, middle-aged man who was clearly hammered, came lurching over to Erra and Ludwig's table and stood over them, swaying. He leered down at Ludwig and pointed at her chest, saying, "You have the prettiest tits I've ever seen." The sentence was barely out of his mouth when that glass pitcher of sparkling water smashed into the man's face, knocking him to the ground. Shards of glass on the floor haloed the man's bloodied face. The room went completely quiet. The maître d' appeared, seemingly out of nowhere. "Mr. Erra, your table is ready," he said.

∞

Robert "Bobby" Louis Erra was born in 1945 in Astoria, Queens, the son of Pasquale "Patsy" Erra, a mid-level boss in the Vito Genovese crime family, one of the so-called Five Families that controlled the New York and New Jersey mafia. According to a US government report on organized crime, Patsy Erra was a hit man and bodyguard for Michael "Trigger Mike" Coppola, a gunman infamous for a bottomless appetite for sadism. By the 1960s, like many soldiers and bosses in the Genovese family, Patsy Erra had moved to Miami, joining the South Florida arm of the family business. He gradually worked his way up the mafia ladder and became a partner in the Dream Bar, a well-known mob hangout, part owner of other clubs and restaurants, and owner of several pieces of real estate in Miami. In 1963, his name was listed on what was known as the "Mayor's List of Hoodlums," which was published in the *Miami News*.

Bobby Erra attended the University of Miami. He was quite preppy—as preppy as the son of a gangster can be—playing golf and tennis and wearing Izod shirts. He attended school with a friend named Gary Teriaca, the son of a Genovese business partner of his father's. Erra and Teriaca, unsurprisingly, entered into the family business after college graduation.

Erra started out with some gambling and bookmaking. He owned pieces of many clubs and restaurants that he'd inherited from his father (who died at the age of fifty-eight, in 1973), and he ran the gambling money through them. Soon, Erra and Teriaca started hanging out with Jon Roberts, better known as the "Cocaine Cowboy," who was a key cog of the Colombian Medellín drug cartel during the height of its most fruitful era of cocaine trafficking to the United States.

A. W. Dimock hooks a tarpon in 1908.

Used with permission from the American Natural History Museum.

Stu Apte landing Joe Brooks's 148-pound, 8-ounce–world-record tarpon in 1961.
Courtesy of the International Game Fish Association.

ABOVE LEFT: Tom Evans (pictured on the right) with his first tarpon, a 56-pounder caught with the legendary guide Jimmie Albright, in 1968. *Courtesy of Tom Evans.* ABOVE RIGHT: A hole in the water produced by a hooked tarpon. *Courtesy of Tom Rosenbauer.* BELOW: Billy Pate. *Courtesy of the International Game Fish Association.*

Bobby Erra (front) in Homosassa.
Courtesy of Dean Butler.

Jim Holland Jr., and his 202-pound,
8-ounce–world-record tarpon,
caught in 2001 in Homosassa.
Courtesy of Jim Holland Jr.

Al Dopirak.
Photo by the author.

Dean Butler.
Courtesy of Dean Butler.

ABOVE: Tom Evans fighting a tarpon in 2019. *Photo by the author.* LEFT: Andy Mill. *Photo by the author.*

ABOVE: David Mangum. *Courtesy of David Mangum.*
BELOW: Nathaniel Linville (left) and Steve Huff in 2020. *Courtesy of Chad Huff.*

Tom Evans's IGFA Hall of Fame induction. Bottom row, from left: Stu Apte, Evans, Bernard "Lefty" Kreh. Top row, from left: Nicky Mill (son of Andy Mill), Tania Evans, Arthur Liverant (an antique dealer friend of Evans), Andy Mill, Jason Schratweiser (now president of the IGFA), Steve Huff. *Courtesy of Tom Evans.*

Erra and Teriaca got involved in that trafficking through an inter-mediary, a Cuban-American drug kingpin named Alberto San Pedro, who was known as "The Great Corrupter of Hialeah" (Hialeah is a city within Miami-Dade County). San Pedro was a short man with the build of a weight lifter who dyed his hair white-blonde. For years, he basically controlled Hialeah's politicians, its police force, and its judges. San Pedro once survived being shot five times by a hit man (one bullet pierced his scrotum). Roberts, according to his book *American Desperado* (which he cowrote with Evan Wright), received the Colombian cocaine, then sent it to San Pedro, who then distributed it to Erra and Teriaca.

Things started to get a little messy, as they tend to do in the drug-trafficking world. In July 1977, Teriaca's brother was murdered. Richard Schwartz, the stepson of Meyer Lansky, the well-known Jewish mafioso who was known as the "Mob's Accountant," was charged with the crime. Three months later, Schwartz was shot to death outside a Miami Beach restaurant. Though the assailant remained unidentified, Roberts claimed that he, Erra, and Teriaca had masterminded the hit.

A few years after that, Roberts said that San Pedro lost trust in Erra and Teriaca and asked him for permission to carry out a hit on *them*. The wish was granted, but the plan didn't come together . . . at least not then. In 1981, Teriaca disappeared suddenly, and the police found his apartment "a bloody mess" according to testimony. A decade later—after serving a three-year prison stint for bribing public officials—San Pedro was charged with conspiracy to commit both Teriaca's murder and the murder of another man in Colorado, in a case that would ultimately sweep in Erra.

∽

Bobby Erra was short and pear-shaped and had "thick, bushy hair," according to Roberts. Erra's friends and associates thought he looked just like the actor Joe Pesci, but they never said it to his face. His laugh, apparently, sounded just like that of Danny DeVito's Penguin character in *Batman Returns*.

Outside of his life in the underworld, Erra was a keen sportsman. He continued to play golf after college and became a low-handicapper. He particularly loved the water. He raced Grand National boats that reached speeds of up to 150 miles per hour. In one race near St. Petersburg, his boat flipped on top of him, and its propeller sliced off every finger on his left hand, save for the pointer and thumb. He continued to play golf at a high level after the accident, and would win huge sums of money using his hand as a prop to hustle his fellow golfers. But he stopped racing boats.

Instead, he directed his vast energies into fishing. Erra loved big fish, and he spent years motoring his boat from Miami to Bimini to fish for giant bluefin tuna. His life back home seemed to accompany him wherever he went, though. There is a story from that time that Erra told Hal Chittum, which may be slightly exaggerated, but also may not. One evening after fishing in Bimini, Erra went to the bar of a game club. There he saw a young woman who was sitting by herself at a table. She looked miserable, her eyes swollen as if she'd been crying for days. Erra asked around about her, and was told that she was pretty much being held hostage by a supposed Bahamian smuggler named Bootie Brown. Erra walked over to her and told her to come along with him. Brown appeared and told Erra that the woman wasn't going anywhere. Just then, Erra was knocked in the back of his head with a blackjack club, presumably by one of Brown's associates, and fell to the floor, out cold.

When Erra came to, he went out to the docks to his Merritt sport-fishing boat and told his crew members to start the engines. He grabbed a machine gun out of the boat, walked into the bar, and began strafing the club—above the patrons' heads—with bullets. Brown jumped out of a window and escaped. "And then Bobby grabbed the girl and took her back to Miami," says Chittum. (As with the Jockey Club incident, there is a smidgen of gentlemanly valor in this story.)

In the late 1970s, when the big bluefin tuna of Bimini had pretty much been fished out, Erra decided to dive into a new fishing pastime. And he found exactly the right man to show him how it was done.

∞

In 1979, between his stint as a banker and his guiding and television careers, Flip Pallot opened a high-end fishing and hunting store, Wind River Rendezvous, in a fancy mall in Miami. The store, which had a four-year run, featured fine sporting art, fly-fishing tackle, expensive British country clothing, and a gunroom modeled after the famous Griffin & Howe room in the old Abercrombie & Fitch* store in New York. Through the store, Pallot also offered casting classes and put together sporting trips to places like Alaska and Argentina.

During the store's second year of operation, a short but purposeful man walked in and asked to see Pallot. It was Erra. "He told me that he'd been an offshore guy, but now wanted to learn how to fish the flats," says Pallot. Erra signed up for personal casting lessons from Pallot. He turned out to be a good student and was good for business. "We sold Bobby thousands and thousands of dollars' worth of tackle," says Pallot.

By the spring of 1982, Pallot had had enough of retail ("I hated that job and it took me away from the woods and the water," he says), and decided that he was going to shut down the store by the summer and start guiding full-time. On the day he received his captain's license, Erra approached him.

"I want to hire you for June. And July," Erra said.

"Okay," Pallot replied. "Which days?"

"June and July," Erra said, then handed Pallot a brown paper bag filled with bound stacks of hundred-dollar bills. Pallot had his very first booking as a guide, and it was for sixty-one days straight.

During those two months, Pallot moved into the downstairs area of Erra's house in Islamorada. Erra's Wind River skiff was docked just outside. Erra and Ludwig occupied the second floor of the house. Erra and Pallot went out on the water every fishable day. Pallot says he was cognizant of who Erra was, but when they were in Islamorada, it was all about the fishing. "I never felt like I had any reason to be scared," he says.

Erra loved the flats, but bonefishing frustrated him. It required a finesse that his marred hand did not allow him to realize. And when Erra grew frustrated, he threw tantrums. "He'd miss a fish or screw up a cast,

---

* Abercrombie & Fitch wasn't always a clothing store for teens.

and then throw a brand-new rod and reel into the water," Pallot says. One day while on the way back to the dock after fishing, Erra grew so angry about his fishing performance that he started thrashing his skiff with a rod and reel. "I calmed him down," says Pallot. "At least I thought I did. He just sat there for a while. But then when we got back to the dock, he stood up and took the rod and hit it against the concrete sea wall." Pallot still has the reel that was damaged beyond further use that day.

Pallot guided Erra for a few seasons, and over those seasons, Erra's focus shifted almost entirely to tarpon. Tarpon required less finesse than bonefish, both on the cast and during the fight. After he cast, Erra would put the rod under his armpit so he could strip the line with both hands. He had custom-made large knobs attached to his reel handles for a better grip. The trouble began, though, when he hooked a fish. Erra would maneuver his rod so it was pressed between his forearm and chest. But there was almost always a glitch. The knob of the reel would catch his shirt and the fish would break off, or he would get slack in his line because he couldn't reel fast enough and the hook would fall out of the fish's mouth. These failures would often lead to frustration, and then to more gear-slinging tantrums.

∽

After those seasons, Pallot left South Florida for good, moving up the east coast to the town of Mims, near the Space Coast, to a house tucked into the woods. "Everything was getting too crowded down there," he says. "The magic of the place was gone." Erra moved on to other guides, notably a man named John Kipp.

Around this time, Erra became truly obsessed with tarpon fishing and all of the gear and tackle the sport required. He tied his own flies and leaders, which had immaculate knots. He fooled around with different fluorocarbon leaders in his pool at home, meticulously noting the sink rates of the different sizes. He hired a man who had made some poles for Olympic pole-vaulters and, with Kipp, brought out a line of composite push poles that were top of the line for their time.

In 1985, Erra and his childhood friend, Stephen Stepner, a real estate developer in Miami, started the Mangrove Boat Company. The skiffs they made constituted a big step forward in design, because, at around 650 pounds, they were much lighter than most others on the water. Mangrove boats were long (seventeen feet) and wide (seven feet, four inches), and they exuded the kitschy-cool vibe of Miami Beach, painted in green and blue pastels, with a mangrove logo (borrowed from Pallot's Wind River Rendezvous store) near the bow. Erra and Stepner spared no expense in the making of the boats, hiring a Naval architect to design them, and importing core foam from Canada and Italy. In all, Erra and Stepner made thirteen boats, some with Kevlar bodies and some with fiberglass ones. (Al Dopirak and his son, Brian, own Mangroves that they still fish out of to this day.) "We really built them for ourselves. We were nuts about the stuff," says Stepner. "It was a great business if you wanted to make two million. You just had to start with five million."

Erra even played a role in the launch of one of the world's most famous fly reel companies.

∽

As a young man, Steve Abel worked in various machine shops and then became a deep-sea diver who specialized in underwater construction. He dove in the Gulf of Mexico installing oil pipelines, and in the Suez Canal salvaging sunken ships. "I did the diving for five years, but it's like pro football. You got to get out before you get hurt," says Abel.

He went home to Camarillo, California, and started his own machine shop, where he made parts for the aerospace, gun, and medical industries. In 1987, a representative from the Stutz Reel Company approached him about building some fly reels. Abel agreed to make three hundred of them. "They were a nightmare, very difficult," says Abel. Just as he finished them, the company ran into some financial trouble. "I never did get paid," he says. Abel attended a large fishing show in San Mateo, California, with the reels, anyway, just to go check out the fly-fishing tackle scene. At that show, he met Erra and Stepner.

Erra was still having his problems with fly reels. It started with the retrofitting he had to do, the large knobs on the handles. But it went deeper than that. None of the models that existed at the time suited his needs. The reels weren't sturdy enough, and their drags weren't reliable (we'll dive a bit deeper into gear in a bit). Erra used Seamaster reels, made by Bob McChristian, considered to be top of the line at the time. But like everyone else, Erra had a difficult time getting through to the notoriously difficult McChristian. One winter, he sent some of his Seamasters to McChristian to get them tuned up for a spring tarpon tournament. McChristian had a fit when he saw that Erra had modified his creations with new reel handles, and he refused to work on them and didn't send them back. Then it was Erra's turn to stew. He sent a man up to McChristian's shop to get his reels back, and to deliver a warning to McChristian, who just shrugged it off, apparently not intimidated by anyone. The point here is that by the time Erra met Abel, he was ready for something new in the reel world.

Erra sent Abel a few Seamasters, with the idea that he could make something else, something better. Abel purchased some of the other reels on the market at the time, as well. "I took them all apart and I figured out what I wanted to do," says Abel. Namely, he wanted to make a big-game fly-fishing reel that was rugged, simple, and beautiful to behold. He built two reels—one red and one blue—and sent them to Erra and Stepner. They fished them and loved them and showed them to other anglers and guides in the Keys, who also loved them. Erra and Stepner ordered fifty more. Abel says it was at this point that he started hearing rumors about Erra. "People told me he was a mafia guy, but I didn't know any better. I was all the way in California, and there was no internet then to check on things."

He got an up-close taste of it, though, on a visit to Florida. Erra convinced Abel to allow him to become the East Coast representative for what were by then known as "Abel reels." Abel went down to see him one spring in Islamorada, and he was in his office one day when Erra was meeting with someone from his push pole company. "He told the guy that he was undermining him and right there in front of me, he took out a baseball bat and started beating him," Abel says. "I told Bobby that if he ever came after me with a baseball bat like that, I'd take it from him and beat his brains out. He had his big bodyguard there, but I didn't care." Erra smiled and told Abel not to worry about it.

Back home, Abel got word that Erra was bending some arms to sell the reels. And then he read an article in the *Atlantic Salmon Journal* in which Erra claimed to be the designer of the reels. It appeared that, as mobsters are wont to do, Erra was beginning to clamp down on Abel to try to take control of his company. "I called him and told him he was fired," says Abel. "He was pissed. And then I hired a clipping service and read about him and got scared."

But Erra wouldn't get the chance to retaliate, at least not for a while.

∞

Erra's obsession with tarpon led him, inevitably, to Homosassa. He first fished there in the late 1980s, and quickly became consumed with breaking the world record.

Evans remembers the first time he saw Erra. Evans and Dopirak were on the Oklahoma flat one afternoon, and there was a boat nearby with two men whom Evans didn't recognize. The man in the bow hooked a nice tarpon and fought it for just a few minutes before losing it. Then the man went absolutely ballistic, screaming and theatrically launching all of his tackle into the water.

Evans and Dopirak watched the entire episode in astonishment.

"Hey, you!" Evans yelled. "Throw some of that tackle over here!" Dopirak was relieved that the man in the bow didn't seem to hear him. "Dawg, that's a mafia dude," Dopirak said. "Don't yell anything else. We ain't touching that stuff."

Soon afterward, Erra would introduce himself on land. He saw Evans at the Bayport Inn one night and asked if the guy in the red hat was his guide (Dopirak did indeed wear a red hat that season). Evans told him he was. "I'm going to take a crowbar and knock that red hat off," Erra said. "The motherfucker cut me off." Evans offered to sit down with Erra and have a drink. Erra soon began to understand who Evans and Dopirak were in the pantheon of Homosassa anglers and guides, and he softened his stance on the crowbar issue.

Eventually, Erra and Evans became cordial, at least socially. Erra would corner Evans at the bar in the evenings and pump him for all of the information he could get about tarpon angling. They shared a few dinners. Evans was wary of Erra because of his reputation, but he found that his huge enthusiasm for tarpon fishing made him bearable. Dopirak remained a bit more skeptical. "You didn't really want to be Bobby's friend, but you felt like you had to tolerate him," he says.

Erra's presence in Homosassa soon became amplified. He went to the Riverside or the Bayport Inn every night and mingled with anglers and guides. He hit Becky's for breakfast in the mornings. Everyone knew him, and everyone gossiped about the rumors they'd heard about his other life. Erra started to demonstrate some of the behavior that, years later, would annoy nearly everyone in Homosassa. A mount of Pate's 188-pound, world-record tarpon hung on the wall behind a bar at a restaurant in Homosassa. One evening, Erra took the plaque off the mount, which read WORLD RECORD TARPON, WILLIAM PATE, 188 POUNDS, took it to the Bayport Inn, and nailed it to a stall door in the men's room. One day on the flat in the late 1980s, Erra got on the CB radio and, for all to hear, began lambasting Pate for his movie and all of the trouble it had caused in Homosassa. "He just lit into Billy," says Lee Baker, who was guiding Pate that day. "The thing is, the movie wasn't even out then and we weren't shooting it anymore. But we weren't going to say anything."

Evans says that around this time, he and Dopirak began to notice that there were cars, black and unmarked, that seemed to be casing the boat ramp on a daily basis.

One morning in 1989, Evans and Tania were in their rental car, driving from the Riverside down US 19 to meet Dopirak for breakfast at Becky's, when they were pulled over by a cop. Evans had been driving over the speed limit, but he was still surprised—there were usually no other cars on the road that early in the morning.

Evans went to reach for his wallet in the glove compartment, but it wasn't there. Tania explained that she had moved everything out of the car because she'd had some groceries stolen out of it the day before. "So all I had on me were my shorts, a T-shirt, and a Rolex watch," says Evans.

The cop approached and asked Evans for his license, which he, of course, couldn't produce. He then asked Evans for his zip code. He couldn't produce that, either. Evans and Tania had just moved their residency to Wyoming, and neither had yet memorized the new zip code. The cop went to his squad car and came back with a written document on a clipboard and told Evans to step out of the car.

"Sign this," he told Evans. "Or you'll go to jail."

Just as Evans looked down to start reading the document, two other cops showed up and came around behind him and lifted his feet out from under him. Evans now had his face in the dirt by the side of the road. Tania tried to get out of the car, but one of the cops slammed the door shut on her. Evans was handcuffed, "stuffed into the back of the cop car like a tuna," and taken to the county jail.

Tania, meanwhile, drove the rental car to Becky's. "She walked in and I asked her, 'Where's Tom?'" says Dopirak. "She raised her finger and told me to 'come here' and said, 'He's in jail.'" She would never again accompany Evans to Homosassa after that year.

At the county jail, Evans was told that he was being held for assault and battery, resisting arrest, and suspicion of transporting drugs. He asked to call his lawyer, but the request was refused, and he sat in jail for two hours. Finally, a cop unlocked his cell and led him to the phone. On his way there, Evans passed a young African-American man in cornrows who hissed at him, "Welcome to the real world, whitey."

Evans's lawyer told him they had to do whatever they could to avoid being charged with a felony. A felony conviction would mean he couldn't work in finance anymore. His lawyer made some calls. Soon, Evans had $18,000 wired into Dopirak's bank account, and Dopirak paid off someone in the county to free Evans and avoid the felony charge. Evans and Dopirak went out fishing later that day.

Evans believes that the cops either thought he was Erra or thought he was one of his associates. "I was clearly not from Florida," says Evans. "I was fishing, like Bobby was, and I sometimes had a drink with him. And I had a Rolex." He'd never know for sure, though.

Erra spent several seasons in Homosassa, getting to know the area and the fish, and was just approaching the point of true infamy himself on the flat before he was forced to leave—when his other life finally caught up with him.

∽

Steven Grabow was born in Brooklyn in 1947. He went south for college, graduating with an honors degree in finance from the University of Miami.* He then went to Aspen, where he became a ski instructor who lived the high life, driving a Porsche and drinking from Waterford crystal, a high life that was made possible, according to federal authorities, because he was a big-time dealer of cocaine.

In December 1984, federal agents raided Grabow's home and charged him with spearheading a local cocaine distribution ring that brought $4.5 million worth of the drug into Aspen every six weeks. While awaiting trial and out on bail, Grabow grew a bit paranoid, carefully monitoring the habits of any newcomers to town and borrowing cars from friends.

On December 8, 1985, less than a month away from his federal trial, Grabow borrowed a friend's Jeep and went to the Aspen Club to play tennis. After his match, he got into the Jeep, turned the ignition, and was instantly blown to pieces by the pipe bomb that had been placed under his seat.

∽

In April 1991, just as tarpon season dawned, Bobby Erra and Alberto San Pedro, along with two other associates, were arrested. They were

---

* Man, a lot of people in this book went to the University of Miami, didn't they?

charged with money laundering, federal drug trafficking, and conspiracy to commit murder while running a drug pipeline from 1975 through 1986 that funneled cocaine from Colombia through the Bahamas and Miami to Aspen. Erra, it was believed, had played a vital role in setting up the Bahamas arm of the operation. He had fished there and had gotten to know Lynden Pindling, who was the prime minister of the country from 1969 until 1992. (Authorities believed that Pindling had been taking millions of dollars from the Medellín cartel to allow his country to be used as a way-stop for their cocaine.) According to newspaper reports at the time, prosecutors also believed they could prove that Erra and San Pedro had orchestrated the murders of Teriaca in 1981 and Grabow in 1985, as part of the drug trafficking ring.

Erra hired lawyer Roy Black, who would famously win William Kennedy Smith an acquittal during his rape trial around that same time. "We told Black and Erra that we could prove all of the things that Erra was accused of and put him away for forty years," says Mike Fisten, who was the lead investigator on the case. Erra decided not to go to trial and took a plea bargain. In March 1992, Erra pleaded guilty to drug trafficking, extortion, and money laundering, and was sentenced to eleven years in prison. He had to forfeit everything he owned, including his house in Islamorada. (The government allowed his girlfriend, Ludwig, to continue to live there. Erra had married Donna Miller in 1991.)

Roberts, the Cocaine Cowboy, believed that Erra had gotten lucky. Grabow's murder, he wrote in his book, got Erra off the hook for crimes that were much worse. "His [Grabow's] arrest was a close call for all of us," Roberts wrote. "I'm sure he would have talked had he lived."*

Erra was released from federal prison on January 27, 1998, having served nearly six years of his sentence. He went right back to Homosassa that spring, this time with a vengeance.

---

* Roberts avoided prison time by becoming a protected federal informant. San Pedro's case was dismissed when a judge ruled that he'd been coerced into lying by the prosecution.

One day while Erra was fishing by himself, drifting with the tide near Pine Island, he spotted a red Silver King skiff running the far edge of the flat. The boat was captained by a man named Steve Kilpatrick, who was a relatively new guide to the area at the time. Kilpatrick cut in toward the flat, turned off his motor, and began poling, hewing to all of the etiquette protocols for approaching a tarpon flat. He then set up some seventy-five yards away from Erra, which, because of the number of boats on the water in those days, would also have been deemed a kosher move by most anyone. But not by Erra. He was incensed, believing Kilpatrick had cut him off. He flung his rod down in the boat, cranked up his motor, sped over to a stunned Kilpatrick, and started doing donuts around his boat while yelling, "Motherfucker! Cocksucker! I'll kill you!" over and over again.

Erra's time in prison had not mellowed him at all. In fact, it appeared to have had the opposite effect. He became more open, more brazen, about who he was. The actor Mark Wahlberg bought the rights to Roberts's *American Desperado* book and was supposed to take the lead role in the film. Peter Berg was signed as the director. But despite some early buzz and momentum, the movie never got off the ground. Erra bragged to Chittum that he'd leaned on the movie folks to have it quashed. Steve Abel says Erra wrote him a letter after he got out of prison that said "he should have taken care of me when he had the chance." Clyde Balch and his wife went to dinner one night with Erra and Ludwig, who was an old high school chum of Balch's. Ludwig got a little tipsy and told Balch, in front of the others, that she could run away with him right now. Balch's wife told everyone at the table that she wasn't the least bit worried about that. "She said that she knew that Bobby would take care of us both," says Balch. "Bobby laughed his ass off when she said it."

Guides and anglers now returned to the Bayport boat ramp only to discover that their tires had been slashed. Erra theatrically started his car remotely, one hundred yards away from the dock as he came in from fishing. He threatened to kill Dan Malzone. He also threatened to kill local guide Earle Waters. Several guides began taking handguns along with them on the water.

Erra was Jekyll and Hyde, charming one minute and insane the next. "It was like a light switch," says Dopirak. "There was normal Bobby and there was berserk Bobby." His wife, Donna, called him one day while he was out fishing. "It was a flat, calm day, so everyone could hear everything on the water. She called to tell him that her mother was in the hospital. And Bobby just started screaming at her on the phone. 'I don't give a fuck about that old bitch! Don't you ever call me during tarpon season!' And then he hung up and started fishing again, like nothing happened," says Evans.

Erra sometimes fished by himself and sometimes fished with guides. He occasionally used locals, like Ronnie Richards, Jimmy Long, Tom Mohler, and Dopirak's son, Brian. Kipp, who came up from the Keys, remained his primary guide. And, according to others there at the time, he sometimes acted as Erra's unofficial enforcer, taking on some of his boss's traits.

There was a market near Homosassa, named Clark's, which had high-quality steaks. Erra and Kipp were giving Evans a ride home from the boat ramp late one afternoon when Evans asked if they could stop at Clark's so he could get a T-bone. Erra thought that was a good idea for his dinner, too, so he sent in Kipp. But Kipp came back empty-handed, telling Erra that the owner wouldn't sell him a T-bone because he didn't like how Kipp talked to him. So Erra went in. "And then he comes out with no steak," says Evans. "He said, 'I'm going to fix that motherfucking cocksucker. He won't be here next year.' And I'm not sure what happened, but Clark's wasn't there the next year."

Erra refused to let anything get in the way of the Homosassa tarpon season. He had a coronary bypass surgery one February and was fishing there three months later. He bought a house in Hernando Beach, near the southern end of the Oklahoma flat and close to the Bayport boat ramp. He still had trouble fighting tarpon. He'd be on the water, seemingly having a good day, and then he'd miss a fish and all hell would break loose. His favorite person to blame was the man above. "God, You motherfucker, why do You hate me?" he'd yell all the time. He complained to Evans and Dopirak constantly, about the number of boats, the deteriorating fishery. He'd stop by, uninvited, to see Evans and Dopirak at their rented house in Hernando Beach. "You'd see that nose pressed against the glass door, and then he'd come in and just bitch about everything for hours, telling us how he was going to fix all the bastards," says Evans. "It got tiresome." It also added to Evans's own growing grouchiness with Homosassa, a state of being borne mainly from the lack of fish around. Evans began putting up a note on the door for Erra, telling him not to bother them because he and Dopirak had gone to bed.

Erra began to think of himself as the sheriff of the flat. "He didn't like what you did, no matter what you did," says one guide. Erra had no qualms about telling everyone else how to fish and to point out what they were doing wrong, even if they weren't doing anything wrong. "He yelled at me once at the dock for running a trolling motor on the flat," says Kyle Staton, a young guide in Homosassa. "I didn't have a trolling motor." Erra screamed at Jimmy Long one day because he didn't like the way Long anchored his boat at Chassahowitzka Point. He banged his push pole in the water as a string of tarpon approached his boat and the boat of local guide Mike Locklear. "He was trying to scare the fish away," says Locklear. "I guess he didn't like having me around."

Erra hated the way the locals fished—how they pummeled the tarpon gathered at Black Rock every morning, blind-casting lures and flies at rolling fish, and how they chased the fish with their engines on the flat in the afternoons. So, in 2013, he decided to try to do something about it. He rented out a conference room at the Holiday Inn in Crystal River and called a meeting with all of the local guides, the idea being that he would educate them about the proper way to fish Homosassa. He asked Chittum, Kipp, and Nat Ragland to come to the meeting and talk to the local guides about proper tarpon-fishing etiquette.

Long, a local guide whose family has been fishing in the area for a half century, didn't like the fact that the meeting had been called in the first place. In the end, he attended it, but he took a special precaution beforehand, hiring an undercover cop to also come along. The cop dressed in a fishing shirt and blended in with the others. "I wanted him there just in case anything funny happened," says Long.

Chittum took the lead for Erra, with Kipp and Ragland seemingly there for moral support. "I talked for about fifteen minutes," says Chittum. "It didn't go over very well."

The locals, as expected, weren't very receptive to being told how to fish their own water. A local guide named John Bazo stood up after Chittum's presentation and asked him what gave him the right to tell them how to fish Homosassa, especially since Chittum hadn't really been there for twenty years. (Chittum had, indeed, left Homosassa in the late 1980s.) "The message was, it was okay for Chittum and those guys to fish Black Rock hard in the late 1970s, but it wasn't okay for us to do it now," says Long. "It was just another example of Bobby just wanting to control everything."

The meeting ended in an uproar—yelling and screaming, but no violence—and accomplished nothing other than deepening the divide between the locals and the outsiders.

∾

The fall of Bobby Erra came rather swiftly. His enemies on the water at Homosassa became legion. And one by one, his few friends, or at least the people who tolerated him, fell off. Evans and Dopirak began avoiding him at all times, and Erra told them that they were "miserable, cocksucking, motherfuckers, just like the rest of the bastards," says Evans. Kipp cut down on the number of days he guided him, and Erra had some difficulty finding local guides to book.

Then, in late 2013, Erra learned he had brain cancer. After that, his behavior grew even more erratic. "He just got batshit crazy, cursing and yelling at God and everyone else all the time," says Kipp, who fired him.[*]

---

[*] Kipp has had his own woes since then. He's had to quit guiding because he says he has swelling in his brain.

"Something was off with Bobby by then," says Kent Davenport. "He didn't recognize me the last time I saw him."

On November 26, 2016, Bobby Erra passed away at his house in Homestead. He was seventy-one. He left behind a complicated legacy in the tarpon world. Many anglers and guides in Homosassa felt what could be described as a sense of relief after he died. "I hated that motherfucker," says Locklear. "He robbed the joy of tarpon fishing here for so long." Another guide says, "Bobby was bad for business. My blood pressure is close to zero without him here." Steve Abel says he "danced on his grave."*

There are many in Homosassa who are still afraid of Erra, even in death. "Don't put anything about me not liking him in your book," one guide told me. Another said, "Do not mention my name with anything to do with his craziness."

And yet, Erra's dedication to the sport—the hours and energy he put into it, his absolute, undying love for it—couldn't be ignored. "I think he loved the sport so much because it wasn't part of his other life," says Harry Spear. Kipp says that he "loved Bobby right up until the end." Evans always admired Erra's knowledge about tarpon tactics and tackle, which was extraordinary. "A lot of people didn't like him, but no one had a passion for tarpon fishing like Bobby did. He lived and breathed it," says Ronnie Richards, who guided Erra a bit in his later years.

The spring after Erra's death, Richards set up a memorial for him on the Oklahoma flat. "No one else wanted to do it, but I thought he deserved it," he says. Richards fastened two PVC pipes together to make a cross, secured the cross to a rock in the water with some concrete, and then stuck one of Erra's custom-made rod and reel outfits into the hole of the vertical pipe. Erra's Rock, as it's now known, is in an area that Erra used to love to fish, not far from Guido's Rock (named after Malzone). Anglers and guides who fish the area on an afternoon

---

* Abel would later survive his own tough bout with cancer and sell his reel company, which, for a time, was owned by Andrew Madoff, son of Bernie, and is now owned by a Colorado company.

outgoing tide set their drifts toward those rocks on what is now known as the "Guido Line."

Erra's rod and the horizontal pipe on the cross were washed away in a storm shortly after they were erected. The vertical PVC pipe is still there, though. It shoots up from seemingly out of nowhere on the vast flat, like a giant middle finger from the afterworld.

INTERLUDE 3
A BRIEF DISCUSSION
ABOUT GEAR

One thing that Homosassa, its tarpon, and the obsessives who chased after them did was help accelerate innovations in fly-fishing tackle and related gear, especially when it came to rods, reels, and skiffs.

Bamboo fly rods were the only ones really available in the earliest days of tarpon fly fishing in the Keys and elsewhere. Flats-fishing pioneer Joe Brooks used Orvis bamboo rods for bonefish in the 1940s and 1950s, because that's what he used for Atlantic salmon. When he and others began targeting tarpon, they naturally continued to employ those rods but had little success in landing many of the big fish because the bamboo was brittle and far too pliant. Though the Shakespeare Company introduced fiberglass into the rod market in the late 1940s, the material didn't make the leap into tarpon rods until the 1970s, when a rod known as "The Great Equalizer" hit the scene. The blanks for that rod were made by a company called Kennedy Fisher, but the rod itself was sold by 3M/Scientific Anglers. The Great Equalizer remained popular among tarpon anglers through the 1980s. It was stout, nearly impossible to break—"As big as a push pole," says Dopirak—and no fun to cast.

The next step in the evolution came with the Lamiglass rod, which was part fiberglass and part graphite. It was easier to cast than The Great Equalizer yet maintained the necessary backbone needed to fight and land big fish. Graphite rods were available by the late 1970s but didn't quite catch on in the tarpon world until the next decade, when the Biscayne Rod Company's one-piece, all-graphite rod became popular. That rod led directly to our contemporary era, which continues to evolve, bit by bit, every year. This is the golden age for fly rods, replete with light-but-strong sticks made by Sage, Orvis, Scott, Loop, R.L. Winston, Hardy, G. Loomis, and others from space-age graphite blanks. They are a true joy to behold and cast.

Interestingly, both Evans and Pate, creatures of habit and, perhaps, superstition, stuck with older rods even as more advanced technology became available. Pate used an old Fenwick rod he called "Trusty Lucky" from the 1980s until 2002. Evans used his Biscayne rod from 1985 until 2014. "I liked that rod because it had a great backbone," he says. "I was never really into gear. I just wanted stuff that worked."*

The earliest tarpon fly anglers also used the same reels they used for Atlantic salmon fishing, which were, in those days, multipliers (meaning every time the handle was turned one full revolution, the spool took up more than one spool's worth of line). The Pflueger Medalist (again, no relation to Al Pflueger Jr., the taxidermist) hit the market in the 1930s and dominated for the next few decades, even though it had some design flaws that became very apparent when fighting big tarpon—namely, its drag wasn't great, and the reel sometimes shuddered nervously and even blew apart when fighting big fish. Many anglers took to jury-rigging their Pfluegers. Jimmie Albright put rivets in the frame to balance out the reel.

---

* This is true. While Evans does have a beautiful old wooden box in which he keeps his tarpon leaders—attached to flies—for his day on the water, he does not have a traditional fly box for his tarpon flies. Instead, he carries them in a black trash bag. Evans does now use up-to-date Sage and Hardy rods, though.

Ronnie Richards epoxied a nickel on the non-handle side of his Pflueger to keep it from breaking apart. Lefty Kreh cut a hole in one side of the spool so he could put his thumb on the drag. Ted Williams did the same thing, but added a piece of leather there so he wouldn't burn his thumb.

The two most popular tarpon reels by the 1960s and into the 1970s were Gar Wood Jr.'s Fin-Nor Wedding Cake (named for its graduated series of layers on the non-handle side), and the Seamaster, made by Bob McChristian (the company was, if you'll remember, once partly owned by Jimmy Lopez). Seamasters were good, reliable reels, but McChristian was a crank who worked at his own deliberate pace, only handcrafting his reels when he felt like it. While a student at the University of Miami, Huff used to hang out at McChristian's shop. "Somebody would call in with an order and Bob would stand there with his eyes closed, not writing anything down. He'd say, 'Yeah, okay. Three wide Seamasters? Yeah, okay. Your name? Okay. Your address? Okay,'" says Huff. "Then he'd hang up and I'd say, 'Wow, you must have some memory.' And Bob would say, 'Oh, that motherfucker will never get a reel.'"

During the early Homosassa years, Evans tried the Fin-Nors and the Seamasters. None of them picked up the line during a fight fast enough for him. So he contacted John Emery, who was then building rods and reels at the J. Lee Cuddy tackle store in Miami. He asked Emery to make a heavy-duty reel with a good drag and large arbor—which allowed for faster line retrieval—and backed him with $10,000. The first Emery reels on the market had a pretty serious problem: the reel seats fell off when fighting big fish. But Emery, whom Evans began calling "John Hemorrhoid," fixed them and ended up making 220 in all. The Emery reels sold out, even though Evans says he "didn't think there were 220 tarpon fly anglers at the time." Emery died before making any more, but the reel he created is considered the precursor to reels like Abels and the large arbor reels of today.

Pate also used a Seamaster for years. He didn't like its double-handle reel, which was shaped like an S, so he cut if off and replaced it with a single handle. (Erra also didn't like the Seamaster reel handles, remember, but for a different reason.) Pate also used Fin-Nors, but he didn't like the drags on that reel, nor did he like the fact that he frequently had his knuckles rapped by the handle as it spun while fighting a fish. By happenstance, the answer to Pate's problems with tarpon reels came walking into his office one day.

∽

Ted Juracsik was born outside Budapest in 1937. He has fond memories of his early childhood, of playing soccer with his friends and fishing with them in World War II bomb craters in the Danube River. As a teenager, he was fascinated with machines and their parts, and decided to study tool and die making. At the age of seventeen, he became Hungary's youngest master of that trade.

Just two years later, though, Juracsik's life, along with the history of his native country, was upended. Fed up with Hungary's oppressive Soviet-controlled Communist government, Juracsik and many young men like him rose up in a revolution and managed to overthrow the government with relative ease and little bloodshed. But, within a few days, the Soviet Army rolled into Budapest and mercilessly crushed the rebellion and reestablished Communist rule.

With the revolution quelled, the Communist government sought vengeance. They sent out secret police who traveled door-to-door to root out the freedom fighters, whom they would jail and sometimes torture. One night, a neighbor of Juracsik's family informed them that the secret police were searching houses nearby. Juracsik's father ordered his son to immediately flee for the Austrian border. Juracsik made it to Austria under the cover of darkness—one of his good friends did not; he was shot and killed just yards away from safety—and entered a refugee camp. There, Juracsik was given the choice to go pretty much anywhere he wanted in the free world. He says he chose the United States because he'd heard that "the streets were paved with gold."

He lived in a boardinghouse in Brooklyn for a while, then moved to Long Island, where he got married and started his own machine shop in his backyard. He fished the Long Island shore for striped bass and bluefish with conventional tackle. In the early 1970s, he and his family began going to Florida in the springtime to visit his in-laws. On one of those trips, he met a man named Tony Lay, who introduced him to the Florida saltwater fishery. Lay worked at World Wide Sportsman, the Islamorada tackle store co-owned by Billy Pate.

One spring day in the mid-1970s, Juracsik stopped by World Wide Sportsman at around 5:00 p.m. He was supposed to pick up Lay to go fishing. Lay happened to be in Pate's office, talking to him and George Hommell, when Juracsik arrived. "Pate was bellyaching about some big tarpon that he'd lost because of his reel," says Juracsik. "And Tony pointed at me and said, 'Ted can build you a reel. He can build anything.'"

Pate showed Juracsik a Fin-Nor reel. Juracsik, who to that point had never fished with a fly, opened it up and identified what he believed to be the problem with it: the drag surface was too small, which meant the angler couldn't get enough tension on the drag when fighting a big fish. Pate asked Juracsik to build him a reel. He wanted the better drag, but he also wanted one more modification: an antireverse system, which would mean that the handle wouldn't turn with the spool (and hit his knuckles). Pate prepaid Juracsik for a hundred reels. And the next spring, Juracsik brought the reels with him to Florida. He named the reel the Billy Pate.

A few years later, Juracsik and his family moved full-time to Florida. His tool and die shop, still in existence in Delray Beach, makes everything from parts for surveillance devices to window shades for private jets. Juracsik has another home in Chokoloskee, on the western edge of the Everglades, not far from Huff's house. (Huff launches his boat from a ramp in Juracsik's backyard.)

In 1995, Juracsik used the Billy Pate reel as the genesis for a fly-reel company that he named "Tibor" (after his childhood nickname). Tibor primarily makes direct-drive reels (in which the handle is attached to the spool and moves with it), but he still sells the Billy Pates.* Ever since its launch, Tibor has been the standard by which all other saltwater reels

---

* Sales of the fly reels make up around 15 percent of Juracsik's company.

are measured, and the go-to reel for the majority of serious anglers of tarpon and many other species.

∽

Of all the gear involved in tarpon fishing, the boat may have gone through the most drastic change, from the beginning up to now. If you'll remember, Dimock rowed around the Homosassa River in a lapstrake canoe. Others used rowboats back in the day. Motors revolutionized boating, allowing people to cruise, waterski, and fish in farther-off places, but true shallow water boats took a while to catch up to deepwater cruisers. Early on, flats anglers and guides repurposed runabouts and ski boats for their skinny-water needs. There were some early versions of true shallow water skiffs, like the ones made by the Terry Bass Boat Company and the Willy Roberts wooden boats. (McGuane says he misses his Willy Roberts and would like to have it back.)

Freddie Archibald used the Willy Roberts as the inspiration for his Shipoke skiff.* Huff was an early innovator in the skiff world. He bought a Sidewinder ski boat and sabre-sawed it apart, removed the leather chairs, and made decks from plywood. Hewes Boats made a skiff called the Bonefisher, which was popular with guides in Biscayne Bay. Super Skiffs and Dolphins had some adherents. A few of Erra and Stepner's Mangrove boats are still around, like the ones that Dopirak and his son use. Silver Kings remain a somewhat popular brand. The angler/ophthalmologist Lenny Berg once owned the Maverick Boat Company, which is also still making boats.

The quantum leap in shallow water skiffs, though, came in 1997, when Flip Pallot, Hal Chittum, and an avid sailor and boatbuilder named Chris Morejohn collaborated on a fiberglass-hulled boat, the Hell's Bay. The boat was beautiful, and sleek, and, at around five hundred pounds,

---

* Archibald originally called his boat the "Shitpoke," after the little green heron of the same name. But, in the end, he removed the *t* from the name so as not to offend anyone, a rare act of conformity for him.

the lightest one on the market, by far. The Hell's Bay was quiet—Morejohn eliminated the wave slap through a hull innovation—and maneuverable and allowed its users to get into shallower water than ever before. Chittum and Pallot left Hell's Bay in 2002 after a nasty dispute.*

Chittum has gone on to found a new eponymous boat company that he says has pushed the technology even further along. Chittum Skiffs are even lighter than Hell's Bays. And through a strategic concavity in the hull and a primary and secondary chine that was developed with the help of contractors in Europe and the US Navy, he says his boats have eliminated "pressure waves," which is the hidden "pressure" that boats produce—which spooks fish—with mere displacement of water. One literally pays the price for these boats, which retail for around $70,000. "Every skiff is a compromise," as Huff is fond of saying. And while that remains true, those compromises are getting fewer and farther between.

---

* Presumably, the dispute was about money, but one can't be sure. Pallot refuses to talk about Chittum or even mention his name. Chittum says he left because he wanted to build bigger and better boats.

11

MR. 200

By the dawning of the new millennium, Homosassa was an afterthought in the world of fly fishing. The great migration of tarpon that once annually came through there was no more. Balch's 177-pound tarpon in 1994 was the area's last significant catch, and record-hunting fever had subsided—not just there, but everywhere. Erra was on the scene, tormenting and terrorizing. The fishing got so slow that one man began bringing a burner on his boat every morning to Black Rock and cooking up eggs and bacon for his fellow anglers. Evans even took to occasionally reading his BlackBerry on the boat as Dopirak poled around the flat, something that would have been unthinkable years before. The white heat of the tarpon fly-fishing world had moved southeast once again, back to the Keys, where the fish were smaller but arrived annually in much greater—and more reliable—numbers. Tarpon fishing there was becoming hipper and younger just as Homosassa had become the province of old men who were haunted by memories, drawn there by the faint whiff of nostalgia.

And yet, Homosassa remained the only place, save for the west coast of Africa, where the truly giant tarpon swam, where fish of two hundred pounds and larger still occasionally made a visit. Even in its severely diminished state, Homosassa was still the spot where true world-record hunters—whose numbers, like the tarpon, had dwindled to a mere

handful—still felt like they needed to go. Among them, of course, was
Pate, who in the year 2000 was sixty-nine years old, and Evans, who
was then sixty-one.

∽

Steve Kilpatrick is tall (6'3") and big (230 pounds). He has chestnut
brown eyes, and his dark hair is in slight retreat. The sixty-seven-year-
old walks as if he's a marionette, his appendages seemingly unattached
to the rest of his body, wooden and stiff and moving to a staccato beat.
There's a reason for that. Kilpatrick has had seventeen surgeries during
his lifetime, including two total knee replacements. That severe wear and
tear is thanks to a working career that began at Georgia Pacific, where
he worked with resins and plywood and particle boards in the company's
chemical department, veered into woodworking, then settled into guiding
wealthy sports, for turkeys and, more notably, for tarpon. Kilpatrick
grew up in Jacksonville and now lives in Chiefland, Florida, a small,
agricultural, inland town that's some fifty-five miles north of Homosassa.

Kilpatrick started tarpon fishing in the mid-1980s. Among his first
mentors was Stu Apte. From Apte, he learned how to both fish for tarpon
and how to guide for them, a valuable dual education. Apte also taught
him about the lore of the sport, which included tales of the giant tarpon
of Homosassa. Kilpatrick made his first pilgrimage to the fishery in
1985, when he, like many others (myself included) with no real firsthand
baseline knowledge from which to judge it, saw a handful of big tarpon
swim by on his first day there and thought he'd "found heaven."

Kilpatrick became a licensed fishing guide three years later. Even with
Apte's training, he found the going in Homosassa very difficult early
on—the vast flats were indecipherable, and the fish were so few, and the
ones that *were* there were so large that it took him thirty-one days over
a span of two years to finally land one. His learning curve straightened
out after that, and by the turn of the millennium he was one of the most
respected of the guides who ventured to Homosassa every May and June
to fish. "He may seem like a country boy, but he's the real deal," Dopirak

says of Kilpatrick. "He's an excellent guide. He ties perfect knots and beautiful flies."

It was Apte—the great connector of the tarpon world—who made the call to Kilpatrick that would lead to the landing of the largest tarpon ever recorded on a fly, an event that would momentarily upend his life and the lives of his clients, and crush the dreams and egos of both Pate and Evans.

"Steve, I have some friends, a father and a son, who need a guide in Homosassa," Apte said. "You available?"

∾

The father is Jim Holland Sr., a plaintiff's trial lawyer from Vancouver, Washington. He is disciplined and driven, fit and bald and bespectacled, and never afraid to voice an opinion, which, one of his friends and long-time guides, Tommy Locke, says, "sometimes rubs people the wrong way." Holland Sr. speaks in the quirky accent indigenous to the Pacific Northwest. He pronounces the name of his former favorite fishery as "Homa-sauce-a."

In the early 1980s, when the famous rod designer Gary Loomis was in the process of forming his iconic fly rod company, G. Loomis, he appeared one day in the offices of Holland Sr., seeking legal advice for his new venture. Holland Sr. helped him out, and the two men became fishing buddies. In 1984, Loomis designed the famous IM6 graphite fly rod and decided that he wanted to put the rod to the ultimate test. So he took Holland Sr. along with him to the Keys to fish with, you guessed it, Stu Apte. Apte loved the rod and sang its praises, and G. Loomis soon caught fire as a fly rod company. Holland Sr. stayed in touch with Apte, and for the following few seasons, he returned to the Keys to fish with him, staying at his house. "We fished all day and then, at night, we'd go over notes and tie flies, and Stu would give me an exam," says Holland Sr.

The son is Jim Holland Jr., who was, at a very young age, included in his father's fly-fishing exploits. Holland Jr. began casting at age eight, under the tutelage of Steve Rajeff, a G. Loomis rod engineer and, arguably, one of the greatest casters who ever lived. Apte and Loomis also served as mentors to Holland Jr.

Holland Jr. took to the sport. He trout fished while in undergraduate school at the University of Washington. He caught his first tarpon in the Keys with his father in the early 1990s, and an obsession blossomed. "And then we naturally heard about Homosassa," he says. The Hollands first fished there with Ted Johnston, the rather enigmatic real estate man who, if you'll remember, fished with Ted Williams and arranged for the baseball great's two houses in the Citrus Hills development in Crystal River. The Hollands began to make Homosassa an annual tarpon trip, mostly for a week at a time. "We went fully in," says Holland Sr. "We were committed to tarpon fishing in Homosassa. We practiced for it all year 'round."*

As the 2001 Homosassa season approached, the Hollands were lacking the one thing they needed most: a guide. Johnston had a conflict, and none of the other good local guides had any openings. So Holland Sr. called Apte, and Apte called Kilpatrick, who just happened to have May 6 though 11 open.

That season, Kilpatrick and Dopirak were sharing accommodations for the tarpon season, a poon shack consisting of two side-by-side dwellings in Aripeka, a tiny town located just a few minutes from the boat launch at Bayport. Their sports would come and stay with them while they fished. This arrangement meant that during their Homosassa week in 2001, the Hollands would basically be sharing a house with Evans.

---

* One thing all great tarpon fly fishermen have in common is a dedication to practicing—casting, tying knots, and attaching tippets to scales to figure out just how hard they can pull on it before it breaks. Once, when I reached Holland Sr. on the phone, he was outside his home, practicing his cast. Apte tied and re-tied knots until they were perfected. Pate constantly worked on strengthening exercises. Evans practiced casting until his back problems made that impossible, and, for many years, he spent two weeks in the Keys each year before going to Homosassa, as a sort of a spring training exercise. In his prime as a tournament angler, Andy Mill spent almost as much time practicing his cast and retrieve, and testing his tippets on weights, as he did actually fishing. Huff still practices casts in his yard every week.

The weather that week was abysmal, with overcast skies and a cold and constant north wind. In the first five days of fishing, only Holland Sr. managed to get a tarpon to bite on Kilpatrick's boat. To that point, the highlight of the trip was the evenings—the big dinners and Evans's excellent wines and the post-meal tutoring sessions that Evans led. "He took us to school," says Holland Sr. "He described to us how he fought big tarpon, and he took out his log book and went through each significant fish he'd caught." The Hollands had decided to use twenty-pound tippet, something Evans—who was using sixteen-pound tippet at the time—wasn't thrilled about, still peeved that Pate had somehow convinced the IGFA to allow it. "But it was legal and it was their choice," says Evans.

On the afternoon of May 10, Evans and Dopirak drifted along with the tide at the Middle Racks. Kilpatrick and the Hollands were nearby. Dopirak spotted a small string of tarpon. Evans picked out the one he thought was the biggest of the bunch and cast to it. The fish ate the fly and went ballistic, zigzagging away from the boat at a tremendous speed. Kilpatrick and the Hollands stood and watched the show from Kilpatrick's boat. Just as Evans worked the fish in close, the fish leapt, or, really, tried to leap; its mass was such that it couldn't quite clear the water. Right at the moment of the quasi-leap, Holland Sr. snapped a photo. The fish, headed away from the boat, is clearly enormous, even though only its head and upper back are visible above the waterline. Dopirak is seen standing on the platform, holding the push pole, calm and attentive-looking. Evans is in the bow, in a short-sleeved polo shirt and shorts, pointing the rod at the fish (known as "bowing" the rod), providing slack for his line so the tippet wouldn't snap if the fish landed on it.

Soon afterward, Evans got the fish to the side of the boat. To that point, Evans and Dopirak had never automatically killed a tarpon, no matter how big they thought it was. Their working agreement was that they would always measure a fish first before striking it with the kill gaff. So Dopirak came down from the poling platform and kneeled down in the boat to grab the fish by the jaw and pull it into the boat to measure it (this was well before the Florida law that prohibited bringing fish of over forty inches into the boat). But just as he kneeled, the fish shot straight up, catching him under the jaw, chipping one of his teeth and sending him sprawling to the boat floor. The fish then sunk down six feet to the bottom. Evans, temporarily forgetting his mounting physical maladies, grabbed the kill gaff and got hold of the fish by its mouth and managed to pull it about halfway up to the water's surface when it freed itself with a shake of its giant head and swam away. "That fish could have been one-eighty or it could have been two-thirty," says Evans. "It could have been whatever you wanted it to be."

There weren't many fish around that season, but one thing was for sure: "The big poon was there," says Evans.

⁓

The next morning, May 11—the last day of the Hollands' trip—Holland Jr. had resigned himself to the likelihood that he was not going to catch a tarpon in Homosassa that year. The weather had been terrible and the fish hadn't really shown up in good numbers. That happened on some fishing trips, and he was at peace with it. He and his father would be back the next year, and, anyway, he had the rest of his life to look forward to. He was twenty-five and in good health. He'd worked as a safari guide in Africa and was a certified airplane pilot and scuba diver. He was a year away from getting his degree from the Willamette University College of Law and then joining his father's practice. He would, within a few years, get married and have children.

Still, on the ride out to the flat that morning, Holland Jr. couldn't help but dream a bit. He kept thinking of that huge fish that Evans had hooked the day before. He mused openly on the boat, not really caring if his father or Kilpatrick was listening. "Can you imagine what it would be like to catch a two-hundred-pound tarpon?" Kilpatrick answered with something like, "You'd be famous for sure."

The morning fishing was slow. They saw a few fish, but nothing within casting range. Later on, they moved down to the Oklahoma flat along with six other boats—including Dopirak's—and they all set up in a line, all at respectful distances from each other. Kilpatrick was the last in line, the southernmost boat. It was Holland Jr.'s turn on the bow. Moments after they set up, Kilpatrick looked up at the boats to the north and saw some activity. Anglers were making casts. Some tarpon were on the move.

It turned out to be a giant school of some three hundred fish. Evans cast at them. So did Bill Bishop and the anglers in the other four boats. But no one hooked a tarpon. Kilpatrick had tied a yellow fly, known as a Lemon Drop, to the end of Holland Jr.'s leader. Holland Jr. threw that fly at the school a few times, but none of the fish were interested. The school swam by.

Kilpatrick told Holland Jr. that he wanted to change his fly. One evening earlier in the week, Kilpatrick had tied a fly with grizzly hackle, polar bear fur, and red-dyed deer hair that was stacked with red and purple fibers. He called it a "confucktion." He now tied that fly to Holland Jr.'s leader. Then Kilpatrick made a wide loop around the flat, with the help of electric trolling motors, and positioned his boat and its angler in front of that same school of tarpon.

When the school was about 120 feet away, Holland Jr. began to false cast. When the school was ninety feet away, he let the fly go. "I didn't purposely pick out the biggest fish in the school," he says. "It was really just a big black mass of fish." On the third strip of his fly, the lead fish in the school charged and ate it, and then violently turned sideways. "For a minute or two, it was utter chaos," says Holland Jr. "My line was hissing through the guides and the fish was running away from us." When the fish paused its run, Holland Jr. cinched the fly in the tarpon's mouth with a few hard pulls. The fish came to the surface twice, showing only part of its body. It was clearly a big fish, but it was hard to tell just how big. Evans, who was maybe a football field away, saw the fish splash and turned to Dopirak and said, "Oh, man. They just hooked a big one down there."

Holland Jr. says that after he hooked the fish and it made its initial run, Kilpatrick told him, "Junior, you've had a tough week. Have some fun with this fish and pull on it with all you got."

"There was no thought that this could be a record fish," Holland Jr. says. "I didn't feel any pressure or anxiety. She was beating on me pretty bad, and I pulled so freaking hard on her, probably a little too hard, in retrospect. I flirted a lot with breaking her off."

The fish dragged the boat north. With each roll and glimpse of the fish, estimates of its weight grew bigger. As it neared Black Rock—the place where, on many evenings, the tarpon had likely sought refuge in the company of hundreds of other tarpon—the fish began to "go crazy," as Holland Jr. recalls. Ronnie Richards, in a nearby boat, warned Kilpatrick that there was a twelve-foot-long bull shark in the area. Kilpatrick spotted the shark and, in an instant, had his big engine on. He ran his boat almost directly over Holland Jr.'s tarpon, put the engine in neutral, and began revving it loudly for about ten minutes. The massive shark finally slid away. "Sometimes that trick works and sometimes it doesn't," says Kilpatrick.

After the shark left, and after the trauma of the revving engine, the tarpon appeared to lose its fight. It sunk to the bottom near Black Rock. Holland Jr., knowing that these respites with tarpon are often only momentary, began lifting the fish with the rod with all of the strength that he had. "I'm convinced that had I not flirted with exceeding the breaking strength of the tippet, I would not have landed that fish," he would write later in an article that appeared in *Fly Fisherman* magazine. "Every tarpon you hook comes with an invisible timer, and you never know when your time is up."

Finally, one hour and fifty-eight minutes after hooking the fish, the tarpon floated up to the surface, lying on its side. The men on the boat now knew that it was exceedingly large. Kilpatrick put a gaff in its lip and held onto its jaw, attempting to hoist the fish into the boat, something he'd done with ease with dozens of other fish. But he could only move the head of this one. The lip gaff bent. Holland Jr. leaned over the side of the boat to help out, and with considerable effort, the two men finally got the fish into the boat. Kilpatrick measured it. The girth was nearly four feet. The length, just a hair over seven feet. Kilpatrick plugged the measurements into a calculator. The weight came out to 204. "I thought I must have screwed it up," he says. So he did it again . . . and got the same weight. "He called out the weight, and you could have heard a pin drop," says Holland Jr.

Kilpatrick got on his phone and made two quick calls. The first was to Dopirak. "I told Al what we thought we had and told him that I was sorry, but that I was going to run the boat through the flat," says Kilpatrick. The next call was to Dan Malzone, who had a certified scale in the back of his truck.

Kilpatrick had never caught a record, or a potential one for that matter. But he remembered what Apte had told him to do in the event that he ever had such a tarpon on his boat.

What happened next might not be suitable for minors or for anyone who happens to be reading this book while eating a meal. Feel free to skip the next paragraph if either is the case.

Just before he began the run back to the boat launch, Kilpatrick reached into his boat's glove compartment and retrieved a box of tampons. Yes, tampons. He unwrapped a few of them and stuck them into the anus of the giant tarpon that was now lying across the boat's floor. He then took a rag and shoved it down the tarpon's throat. He also draped some wet towels over the fish and, now running back, continuously poured water over the top of it. "Stu always told me that while in transit, a tarpon can lose up to two pounds in fluids," says Kilpatrick. "You have to stop them up."[*]

At the boat launch, Kilpatrick hooked up the boat—with the fish still in it—to his Ford F-150 and drove to the Aripeka compound. Chickens and lizards scattered about the grounds as they arrived. Kilpatrick hoisted a rope over a big branch of an oak tree and, with the help of the Hollands, tried to pull the tarpon up but couldn't. It was too heavy. So they propped the fish on the hood of the Hollands' rental car and secured the rope to Malzone's scale. Only then could they finally hang it from the tree and properly weigh it. The scale read 202 pounds, 8 ounces. Jim Holland Jr.—a young man and relative newcomer to the Homosassa

---

[*] Kilpatrick told this story to Evans, Butler, Dopirak, and me one night in Evans's rented poon shack. It was after dinner—thank God—and many glasses of wine. When Kilpatrick mentioned the tampon part, Butler turned to Evans and said, with an impish grin, "Tom, I reckon we may need to go to the pharmacy tomorrow for some supplies."

record-chasing scene—had finally eclipsed the mythical 200-pound mark for tarpon on a fly, the Holy Grail that had been chased obsessively for four decades. "I was walking on cloud nine. It was one of the best days of my life," says Holland Jr. "But then things started getting weird."

∞

The cloud nine part is captured in a one-minute-long video from that day that was posted on YouTube in May 2019 by a fishing guide from Tampa. In the video, shot outside of the Aripeka house, a boyish, beaming Holland Jr. stands beside his enormous, glistening fish. The sleeves of his shirt are rolled up around his biceps. Milling around him, occasionally offering congratulations, are smiling men twice his age—Kilpatrick, Malzone, Dopirak, and others. It's as if Holland Jr. is a young member of the tribe who has returned from his first hunt and proven himself well beyond expectations, making his elders happy and proud.

They had a party that night at the poon shack. Evans procured some expensive rum. Calls came in from around the country, from Pate, Pflueger, Apte, and Andy Mill. Things began to get a bit blurry. A small crowd broke off from the party and started whispering about the catch, questioning its legitimacy because of the still somewhat controversial twenty-pound tippet size. Evans got word of what that group was saying. He bowled over, swallowed all of his feelings about that particular tippet size and the man who had championed it, and said, loud enough for most everyone to hear, "Shut the fuck up. This is a great catch."

The drinks continued to flow and things got even blurrier. Late that night, Holland Jr. found himself sitting across from Evans at a table. Evans drew in a breath. His eyes were rimmed red. He looked straight at Holland Jr. "Good job, kid." He paused, tapped the table twice with his rum and Coke. "You know you broke my heart today."

It hurt for Pate, too. His 188-pound tarpon was no longer the biggest tarpon ever officially recorded on a fly. His years-long, ultimately successful campaign to get the IGFA to certify twenty-pound tippet had blown up on him unexpectedly. He would express his pain in a different manner.

⧜

The weirdness for Holland Jr. started pretty much the morning after his catch. It came in a few different parts: One had to do with questioning the legitimacy of his catch. Another had to do with a total breakdown of the relationship between the Hollands and Kilpatrick. And yet another had to do with the reaction of the general public to his catch.

As happens with any monumental feat, there were attempts to belittle it. Holland Jr. was initially painted by some as just some lucky young kid, a newbie with little experience. And while it was true he was relatively new on the Homosassa scene, he had, with the mentoring quartet of Apte, Loomis, Rajeff, and his father, one of the strongest tarpon fishing pedigrees—perhaps the strongest—of any twenty-five-year-old in the world. There was also more grumbling from the old school, which still didn't like the twenty-pound tippet and didn't think it was true "fly fishing." But that, too, was easy for Holland Jr. to handle. It was legal tippet, so the old-timers would just have to suck it up.

The rumors that began to circulate about his catch, however, were a bit harder to deal with. It was whispered that he had been trolling his fly when he hooked the fish, which would have invalidated his catch. There were insinuations that because of the duration and difficulty of the fight with the tarpon, the son had handed the rod off to the father at some point to take a breather, which, again, would have made the catch illegal under IGFA rules. Neither of these rumors was true, according to the Hollands, Kilpatrick, and the other anglers who witnessed the fight. Nevertheless, they hung over the catch for a while like an unhealthy haze.

Kilpatrick, right away, believed he knew exactly who had started the rumors. "It was Pate," he says. Jodi Pate Ahearn, Pate's wife at the time, says that Pate did indeed "have a strong reaction" to the fish, mainly because Holland Jr. "wasn't one of the main guys after the record." Pate's former guide, Lee Baker, who says he and Pate were "like brothers," takes it a bit further. "That fish really ticked him off," he says. "He protested it. He did everything he could to try to make it go away. We had outdoor writers on the boat one day, and he told them that it was an illegal catch.

I said, 'Billy, what are you doing?' It was embarrassing then to be a good friend of his."

Those protestations seemed to be at least listened to by those who mattered. Kilpatrick says the IGFA asked to actually see the fish, likely a precaution, given the magnitude of the catch, but still an unusual step, since the organization rarely laid direct eyes on any potential record catch (anglers usually sent the IGFA the application, pictures, tippet, and fly, but not the fish). So, the day after the catch, Kilpatrick packed the fish in ice, wrapped it in a tarp, put it in the back of his truck, and drove the four and a half hours from Aripeka to the IGFA headquarters in Dania Beach, just outside Fort Lauderdale. When he arrived, Kilpatrick says, he was met in the parking lot by someone from the IGFA, who inspected the fish and measured the tippet. Over the next twenty minutes, a few more IGFA representatives came out of the building to take a look at the tarpon.

The next morning, Kilpatrick says, someone from the IGFA asked him to stop by. "They interviewed me and asked me if I caught the fish, if I touched the rod, if the rod had been swapped," he says. "The answer to all of that was no. It was a totally legitimate catch."

In the end, the IGFA was satisfied by what it had seen and heard. Within months, Holland Jr.'s tarpon was certified as the biggest recorded tarpon ever caught on a fly. But the drama didn't quite end there.

Kilpatrick took the fish to King Sailfish Mounts, a well-respected taxidermy shop in Fort Lauderdale. He did this with the explicit permission of the Hollands, who had tipped Kilpatrick $10,000—industry standard for a major world-record fish—and promised him a free mount of the fish. Kilpatrick says he gave King Sailfish a $1,500 down payment for a mold, and believed he was the point man for any mounts to be done—that the Hollands didn't want anything to do with them. The fissure between guide and clients appeared a few days later, though, when Kilpatrick received a call from a representative from King Sailfish, who said that they'd received a legal notice from the Hollands proclaiming their rights to the fish and said that Kilpatrick should no longer have anything to do with it.

According to Holland Jr., he and his father did this because they believed Kilpatrick was trying to exert total control over the fish, which included any stories and photos of it. "I got some emails from outdoor writers that just read, 'Who the fuck do you think you are?'" says Holland Jr. "When I called them up, they were pissed. 'You think your story is worth ten thousand dollars?' they asked me. When I asked them what they were talking about, they told me Kilpatrick was asking for ten thousand dollars to release the story and the photos. I couldn't believe it." (Though reports of the catch appeared on the Associated Press wires and in various newspapers, magazines, and on various internet sites, Holland Jr. would tell the official firsthand story in the piece he wrote for *Fly Fisherman* magazine.)

Holland Jr. believes that Kilpatrick thought some serious money could be made on the fish, somehow, through the stories or pictures or just by being the guide who led his client into the fish. (At the time, $8 million was being offered by a company to the person who broke the world record for largemouth bass, so money for records seemed to be in the air.)* Kilpatrick says it was all a misunderstanding, and that he wasn't trying to take ownership of the fish or make any money from it. Nevertheless, the trust between guide and clients had been breached. "At that point, our relationship with Steve was totally broken," says Holland Jr. "I don't bear Steve any animosity anymore. It was a long time ago. I think there was a lot of stuff going on and he was trying to make a living. I've let it go."

The last of the weirdness for Holland Jr. came with some of the general public's reaction to his fish. Many of the stories in the newspapers, magazines, and on the internet were followed by indignant letters to

---

* Bass fishing was then, and remains now, a much more popular sport than fly fishing for tarpon, due mainly to its ubiquity. There are bass ponds, lakes, rivers, and streams in every state in the nation, save for Alaska, and there are currently 9.6 million bass anglers in the country. Though there is no official count of US tarpon fly anglers, some reports suggest that there *may* be twenty-five thousand of them. So it's highly unlikely that the world-record tarpon would be worth much at all. The Big Bass Record Club—the outfit that promised the $8 million for the world-record largemouth bass—turned out to be a house of card anyway, and collapsed before doling out any significant money.

the editor and comments, and he began to receive hate mail. "People asked how dare I kill an animal like that," says Holland Jr. "I get it. I understand. But I made a conscious decision to kill that fish and I don't regret it. Unfortunately, there is no mechanism to weigh a tarpon for a world record without killing it. If there was, I would have done it." Holland Jr. also believes that, at fourteen-and-a-half pounds bigger than the previous world record, his fish probably saved the lives of two or three incremental fish. This defense, however, was not good enough for some and never will be.

And anyway, there were tougher issues Holland Jr. had to face just a year after his catch, when he was diagnosed with Crohn's disease, which produces inflammation and pain in the bowels, and ankylosing spondylitis, an autoimmune disease that is a form of arthritis, which causes him sometimes debilitating pain in his back and other joints. "Things have gotten bad, but I've tried to manage my health as best I can," he says. "That year I caught the record was my last full year of good health. I guess I was at my official peak."

Kilpatrick still returns to Homosassa every year, guiding clients, still after another record fish. He and the Hollands no longer speak. The Hollands continue to fish for tarpon, in Boca Grande, Cuba, and Belize. Holland Sr., the more outgoing and outspoken of the duo, went back to Homosassa for a few seasons after the world record was set, mainly fishing with Tommy Locke. For whatever reason—perhaps, as Locke has said, because of his outspokenness—Holland Sr. has never really fit in with some of the more curmudgeonly members of the tarpon-fishing scene. "He's kind of obnoxious," says Evans. No one, it appears, bears any such ill will toward Holland Jr. Nevertheless, he has never returned to the scene of his world-record fish and says he never will.

12

THE ASHES AND
THE PHOENIX

On the late afternoon of May 11, 2001, Robert "Bobo" Cunningham landed his plane at the small airport in Hernando County, kicking off his annual Homosassa fishing trip. At the time, he was attempting to break the world record for tarpon on eight-pound tippet with his guide, Steve Kilpatrick, whom he'd booked for the coming weeks. Cunningham drove the twenty minutes or so from the airport to Aripeka, and then turned into the driveway of the compound that Kilpatrick and Dopirak were sharing that season. As he pulled in, Cunningham was greeted with the sight of a 202-pound, 8-ounce tarpon hanging from an oak tree—Holland Jr.'s record. He got out of his car and walked up to the fish and touched it, almost as if to make sure it was real, and then fell in with the party at the compound, which was already well under way. "I wasn't fishing twenty-pound tippet, so I didn't really get upset about it," says Cunningham. "In retrospect, it was such a perfect example of the way things go in life. Somebody who was not that serious about the world record actually catches the thing and then goes home and never comes back."

Cunningham was born and raised in Mobile, Alabama. As a child, his parents nicknamed him "Bobo" (pronounced "Bob-oh"). "I never really shook it," he says. "It kind of gets silly at my age [seventy-two], but you just put up with it." Before going to college, Cunningham enlisted in the US Marine Corps. He became a helicopter pilot and was sent to the Vietnam War, where he flew on more than five hundred missions from 1965 to 1970. During the Tet Offensive in 1968, Cunningham was in the process of evacuating some injured US soldiers from the side of a mountain when he was hit in the calf by a round that pierced the armor of his helicopter. His co-pilot took over the craft as he bled all over the floor. Cunningham was sent to a hospital in Japan for a few months, then returned to Vietnam to finish out his tour. He earned both a Distinguished Flying Cross and a Purple Heart for his service, and he still has the AK-47 round in his leg. "It's my memento," he says.

After receiving his JD from the University of Florida in 1975, Cunningham was admitted to the bar in Alabama and began a long, distinguished, and profitable career as a plaintiff's attorney. In 2002, on a pro-bono basis, he represented the University of Alabama's football team in its appeal of sanctions placed upon it by the NCAA. A year later, he was the lead attorney in a twelve-billion-dollar judgment against Exxon-Mobil for withholding gas well royalties from the state of Alabama. In 2012, he was appointed the leader of the trial team for the multi-district, class-action lawsuit against BP for the Deepwater Horizon oil spill. After settlements and a trial, the plaintiffs were awarded more than $14 billion. "That was really the culmination of my career," says Cunningham. "I had a personal connection, too." That personal connection was the Gulf of Mexico.

The grey-eyed, trim Cunningham had kept himself in good shape after his stint in the military, participating in triathlons and, later, breaking two Alabama state records for the bench press at the Masters level. But he felt that something was missing, something that not only allowed him to escape the pressures of work but also provided the sort of adrenaline rush he'd experienced back in that helicopter in Vietnam.

He found it on the water. Cunningham had always been a fisherman—his grandfather and father fished, and often took him along as a boy. But it wasn't until a fishing trip in 1989 to Costa Rica, where he first laid eyes on an IGFA record book, that some focus came to his fishing. He decided to comb through the book and chase after the records he believed he could break. (Cunningham wrote a book about his personal quest, called *Chasing Records*, which was published in 2012.) A lot of the fish he targeted were in the Gulf, where he broke records for redfish, mahi-mahi, cobia, and yellowfin tuna. In the Mississippi Delta, he broke records for freshwater fish, like the bowfin and the spotted gar. In all, he set fifty-nine IGFA records, on both fly and conventional tackle.

Those records acted as sort of a gateway drug. Tarpon, he soon came to realize, were the ultimate, the fish that, on the fly at least, rose above all others. He broke the Louisiana state record for a fly-caught tarpon. And then, soon enough, he was headed to Homosassa, the biggest stage. He first fished the area in 1999. "My advantage is that I wasn't there when it was so great," Cunningham says. "The first time I saw one of those big tarpon, I was hooked."

Kilpatrick became his guide. Because of Kilpatrick's relationship with Dopirak, this meant that Cunningham and Evans were in close contact for his first few seasons in Homosassa. The two men mixed, well, like oil and the Gulf of Mexico. Evans, ever the wrestler, always seemed to find a rival on the water, someone to stare down. He called Cunningham "Boo-Boo," like Yogi Bear's pal. The brusque, forthright Yankee-born-and-bred Evans had always had a bit of trouble stomaching the Southern gentleman type. And, as a former Wall Streeter and anti-regulation kind of guy, he had no love for plaintiffs' lawyers to begin with. ("Evans would always bring up the plaintiff's lawyer thing whenever I saw him," laughs Cunningham.)

The feeling was mutual. Cunningham spared no mercy on Evans in his book, describing him as "Gruff. Profane. Curt. And did I mention arrogant?"

Still, there was a begrudging mutual respect. Evans admires Cunningham for his military service. And though he is no fan of people who chase what he deems to be "minor" records, like the bowfin and the spotted gar, Evans says that it is "a good thing that someone is into the tarpon record." Cunningham says he's always been impressed with Evans's continuing desire to show up in Homosassa after seeing the great years and then the great decline. "Most people would have given up a long time ago," says Cunningham. He wrote in his book that he learned to "respect Evans for his undeniable angling ability." He described Evans sitting in the boat, reading his BlackBerry as Dopirak looked for fish as "a statement . . . unconventional and eccentric, and a sort of flamboyant gesture like a great, hot-dogging athlete might make to show he is so good that he can get away with being unconventional and almost disinterested." Cunningham added that he also learned to "avoid overexposure to [Evans's] caustic personality. Life is too short to spend much of it listening to him bitch."

"Dopirak deserves a damn medal for putting up with him for that long," he says.

Dopirak and Kilpatrick, sensing their clients' thinly veiled animosity, started renting different houses after a few seasons. Evans and Cunningham now see each other on the water and, on the very rare occasion, for a quick drink, when the antagonisms usually don't stay under the surface for very long.

∞

One might have reasonably thought that Holland Jr.'s world-record fish in 2001 would have sent a jolt of needed energy into the Homosassa fishery. Instead, the opposite happened—it laid an enervating haze over the entire scene. The record was now, it seemed, out of reach. Pate kept coming back for a few more years. Balch hung around until he was no longer physically able to fish for tarpon. Evans never stopped. But there weren't really any dedicated newcomers who came in solely to try to top Holland Jr.'s mark, or the records for the sixteen- and twelve-pound tippets. The newcomers, like Cunningham, aimed, at least at first, for other records, and in particular, the eight-pound tippet one, which was held by a man named Del Brown, who caught a 127-pound tarpon in 1985 with Steve Huff. Targeting that record made logical sense. There were more 130- to 150-pound tarpon in Homosassa than those in excess of 203 pounds. Logic didn't make the task any easier, though.

∾

There was another record chaser on the scene by this time, a relative newcomer who started in the 1990s. He was very different from the rest of the gang, very Zen about the whole thing. I say that knowing that I'm at risk of falling into the hole of a racial stereotype. But it is true. He is a family physician from Palos Verde, California, now seventy years old. His name is Brian Tang. Evans, of course, immediately started calling him "Poon Tang."

Tang came to Homosassa the first time having never fly fished before. "I did practice with a fly rod for a few months before I came," he says. "I'm still a terrible caster, but I was much worse then." Tang decided that going after the eight-pound tippet world record "seemed like fun." He fished with Ray DeMarco and Mike Souchak and Dan Malzone before settling in with Dopirak every June, after Evans had left for the season. While May was traditionally the month when the truly large tarpon migrated through Homosassa, there were always some fish that hung around until July. They were usually smaller than the May fish, but plenty of them exceeded 127 pounds.

From the beginning, Tang had a different mind-set than the other record chasers. "It's all pretty foolhardy," he says. "It's just fishing." He's well aware of the history of Homosassa and the record chase and the toll it took on some lives. "Most of these guys are divorced," he says. "I don't want that." Tang takes long, leisurely naps on the boat daily. He brings his wife of forty-three years along with him in the boat, and she fishes as the primary angler for a week. He says he has no illusions about the sport and his position within it. "The only reason I'm in the bow of the boat and not the back is because I have a bigger credit card," he says. "Al [Dopirak] is a much better fisherman than I am." He likens world-record tarpon fishing to bullfighting. "I'm the guy who sort of weakens the bull, who puts swords in it," he says. "Al is the guy with the cape."

Tang says he's come close to the record a few times. A few years ago, he submitted a 147-pound tarpon—which would have topped Del Brown's record by twenty pounds—to the IGFA, but the catch was disqualified because his eight-pound tippet tested at 9.1 pounds. "That broke my heart, but I got over it quickly," he says. "If I don't win, if someone beats me, I don't really care. I'm just happy to have played the game."

In the end, Tang and Cunningham may represent some evolutionary step in the world-record chase. While they are still deeply involved in what many would characterize these days as a rather anachronistic pursuit, they are both outwardly happy and content people.

Evans was becoming, it seemed, the opposite. His physical decline—which started slowly at first, with the old football injuries and the torn rotator cuff and the back problems from the bike crash in 1996, then happened all at once, with the botched back surgeries in the 2010s—mirrored the decline of the Homosassa fishery. His mood had grown darker. "I hate the fucking poon," he would say on nearly a daily basis. "He doesn't play fair anymore." Evans was not going gently into that good night. He no longer cared much what other people thought of him. He tells a story from around that time, of being invited to a dinner party and meeting a new couple, a husband and wife who had recently moved to his Vermont town. At the party, Evans realized immediately that he didn't much like the husband's politics, and he let him know it. Evans and then Tania argued with the man, which quickly grew into a shouting match. As Evans and Tania got up to leave the party early, the husband told them, "I hope you hit a patch of ice on the way home and run into a tree and your seat belts and airbags don't work."

The death of his favorite fishery, the physical decline, the darkening mood . . . all of it made what he accomplished in the first decade of the new century that much more impressive.

∞

The 2003 tarpon season in Homosassa was pretty much like the previous decade before it. "Really shitty," says Evans. A few fish showed up in the first few days of May, maybe a dozen or so, and they were hounded by anglers in Black Rock in the mornings, and on the Oklahoma flat in the afternoons. And then, from May 5 through May 12, the fish disappeared.

Not one was caught. In fact, not one was spotted. "They just weren't there," says Kent Davenport, who was at Homosassa at the time.

Evans was sixty-four years old in 2003. Despite his repaired rotator cuff and bothersome back, he believed he could still wrestle in a big tarpon on sixteen-pound, using all of his old fighting tricks and pulling as hard as he could.

On the afternoon of May 13, Evans and Dopirak were floating near the Eiger Rocks, the place where Evans had first fished Homosassa twenty-seven years earlier. Neither man had much faith in the day. It had started out just like the previous eight days before it, with no fish seen. Evans sat amidships, looking out over the water and occasionally taking a peek at his BlackBerry. "I really admired Tom for his dedication at this point," says Dopirak. "It had been years, more than a decade, since we'd boated a possible record fish. If I had been in his shoes, I'm not sure I ever would have come back."

Just after they had eaten lunch, Dopirak spotted something coming from the north, a little glitch in the matrix of flowing water, white sand, and the occasional pile of black rocks. That something was three tarpon. "Here they come, dawg," Dopirak said. "You better get up there," referring to the casting platform on the bow. Evans grabbed his rod and huffed and puffed his way to the bow. He spotted the fish. Dopirak pointed with his push pole. "Thomas, that one in the back, that's the biggest one," he said.

When the string of fish came into casting range, Evans laid out a cast, placing it just off the tail of the second fish. He made three strips, and the last fish in the group turned and swallowed the fly. Evans, knowing he was not fit for a long fight, "put the wood" to the fish, according to Dopirak. Just half an hour later, the fish was to the boat.

By this time, Evans had decided that with so few fish and so few opportunities, he was "too old to be nice" and he would "put a hole" in any fish that looked like it could be a record. Dopirak did just that, and wrestled the fish into the boat. The fish bled as they raced back to the boat ramp. (They did not use any rags or tampons to try to staunch the loss of fluid.) Back at the poon shack, the fish weighed 190 pounds,

9 ounces. A few months later, the IGFA approved the catch as the new world record for sixteen-pound tippet, eclipsing Pate's iconic record from twenty-one years before. "The curse was over," says Evans. He did not write Pate a letter to inform him that his most treasured record was no more. Evans did call Ted Juracsik, though. He had caught the fish on a Tibor reel and wanted to let him know. "Oh, man," Juracsik said. "That's going to kill Billy."

∽

Some of the intervening years that followed that catch were the worst Evans had ever experienced in Homosassa. He landed just two fish in both 2004 and 2005. In 2006, he landed three. He had one decent year in 2008, when he landed ten tarpon. But that turned out to be an outlier. The next year, he managed just four fish. "We had a whole lot of days—seasons, really—of just staring out at an empty sea," says Dopirak.

The year 2010 was another tough one. Evans managed only three tarpon. One of them, though, turned out to be momentous.

On the afternoon of May 10, 2010, Evans and Dopirak were again on the Oklahoma flat, this time on the southern end. They'd seen a few fish the previous day but hadn't gotten any good shots. With the sixteen-pound tippet record in hand, Evans had gone down to twelve-pound, to target Clyde Balch's 1994 world record of 177 pounds.

The scene that day played out much like it had in 2003. Dopirak spotted two tarpon swimming quickly toward them. Evans went up into the bow, settled himself, and picked out what he determined was the bigger of the two fish. He made a cast with a brown bunny fly. The fish ignored it. So Evans made another cast, and hooked the tarpon and let it run, knowing he had to use a bit more care with the twelve-pound tippet. The fish leapt. Evans didn't see it; he was focused on clearing his line. Dopirak did, though. "*Damn*," he said. "That's a two-hundred-pounder."

"I don't know, Al," Evans said. "I don't think this fish is big enough." Maybe Evans's low reserve of energy was sapped. Or maybe it was just impossible to tell just how big a tarpon was in the water. But Dopirak had a feeling about this one. "I guarantee you this one is big enough, Thomas," he said. "Let's get it."

Thirty-five minutes later, Dopirak gaffed the giant tarpon. The fish weighed 194 pounds, 8 ounces, obliterating Balch's record by seventeen and a half pounds. The catch was astonishing, given the size of the fish and the featherweight tippet with which it was landed. "It's the greatest fly rod catch ever," says Huff. Andy Mill, Stu Apte, and many others agree. (That it was caught on the old-school, original largest tippet size for fly records—the twelve-pound—also satisfied the hard-liners within the tarpon world.) There was one other element, in addition to the size of the fish and the tippet, which made the catch particularly remarkable: "He caught that fish when there were no fish around," says Dopirak.

At the age of seventy-one, thirty-four years after first visiting Homosassa, Evans caught the fish of a lifetime. It wasn't the two-hundred-pounder that he had sought for so long, and the sting of watching someone else hit that mark would never truly be salved for him. But he had accomplished something with a fly rod that a certain select group—really, the only people whose opinions mattered to him—believed was equally impressive as, if not more than, the two-hundred-pound mark.

Of course, every new world-record holder creates a former one. For more than a decade and a half, Balch, according to Dan Malzone, had never shaken his worry about Evans breaking his record. And now it had become reality. "Clyde called me," says Malzone. "He was really mad and said that he hoped Tom's line wouldn't pass at the IGFA." But it did.

⁓

Another former world-record holder likely had no idea that Evans caught a significant fish in 2010. Billy Pate, by that time, was deep in the throes of his battle with Alzheimer's disease, the illness that had taken the life of his mother, and the one he had feared and worked so hard to prevent with his rigorous workouts, innumerable daily vitamins, and chelation therapy.

Pate's final world-record tarpon had come in 1982. But he never stopped his pursuit of the two-hundred-pound tarpon in Homosassa until he was mentally and physically unable to do so. In the Homosassa movie he'd done with 3M, he'd claimed he'd come tantalizingly close to consummating his nearly lifelong obsession on many occasions, hooking at least fifteen tarpon of more than two hundred pounds. "You can be sure that I'm going to land one of these son-of-a-guns one day," he declared in the movie, and there really was no reason to doubt him. He was among the very best tarpon fishermen of his era, and remains a legend to this day.

His fishing regimen began to change a bit in the early 1990s. He met a woman named Jodi while on a steelheading trip in the Pacific Northwest, after putting an ad in the local paper for a housecleaner. She was smart and attractive and could cast a fly (indeed, she would go on to set sixteen world records in the IGFA's women's category). They were married in 1992 and traveled the world fishing together, including an annual five weeks in Homosassa.

A year after he and Jodi were married, Pate decided that he no longer needed guides in Homosassa. He would now fish alone, maneuvering his boat with the foot pedals he'd installed on the massive platform, or go out with his very capable wife. Despite the parting of ways, Pate remained beloved by his Homosassa guides Ragland and Baker. "He was always very conscious of his guides and their welfare," says Ragland. Pate paid his tarpon guides for seven straight days, even though he usually only fished six of them, which provided his guides with a rare, but much appreciated, day off every week in the middle of the grind of the tarpon season. "I really enjoyed fishing with him. I always looked forward to it," says Ragland. Baker says he felt the same way.

Though he would never again land a world-record tarpon, Pate did find some success fishing without guides. One day in Homosassa in 1995, Pate headed out to the flat by himself. He positioned his boat away from the scrum of the others there, playing a hunch that some fish would swim his way. His hunch proved correct. He spotted a school to the outside of his boat and hooked what looked like a massive tarpon. He fought the fish away from the other boats for half an hour, but it eventually dragged him right into the middle of them. The tarpon leapt among the boats, as if putting on a show. Guides on the other boats chatted on the radio about the fish, which looked like a potential world record. Several of them offered to help Pate land the fish, but he turned them all down. Finally, after a few hours, Pate lip-gaffed the fish and dragged it into his boat by himself. "The entire thing was pretty impressive to watch," says Gary Merriman.

Pate took the fish back to the shore to have it weighed. While it was certainly long enough to break the record, the fish was fairly skinny by Homosassa standards. Pate told anyone who'd listen that the 173-pound tarpon he caught that day was the most satisfying one he'd ever landed.

∽

Tarpon and women. Those were the two subjects that Pate always liked to talk about, according to his friend, the outdoor writer Doug Kelly. Kelly says he helped Pate set up his internet dating profile when the World Wide Web started to become ubiquitous. In 2005, Pate—by then divorced from Jodi—went to Ukraine "on a junket where you meet women," says Kelly. He was there for a week and was not having a very good time. "All of the women he met wanted children, which he didn't want," says Kelly. So Pate decided one day to make the long drive to Kyiv, to do some sightseeing.

In Kyiv, as he left a restaurant one day after eating lunch, he walked by an attractive, full-figured woman. He introduced himself. Her name was Tetyana Kushynskaya, but she went by Yana. She was a classically trained pianist. "Billy asked me to help him learn piano," says Yana. "And he started showing me pictures of fish." Pate stayed in Kyiv and proposed to her three days later.

After he got back to the United States, Pate continued to correspond with Yana via phone and email, and helped her get her papers squared away for the move to the United States. A few months after they first met, Yana arrived in the Keys. Soon afterward, Yana became Pate's fifth and final wife. He was seventy-five at the time.

"Billy was very kind to me," says Yana. "He treated me like a queen." Pate had a mock IGFA world record certificate made of his 188-pound tarpon with her name and the words MY TRUE WORLD RECORD written on it. Yana quickly became involved in the Islamorada community, becoming the pianist at a local church.

Pate and Yana fished a few times together as he made some of his last casts in his pursuit of a world-record tarpon. When they were first together, Yana says, Pate was fanatical about keeping his boat, his gear, and himself in top shape. But, just a year or so after they were married, "he grew less and less interested in fishing, and I started to notice that he had trouble with his memory," she says.

She wasn't the only one who noticed. In the late 2000s, the IGFA asked Pate to do a tarpon film. In a reunion of sorts of their Homosassa/3M film, Baker served as Pate's guide, and Ragland manned the camera boat. They went to Buchanan Bank, long Pate's favorite spot in the Keys. "The fish would come down on the northwest side, in the basin," says Baker. "I set us up so that Billy had a head-on shot at the oncoming tarpon."

Baker says he spotted the fish, then alerted Pate about their imminent arrival. But Pate kept doing a curious thing. "The fish would get into casting range, and instead of fishing them at twelve o'clock, Billy would cast away from them, to nine o'clock," says Baker. "School after school came at us, and he kept doing the same thing. I kept telling him to take the straight shot. He'd say, 'Okay,' and then he'd throw it at nine o'clock. I had no idea what was going on."

The shoot was somewhat of a disaster, saved only by a few fish hooked on the seventh, and last, day of shooting. "Later on I realized that Billy was probably in dementia at the time," says Baker.

Some time later, Baker and Ragland went to Pate's house in Islamorada for a visit. "It was a bad time," says Ragland. "It was obvious that Billy had no idea who we were. His house was filled with mounts and pictures. I pointed to a picture of me and asked, 'Do you remember that guy?' and he said, 'No.' I was really sorry to see him that way."

Sometime in 2008, Pate made one last trip to Homosassa. He'd been invited to a banquet held by a local fishing group. He planned to take

Yana out on the flat the day after, just to motor around and see it. Pate was fine on the night of the event, but the next day he woke up and didn't feel good. "He said, 'Let's go home,'" says Yana. Pate would never see Homosassa again.

Yana soon became a full-time nurse to her bedridden husband. Near the very end of his life, Pate was noncommunicative, save for one word—the name of his hometown. "He would just say 'Greenville,'" says Yana. "He repeated it hundreds of times a day."

On April 18, 2011—fittingly, during the beginning of tarpon season in South Florida—Billy Pate died at the age of eighty-one. He left behind a complicated legacy. He was, undoubtedly, one of the greatest fly fishermen who ever lived, especially when it came to tarpon. (By his own estimate, he caught five thousand of them during his lifetime.) He was, by many accounts, a Southern gentleman—quiet, soft-spoken, well-mannered—and was, and remains, fiercely loved and protected by his friends. "He was a fine man," says Tom Gibson, who accompanied him on his tarpon trips to Africa. Though Pate disliked Evans, he never disparaged him publicly. But Pate also pushed the envelope of seemliness when it came to his ardent womanizing, and he fell prey to his own ego, which would metastasize in instances like groundlessly disparaging Holland Jr.'s catch. In the eyes of many of his contemporaries, he brought much unwanted attention to the sport and spoiled it, all for the sake of self-promotion. He was, in the end, a flawed human, like the rest of us.

Just a little more than a month after his death, Pate's funeral was held at World Wide Sportsman (which was, by then, owned by Johnny Morris, the founder of Bass Pro Shops). After the ceremony, a fleet of thirty boats—mostly shallow water skiffs, but also some bigger crafts—left the World Wide marina and headed for Buchanan Bank. There, the boats anchored around a little thirty-foot-by-thirty-foot area known as the "Pocket," the best fishing spot on Buchanan Bank, a sort of cul-de-sac where, for some mysterious reason, the tarpon loved to hang out. Green carnations were dropped in the water and quickly swept away by the strong outgoing tide. ("Green was his favorite color," says Yana.) A priest said a few words. Pate's ashes were poured into the Pocket, as he had directed in his will.*

And then Ted Juracsik stood up in his boat. "Billy was a great friend of mine, a nice and honest guy," he said in his Hungarian accent. "When he asked me to make him some reels, I built two prototypes. I gave one to him, and I kept the other." Then Juracsik reached into his pocket. "Here's mine," he said. "I figure Billy should have both of them." And with that, Juracsik hurled the reel into the water.**

∽

In 2011, with the sixteen- and twelve-pound tippet records in hand, and with no desire to try for the twenty-pound record, Evans switched up his game. He would now, he decided, go after the eight-pound record, Del Brown's 127-pound tarpon. It would present an enormous challenge for him—his age, physical state, and the lack of fish in Homosassa were serious impediments. More than that, though, the eight-pound tippet—which an angler might use for largemouth bass fishing—required a type of finesse that Evans had never demonstrated in his fishing career, much less his life. All of those angles and that leverage that he had used to quickly subdue large tarpon were of little use. Pulling hard on eight-pound tippet pretty much guaranteed a break. The tippet class required nearly endless patience, and it was much more a team effort than the larger tippet sizes, with the maneuvering of the boat and the gaffing of an often "green" fish (meaning one with a lot of energy and fight left).

---

* The guides Jack Brothers, Jimmie Albright, and Cecil Keith also had their ashes spread in that spot.

** An estate sale of Pate's belongings—rods, reels, flies, mounts—raised around $150,000. His famous boat, with its large platform, was bought privately before the estate sale, by a collector from England and a Keys guide named Mark Cockerham, with the idea that it could one day be included in a fishing museum. "It had been sitting out for years by the time I got it, and the bull ants and rats had pretty much destroyed it," says Cockerham. "I fixed it up and was able to get it running." The boat hasn't found a home in a museum yet, and still sits in a yard in Islamorada.

"A big tarpon on eight is really landed by the guide and not the angler," Evans says.

Evans's first attempt at the eight-pound record came in the Keys, during one of his warm-up trips before Homosassa. He was fishing with the well-regarded Keys guide Tim Klein when he hooked a fish that they estimated was 140 pounds, well clear of Brown's record. Evans played it well, slowly and gently. When he got the fish to the boat, it was still somewhat green. As Klein reached for his gaff, Evans couldn't believe his good fortune. "I'd only been at it for a few hours," he says. "It was too easy, too fast. I didn't think I deserved it. Little did I know I was in for more torture."

Klein hit the fish with the gaff, and it pulled him into the water. "I looked up and saw my boat floating away and I knew that Tom didn't really know how to run it," says Klein. He was standing in five feet of water. The bottom was mushy. He managed to work his way back to the boat, dragging the tarpon. He handed Evans the gaff and pulled himself back in the boat. Somewhere in that transition, though, the tension on the gaff went slack, and the possible eight-pound record wriggled free and swam away.

Evans realized after that trip that the pursuit of the eight-pound record would require more help. He needed a third person on the boat, someone who could act as a gaffer, someone with loads of experience with big fish. He knew just the guy to call.

⁓

Dean Butler grew up in Melbourne. He played Australian rules football as a youth, and got a job selling ball bearings when he was out of school. "It was a good job. I was in charge of some people and I was good at managing them and I was well looked after," says Butler. "But all I really wanted to do was fish."

He quit that job and, with a man named Rod Harrison, started a sportfishing travel and production company. They ventured to the remote corners of Australia, developing fisheries, shooting videos, and promoting trips for potential clients.

In the early 1990s, Butler and Harrison, looking to break into the US market, invited Lefty Kreh to fish with them in Oceania. Kreh was the most famous fly fisherman in the world at the time, and the sport's biggest promoter, something Butler, a student of the sport and a fledgling outdoor writer, knew well. Kreh accepted the invitation, and the three men went to Papua New Guinea and fished for that country's native black bass, a species that Kreh would always recall as one of his favorites. Kreh stayed at Butler's house for a few days before going back to the United States. After the legend had departed, Butler realized that Kreh had left behind a pair of his tighty-whitey underwear. Ever the fly-fishing history geek, Butler mounted the underwear in a frame, which he hung up in his home.

By 1995, Butler and Harrison had split the business. Butler got the travel side. He heard about some good striped marlin fishing off the coast of Australia, and he decided he would try for them with a fly. "I knew that Pate had been down here fishing for marlin with a fly, but no one was really doing that at the time anymore," says Butler. "I wanted to create a little niche."

Butler did more than that. Within just a few years, he'd become one of the most respected marlin fly-fishing guides in the world.

∞

When Evans decided to add a billfishing trip to his annual Homosassa one, he initially went to Costa Rica. And while he found some success there, he sensed that he was missing out on something. "I felt like I was just dicking around," he says.

One year in the early 2000s, his stepson, Chan Morgan, showed him a guide he'd found on the internet: Dean Butler. "Dean had some pretty impressive-looking stuff on the web, so I gave him a call," says Evans. When he called, Butler was away on a trip. Evans spoke to Butler's wife, Corinne, telling her that he wanted to book her husband for a month to try to break the world record for striped marlin on twelve-pound tippet. When Butler got back home from his trip, Corinne handed him some

Post-It notes on which she had written down his phone messages. One of them read, simply: "Tom Evans—sounds like a big fish."

Evans flew down to Australia, and he and Butler fished the Port Stephens area, a couple hours north of Sydney, for that month. They had terrible weather, with the wind howling at thirty miles per hour each day, and Evans only caught one fish, a small black marlin. But they had a blast and discovered that they were kindred spirits. "I knew Dean and I were on the same page," says Evans.

Marlin fishing with a fly is not a sport for everyone. The marlin are teased up from the depths with a hookless lure attached to a spinning rod. Once a marlin shows interest, the lure is reeled in—with the marlin hopefully following—close enough to the boat for a cast with a fly rod. Working in coordination, the guide (Butler) yanks the lure out of the water, and the client (Evans) attempts to throw a giant fly right onto the spot the lure has vacated.

It is not an easy sport and, to some purists, it's not a very sporting way to fly fish, either, because of the teasing lure that's used to attract the fish and the way the captains use their boats and big engines—especially when not fishing for records—to help fight the fish. ("Tarpon is more one-on-one," says Butler.) It's also a sport that can drive deep-sea fishing captains mad, because of the long periods of not seeing any fish and the extreme difficulty of not only getting a marlin to bite a fly but also fighting it to the boat once it's hooked. "Fishing for marlin with a fly rod is really a stupid idea," says Butler. "You find out quickly who is up for it and who is not." Adds Evans, "We put three diesel captains into the cuckoo house. Most marlin stories are torture stories," which seemed to be something that he was extremely attracted to. Over the next decade, fishing off the coasts of Australia, New Zealand, and Vanuatu, Evans and Butler managed to break nine marlin world records.[*] (Butler has thirty-one big-game IGFA records in total.) Evans believes that his marlin fishing made him a better tarpon angler.

---

[*] These marlin feats were made even more remarkable by the fact that longliners had pretty much wiped out most of the populations of marlin in those areas by then.

So when Evans decided in 2011 that he needed help with the eight-pound tarpon record—very likely the last of his tarpon quests—he hired Butler to come to Homosassa. Since that season, Butler has nominally been the gaff-man on the water. But he's much more than that. Butler has become somewhat of a caretaker for Evans. He makes sure the poon shack and all of Evans's gear is squared away. He gets the groceries. He fixes Evans's drinks and makes sure that he takes all of his prescribed meds. Butler makes his breakfasts and lunches, and cooks dinner for all in the poon shack on most nights. Dopirak describes Butler as "Mr. Whatever-It-Takes." Like Dopirak, Butler is highly competent with boats, engines, rods, reels, gaffs, flies, and knives, and the duo—with all of the significant records between them—may be the best big-fish, fly-guiding team ever assembled. More than that, though, Butler's presence injected a much-needed strong dose of energy and that native Aussie love of fun into what had begun to become a rather glum endeavor.

INTERLUDE 4
THE LOG BOOK

From 1989 until 2013, Evans kept a daily log during his Homosassa tarpon trips. Within his log book, he jotted down the dates and usually a line or a phrase describing the conditions or the fishing. The entries are, at once, a master class in the caustic minimalist poetry that is Evans-speak, and also a year-by-year documentation of the precipitous decline of the Homosassa fishery, interspersed with a few fleeting moments of triumph.

In the late 1970s and early 1980s, Evans was landing—that is, fighting the fish to the boat and removing the fly—one hundred to two hundred tarpon a season. In 1996, he did not land a single fish in thirty days. From 2004 until 2006 (roughly ninety days of fishing), he landed seven fish in total, averaging just more than two fish a year. From 2009 to 2013 (roughly 150 days on the water), he landed sixteen fish in total, just more than three fish a year. Evans's world records in 2003 and 2010 suggest that the decline in catches had little or nothing to do with any deterioration in his angling skills, despite the fact that he was getting older and more broken down as the years went on. There just weren't any fish around.

Homosassa had become, by this time, like a bad drug habit that Evans couldn't shake. He kept going back for another dose, hoping to recapture that initial high. A therapist would likely have a field day with his log book, which can be read as the very definition of insanity that obsession can lead to, recalling that famous phrase supposedly uttered by Albert Einstein.

I read through all of the log entries and jotted down a few of my favorites. (Note: I have included some of my comments in brackets after the entries for clarification.)

5/15/91—"Front blow out—or perhaps poon God?"

5/18/91—"El sucko huge."

5/14/94—"Balch 177 on #12. Ouch." [This is the day when the plastic surgeon-turned-Ukrainian-skirt-chaser Clyde Balch broke the tarpon record for twelve-pound tippet.]

5/16/95—"173 Pate strikes again." [Evans was infuriated every time Billy Pate killed and weighed a tarpon that was well under the record weight, seemingly just for the publicity, as he did on this day and others.]

5/20/97—"Pulled on Mr. Poon. Took out hook, patted him on head. Told him he was a good poon."

5/11/01—"Steve Kilpatrick + Jim Holland Jr. make poon history." [The day of Holland Jr.'s world-record catch.]

6/3/01—"Escaped!" [The final day of a terrible season for him, made more terrible by Holland Jr.'s catch.]

5/19/02—"Worst poon season ever. Need new hobby."

5/13/03—"190.6 #16. How sweet it is. 21 years." [This refers to Evans's tarpon, officially recorded as 190 pounds, 9 ounces, that broke Pate's twenty-one-year-old record on sixteen-pound tippet. A rare moment of joy in the log.]

5/18/05—"Poon being a prick."

5/15/08—"Jaws got him." [A shark ate his tarpon.]

5/10/10—"194 #12. Had two shots." [A strangely underplayed entry for the day that Evans broke the twelve-pound record with a 194-pound, 8-ounce tarpon, which some believe is the greatest fly rod catch ever.]

6/2/13—"Worst ever." [End of the 2013 season, which, in fact, wasn't the worst ever. He landed three fish that year, which was more than he did in 1996, 2002, 2004, 2005, and 2012. This is the last entry in the log, which he stopped keeping after that year because, he says, "it was too depressing."]

13

TOO MANY MOTHERF*%CKERS

est the final entry in Evans's log book give the wrong impression, however, fly fishing for tarpon has never been more popular than it is right now. We lack hard numbers on tarpon anglers, so there is no way for me to prove this assertion. But I am certainly not the only one who believes this is so—it is the consensus among anglers, guides, and industry types. Any guide in the Keys, the Panhandle, or the Everglades will tell you that there are more people on the water fishing for tarpon than ever before.*

In a symbiotic phenomenon, tarpon are also written about, photographed, and filmed more than ever before. It helps that the fish make for stunning models on the covers of glossy magazines, and happen to be excellent TV and film stuntmen and women, with their acrobatic leaps and mad dashes and general thrashing about. For six seasons now, tarpon have even had their own television show, *Silver Kings*, which is hosted by the young and respected tarpon guide Jared Raskob. The show

---

* The Keys were once *the* spot to target big bonefish. The area's population of bonefish has plummeted in recent years, which has contributed to the growing popularity of tarpon fishing there.

is set mainly in the Keys and has aired on the Discovery Channel and the sports channels owned by NBC, CBS, and Fox.

Underlying and boosting this popularity in fly tarpon angling is the concurrent transformation of fly fishing as a whole. The sport has been infused with youth. The movie version of Norman Maclean's autobiographical novella, *A River Runs Through It*—which was released in 1992 and was directed by Robert Redford and starred a young Brad Pitt—is often credited with kicking off a massive boom in the popularity of fly fishing. That boom had major aftershocks. Sometime in the mid- to late-2000s, fly fishing morphed from a somewhat staid sport dominated by middle-aged to older men who geeked out over the Latin names of the insects that trout ate to a hip and cool one that mirrored, in some ways, the surfing and skateboarding cultures. The gear—the rods and reels and skiffs—was immaculate, beautiful to gaze upon and, with its advanced technology, performing at a level higher than ever before. The clothing suddenly became more fashionable, too. Gone (for the most part) were the oversized fishing shirts with their big, ungainly chest pockets, the fishing equivalent of the old boxy Brooks Brothers suits. In their place came tight-fitting, sweat-wicking performance shirts. Buffs—those cylindrical pieces of fabric that protect the neck and face from the sun, that example of "Guru Shit" that Dopirak talked about—became ubiquitous in the fly-fishing world. When pulled up over the nose, they convey the look of a bandito, and the feeling that, just maybe, you are getting away with something.[*]

Lifestyle brands oriented around fly fishermen have taken off in recent years. Yeti, a cooler company founded by fly fishermen, is one of the hottest young brands in the United States. Patagonia, Simms, and Orvis now create articles of clothing—shirts, jackets, pants, hats—that work both on and off the water. Other companies founded by fishermen make lifestyle clothing that runs the gamut, from the edginess of Austin's Howler

---

[*] Buffs also provide the odd, tangible, and somewhat pleasing effect of closing off the rest of the world when lifted over the face, nose, and ears. It's almost meditative. You can hear your own breathing.

Brothers to the northeastern prep of Vineyard Vines to Poncho Outdoors, which occupies the space in between. Costa del Mar's polarized fishing glasses have made the leap into the nonfishing world.

Media have evolved, too. New fly-fishing magazines, like *The Drake* (founded by a former *Powder* magazine editor), *The Fly Fish Journal* (an off-shoot of a surfing magazine), and, more recently, *Anglers Journal* (which also features some spinfishing), concentrate less on the "how-to" in fly fishing, as their hook-and-bullet forefathers had, and more on the experience of the sport.* These magazines eschew the once typical grip-and-grin photos, opting instead for stunning scenery shots or portraits that describe a state of being, the "feel" of the sport. The prose within them, much of it written by and about younger anglers with facial hair and tattoos who love craft beer and weed, flouts some conventions with its style. It's cheeky, ironic, and experiential, sophisticated but not snooty. Many of these younger anglers live online, of course. There are numerous excellent fishing blogs/digital magazines on the internet, including *Midcurrent, Gink and Gasoline, Moldy Chum, Southern Culture on the Fly,* and *Tail* (which also has a print component). Instagram has become the visual medium of the sport, with a voluminous number of anglers and guides providing daily accounts of their fishing exploits.** Some influential media enterprises, like *Fly Lords*, were started, and have prospered, on that social media site.

One of the biggest leaps forward in fly-fishing media was made in film. The quality of the new films—with the help of editing technology, drones, and cool music—has never been better. There is an international fly-fishing film tour that makes its way across the United States and Canada every year, showcasing the work of several companies that specialize in fly-fishing films, as well as that of some high-quality amateurs. *The Drake* has sponsored a fly-fishing video

---

* Some not-so-new fishing magazines, like *Field & Stream, Fly Fisherman,* and *American Angler,* have evolved a bit this way, too.

** Some old-timers worry a bit about constant connectivity of the iPhone generation. David E. Petzal, a longtime contributor to *Field & Stream* and self-described curmudgeon, wrote in 2019, "Hunting and fishing are, at their core, sports of solitude, and they will end when enough shitheads decide that nothing is worth Being Out of Touch."

award show for the last fifteen years. Yeti has produced several excellent short films, including its acclaimed *120 Days*, which is about fly fishing for tarpon.

Part of the reason for this popularity, lifestyle brand expansion, and new media is that fly fishing hasn't just become younger—it's become more female. In recent years especially, women have increasingly made their way into what was previously a male-dominated sport, following in the footsteps of Joan Wulff, an early icon. Dotty Ballantyne holds five tarpon world records in the IGFA's women's division, making her by far the most decorated woman tarpon angler ever (her husband, Fitz Coker, is also a well-known tarpon angler).* Hilary Hutcheson created a fishing-related company, called Outside Media, and cofounded and hosted the show *Trout TV*. Stevie Kim-Rubell is a fourteen-year-old tarpon fishing phenom who was the subject of an episode of *Silver Kings*. April Vokey, who has mastered the art of Spey casting, is the host of arguably the sport's most popular podcast. Fifteen-year-old Maxine McCormick has won two women's Flycasting World Championships (the first at age twelve) and is, inarguably, one of the best fly casters in the world right now. Diana Rudolph is a total badass, a world-record holder in many species, and the only woman to ever win a major tarpon tournament in the Keys (she beat an all-male field in the 2004 Don Hawley tournament). Jen Ripple created *Dun Magazine*, the first women's fly-fishing publication. Meredith McCord holds nearly two hundred IGFA world records and counting. Alex Lovett-Woodsum is an up-and-coming talent on the flats and starred in a Ram Trucks commercial about her fishing passion. Kate Taylor is a famous guide, and it is no longer that odd to see women fly-fishing guides on American rivers.

∽

---

* When I asked Ballantyne if she would prefer that there *weren't* separate IGFA divisions for men and women (after all, women are just as capable of catching any fish a man is), she told me that she liked the fact that there are different categories. "It builds community and promotes fishing among women," she says.

The person most responsible for helping to usher in this contemporary era of fly fishing for tarpon is a man named Andy Mill. Mill has lived an interesting life—US ski team member, television host, former husband of tennis great Chris Evert, and the tarpon tournament world's Tiger Woods.

For a period in the 1970s, Mill was the best downhiller in the United States and one of the best in the world. He competed in two Olympics and two World Championships. His sixth-place finish in the downhill in the 1976 Olympics—accomplished on a badly injured lower right leg, which he stuck into the snow moments before his run in order to dull the pain—is still regarded as one of the more legendary runs in US skiing history. (In 1988, Mill was given a US Olympic Committee's Spirit Award for that run.) Though he frequently had some of the fastest times on the hill during his training runs on the World Cup circuit, Mill never won a race.[*] That was due mainly to his style of racing. He started in fifth gear and never shifted down. And, as a result, he crashed a lot, and usually hurt himself in the process (over the course of his skiing career, he broke his arm, wrist, neck, back, and both of his legs). The Europeans adored him, nicknaming him the "*wilde hunde*" (wild dog) for his on-the-course ballsiness and off-the-course appetite for fun. His skiing career ended in 1981 with a crash on the Lauberhorn in Wengen, Switzerland, which resulted in a broken back and neck and torn ligaments in one of his knees. "I just ran out of body," Mill says.

His ski-racing career left him frustrated. "I just didn't have the composure to win when it counted," he says. "I was a bit too emotional, and I didn't know how to contain it. I choked a bit on race days. I don't think my potential was fulfilled." He wouldn't have those issues when it came to his next sporting endeavor.

Immediately after the end of his racing career, Mill entered into the world of broadcasting. He created a show, *Ski with Andy Mill*, which aired at eighty-three ski resorts across the country. He became a special correspondent for *Good Morning America*, and worked for ESPN and NBC. He covered the 1992 and 1994 Winter Olympics for CBS. And he

---

[*]   He did have seven top-ten finishes.

hosted a fishing show, called *Sportsman's Journal*, on the Outdoor Life
Network, for seven seasons. In all, Mill carved out a twenty-two-year
career in broadcasting. The television work was good, he says, but it left
him feeling unsatisfied. Mill missed the competitive rush that ski racing
had provided him. He found it in tarpon fishing.*

∽

Mill hooked his first tarpon on a trip to Belize in 1986. Though he failed
to land it, he says he felt like "a bolt of lightning had struck me and I had
survived." He dove completely into the sport, fishing for at least forty
days a season for the next seven years.

He heard about Homosassa and went there in the late 1980s. He met
Evans on the water one day and later had dinner with him, picking his
brain for everything he knew about tarpon. Still, Mill found that Homosassa, with its many fishless days, didn't suit him. "I'm a pretty hyper
guy," says the former quick-twitch ski racer. "I was bored as fuck there."

So he headed to the Keys, where he got his action, along with a big
challenge. On the ocean side of the Keys, he found hundreds of tarpon
each day. The problem was that they were extremely difficult to entice
with a fly. The tarpon on the ocean side are generally thought to be
uninterested in eating, on the move to some unknown destination. Mill,
with the help of his guides, Harry Spear and Tim Hoover, made it his
mission to crack their code.

He eventually did, but it took time and much scientific inquiry. He
started with experimentation. He fished what, at the time, were considered to be tiny flies (tied on 1/O hooks). He lengthened his leader
to fifteen feet (nine feet had been the standard). He tried unorthodox
retrieves with his fly, like wiggling the rod tip to impart motion. He tested
the breaking limits of his tippets by tying them to car bumpers, or using

* You'll remember that Evans (football and wrestling) and Cunningham (flying helicopters in Vietnam) also came to tarpon fishing searching for the rush from a former
life.

a weight-and-pulley system to figure out exactly how hard he could pull so he could get fish in quickly.

And he studied the fish. Most anglers, when confronted with a school of oncoming tarpon, naturally cast for the lead fish. Mill waited and analyzed each individual fish in the school, looking for one that showed signs that it might be more willing than the others to take a fly. Sometimes it was the flare of a gill, or the depth at which the fish was swimming. Sometimes it was the way a fish "looked" in the water (fish that appear brown in the water are more apt to bite than those that appear black, according to Mill). And sometimes it was just some ineffable "feel" that came from instinct as he gained more experience.

In the late 1990s, Mill began to enter tarpon tournaments in the Keys. The tournaments provided him with a way to measure just how good he was at tarpon angling. They also provided him with something else. "They gave me a second chance to prove that I could be great at something," he says.

And great he was. Starting in 2000, Mill (with Hoover) won five Gold Cups—the most prestigious tarpon fly tournament in the world—in a span of six years, and he completed the tarpon tournament world's career triple crown (winning the Gold Cup, Golden Fly, and Don Hawley tournaments). He retired from tournaments in 2006, walking away at the very apex of his game. "The tournaments were beginning to drive me nuts," Mill says. "I'd find some satisfaction on the last day when I held the trophy. But then I'd immediately start driving myself crazy about the next one." (Mill would come out of retirement once—for the 2015 Golden Fly tournament—and win it.) He's now settled into fishing for fun. Each season, he rents a house in the Keys and fishes for a month or so, usually with his son, Nicky. He says the key to tarpon angling is found in a Zen-like koan: "You have to show the fly to the fish without him seeing it."

Mill was—and to a certain degree, remains—perhaps the best tarpon angler of his day, "so much better than anyone else it seemed unfair," as one of his contemporaries described him. He is the sport's great modern-day ambassador. In 2010, he put together an excellent book about fly fishing for the species, *A Passion for Tarpon*, in which he interviewed most of the sport's legends. As an endorser and co-designer, he helped put Hardy on the map as a maker of high-quality tarpon rods and reels. He is a frequent lecturer and master of ceremonies at angling events, and he and Nicky launched a popular podcast, *Mill House*, in 2020. He is the progenitor of some of the sport's most innovative anglers of today, like David Dalu and the guide Scott Collins, who dominated tarpon tournaments in the late 2000s. At sixty-six, Mill still has his Prince Valiant–like long black hair (he was recently named to the AARP's "top twenty hottest men over fifty" list), his quick smile, his heartfelt emotions worn endearingly on his sleeve, and the ability to punch a perfect cast through a 25-mile-per-hour wind, manipulate the fly invitingly, hook a fish that doesn't want to eat, and play it to the boat in less than thirty minutes. He helped make the sport of fly fishing for tarpon popular because he made it look easy. He also made it look cool and fun as hell.

∞

The popularity of a particular species of fish is, generally speaking, a very good thing for the sport in general and for the fish. The more people fish, the more they care about the species they fish for, which can provide political heft when it comes to conservation. It is believed that groups like Now Or Neverglades, Bullsugar, and Captains For Clean Water—nonprofit advocacy organizations that were founded by fly fishermen—tipped the ultra-tight 2018 Florida gubernatorial election in favor of the candidate who had disavowed taking any money from the sugar companies that had long fought *against* proper conservation and restoration measures for Lake Okeechobee and the Everglades (the latter being one of the world's great tarpon spots).

Popularity, though, can also have some downsides.

∞

Most anglers who have dedicated themselves to the sport have had, at one time or another, a spot that they would consider a secret. Finding these spots requires time on the water, intuition and hard work, a willingness to leave the crowds and explore new territory—which can mean many fishless days or weeks—and the utmost discretion (something that Harold LeMaster and Kirk Smith learned the hard way). These spots can be well off the beaten path and hard to get to. They can also be hidden in plain sight (as Homosassa was for many years). To be sure, there are serendipitous discoveries of new secret places. But that good luck is usually earned.

One thing that's also almost always true about these spots: they rarely remain secrets forever. It's hard to describe the utter despondency that accompanies the loss of a secret fishing spot. Every time one of them is found or discovered by others, it feels like a mini reenactment of the Fall of Man, like you've been kicked out of Eden, your naked covetousness painfully revealed.

There are, by my reckoning, three potential responses to the discovery of your spot by others. You can suck it up and just keep fishing it, sharing the spot with the newcomer or newcomers. You can be confrontational and try to exert some sort of ownership over the spot and try to chase the interloper away. Or you yourself can walk away, shoulders slumped, toe-stubbing the ground, knowing that nothing in this world lasts and that, maybe, if you're lucky, and if you're willing to go through all of the pain again, you just might find a new secret spot again someday.

My approach has always been the latter. I usually cannot stand to fish a formerly secret spot with another, and I am no fan of confrontation on the water. But then again, I do not fish for a living.

∞

David Mangum does, though.

Mangum is based in the Florida Panhandle. He is one of the country's most highly regarded tarpon guides, and is one of the faces of the newer generation of tarpon anglers. He is forty-seven, lean and bearded, with sun wrinkles around blue eyes that blaze with intensity. He is sponsored by Simms, Orvis, Costa del Mar, Mako Reels, and Yeti, for whom he starred in the film *120 Days* and put together (and did most of the photographs for) a beautiful coffee table book about tarpon fishing (called, simply, *Tarpon*) that came out in late 2019. He is known for his passion for tarpon angling, and for sometimes going a bit overboard with said passion. Tom Bie, editor of the *Drake* magazine and a client of Mangum's, has a cameo in *120 Days*, which is about Mangum's obsession with tarpon angling (the "120" in the title references the number of days he guides in a given year). In Bie's interview, which is cleverly spliced in with footage of Mangum in his boat, firmly chastising a client for missing a tarpon, Bie says, with a grin, "I don't think he's *overly* a dick." When Harry Spear is asked about Mangum, he answers, simply, "Talk about tight rubber bands!" But those rubber bands are part of what make Mangum so great at what he does.

Mangum grew up in Destin. He says he saw his first tarpon when he was seven years old and was immediately intrigued. "I was baitfishing out of a johnboat with my dad, and I saw this thing that I thought was a sea serpent. My dad didn't see it. Years later I'd realize that it was some rolling tarpon."

He went to Austin, Texas, in the early 1990s, supposedly to go to college, but he ended up bartending and doing "some pretty serious drinking," he says. He quickly deduced that he needed a change of scenery. In the back of an angling magazine, he saw an ad for a fishing operation in Alaska. He called and got a job as a fishing guide and moved up there for the summer. It turned out that the boss of the fishing operation was also a flats guide in the Keys for part of the year. He told Mangum all about tarpon.

Mangum moved back home and started scouting the flats in the Panhandle for tarpon with a friend who had a boat. In 1998, Mangum got his captain's license. A year later, with a loan from his father, he purchased a Hell's Bay skiff. For a while, his daily routine included waiting tables at a restaurant in Destin until late at night, sleeping for a few hours, then running out to the flats in the dark and sitting on a shoal. After the day broke, he would study the habits of both the fish and the other anglers on the water. The Panhandle tarpon fishery at the time was relatively unknown, fittingly located in an area of Florida called the "Forgotten

Coast." Though no longer a secret these days, the Panhandle remains a less popular destination for tarpon than some of its counterparts to the south, like the Keys and Boca Grande. The fish in the Panhandle area tend to bite well, thanks to a slight tint in the area's water (myriad muddy freshwater rivers drain into the Gulf there). But there are fewer tarpon in the Panhandle than in the Keys, and they can be very difficult to find for nonregulars, swimming hidden shoals and banks and camouflaged by the stained water. Most of the tarpon appear merely as bulges in the water until they get right next to the boat.

By 2002, Mangum was guiding full-time in an area to the west of Apalachicola. At the time, the guides there fished only a handful of spots, lining up on them roughly in the order of seniority. Mangum decided he would try to find some new spots. And by 2005, after scouting for years, he had. He gave each of his new spots names, like Wake and Bake, Dreamland, and North End. He guarded them fiercely with a firm confidence in his personal philosophy, which he laid out in *120 Days*. "Nobody owns the ocean," he says in the film. "But you own the intellectual capital that you earned with your blood and sweat over the years." At his spots, Mangum anchors up on a buoy with a skull design on it. If an intruder doesn't get the message from that, Mangum resorts to other measures.

Mangum says he rarely comes upon someone else in one of his spots, but if he does, he usually leads with civility. "I'll tell the guy that I've been fishing here for a long time and that he's welcome to get in behind me," he says. "If that doesn't work, I'll just pull up thirty feet in front of him and anchor." As one might suspect, that move sometimes leads to anger. "If someone starts yelling at me, I'll point to the beach and say, 'Let's go,'" says Mangum. "When I start idling to the beach, that's usually it. It's over. They don't follow and they leave."

One time, though, things went further than that. Mangum arrived at one of his spots one morning halfway through the tarpon season in 2008, only to find a man he knew—a friend, actually—already there. They screamed back and forth at each other for a few minutes. His friend, whom Mangum identifies only as G.J., didn't think Mangum was entitled to the spot. Mangum thought he was. Neither budged. Because they each had other people on their boats, things on the water never got physical. But that changed later that night.

When Mangum got home that evening, he was still fuming. He sat on his couch and downed a few beers. He heard a car come to a hasty stop in his driveway. His front door swung open, and there stood G.J., breathing heavily, full of rage as well. They stood face-to-face for a moment, then G.J. tackled Mangum into the kitchen, grabbed his head, and started pounding it against the floor. "I saw nothing but white stars," says Mangum.

G.J. relaxed for a moment, apparently thinking he'd won the fight already. But Mangum shot up, with G.J. draped on his back, and slammed him into the kitchen counter. G.J. fell off his back, and Mangum then grabbed a hold of *his* head and started banging it on the floor.

And with that, finally, they both collapsed from exhaustion. G.J. left. They talked on the phone a few hours later, to check in on each other. They remain friends to this day. "I guided the next few days, but I was in a haze," says Mangum. "I definitely should not have been out on the water."

According to Mangum, the core problem with the tarpon world—hell, the core problem with life on this earth—is that "there are too many motherfuckers." Meaning: too many people.

The fight that Mangum got into is by no means something new in the tarpon world. "I've always thought that the big tarpon world is the equivalent of big game hunting (trout and salmon anglers are more like bird shooters), with all of its ego and macho posturing and blood feuds," author (and my uncle) Charles Gaines once wrote. Tarpon guides and anglers are a territorial bunch, anxious and protective of their turf, and prone to bouts of temporary insanity. They find secret spots and want to keep them that way, and will go to great, sometimes over-the-top, lengths to try to do so. Huff says he used to instruct clients to sit down while in the midst of fighting a tarpon if another boat was passing by so it appeared as if he and his client were just having lunch. Guide Ralph Delph once made his client, Joe Robinson, wear a blindfold as he ran and then poled into one of his secret spots. Other supposed infractions have provoked even nuttier behavior. Bill Curtis once cut off McGuane on the water in the Keys in the 1970s, and the two very nearly came to blows back at the dock. In "The Longest Silence," McGuane wrote about on-the-water disputes being "settled with gaffs, or barbed wire strung in guts and channels to wreck props and drive shafts." In his novel *92 in the Shade*—which was basically a roman à clef—one guide shoots and kills another with a handgun. Archibald and Chittum's brawl in Homosassa in the late 1970s fits in here, as does the wholly destructive sarcophagus that was applied to the boats of anglers and guides who didn't play by the unwritten rules.

Mangum says he "had a lot of venom" as a young guide. Though traces of it remain, he's known more these days for his innovations. He was among the first guides in the Panhandle to instruct his clients to use short, quick strips of the fly to entice tarpon to bite, as opposed to the traditional long, slow strip. Indeed, when you fish with Mangum, as you retrieve your fly, he says, "tick, tick, tick, ticK, tiCK, tICK, TICK!" in a growing crescendo, as a reminder of how you should retrieve the fly. (He describes the hand movements of the desired retrieval action as "jerking off the hamster.") He frequently uses drones for photographs. He created a new tarpon fly, called the Dragon Tail, which sports an alarmingly lifelike appendage for which it's named and is now commercially available through Orvis (and used in places like Homosassa).

But his most interesting innovation is in his boat. On its bow is what appears to be an extra-tall casting platform. In reality, that platform—which he custom-made—is for him and not the angler. After his boat is anchored to a buoy in one of his spots, Mangum ascends the platform, which situates him right over the angler's shoulder. From there, he provides instructions and, sometimes, takes hold of the rod to point out an oncoming fish. "For a while, I was standing in the bow, right next to my client, which worked pretty well," he says. "But then I thought, 'Why not add some elevation?' Now I can see the fish and relay information really quickly and it gives us an extra five seconds to get ready for a fish." He dreamed up the idea in 2013, and it has since spread to some of his guiding brethren. The setup takes a little time getting used to for the angler. Mangum literally hovers over you, to the point where you can smell the shampoo in his hair. But it is mighty effective.

Mangum, like most of his generation and the younger ones coming along, abhors fishing for world records. "I think all of those guys who are going after records are doing it just to get their dicks in a book," he says. "They just want to be remembered when they're dead. I don't care about getting my name in a book." It was all about the experience and the now.

∞

As discussed before, fishing for world-record tarpon, for all intents and purposes, is no longer really a *thing*. Not in this day and age. There are no newspaper stories about the quest anymore. *Sports Illustrated* hasn't written a story about angling world records in many decades. *Fly Fisherman* magazine printed a picture of Holland Jr.'s catch a few years ago accompanied by a caption that read, in part, "Let's hope that's the last tarpon we ever see hanging in a tree." The tarpon television show *Silver Kings* never mention records. Mill, Dalu, Collins, Raskob, and the vast majority of the newer generation of fishermen and guides do not pursue records. Though the number of anglers in the United States has increased by 14 percent in the last ten years, to 41.4 million (according to the US Fish and Wildlife Service), that growth has not resulted in more world-record hunting, for tarpon or any other species. It's just not an activity that's captivated the newer generation of fly anglers. A big reason is the evolution mentioned before, that growing awareness of conservation issues and of the limits to the bounty of the sea. The specter of the shaming on social media that would undoubtedly be unleashed by a photo of a big tarpon hung in a tree must also factor in here. One can only imagine the negative reaction to a photo of Holland Jr. and his world record circulating on Twitter nowadays. It doesn't help matters that the optics of a tarpon weighed for a record are rather disturbing: a human-sized fish hung from a tree conjures images of lynching.

But there are still some young world-record chasers out there. Among the most thoughtful of them is Nathanial Linville, the thirty-seven-year-old owner of The Angling Company, a fly shop in Key West. He has set world records for permit with his primary guide, John O'Hearn, who is forty-six. And, for the last eight years, he has sought to break the six-pound tippet world record for tarpon with, of all people, Steve Huff.

Linville took a rather tortured path to Key West. He was born and raised in Connecticut, and was introduced to fly fishing in the late 1980s by his mother, who was the president of the Woman Flyfishers Club. His father ran a successful sailcloth business.

Linville had an unsettled childhood. He was expelled from high school and never completed his degree. In his early twenties, he found his way to New York City, where, he says, "I pretty much concentrated full-time on the destruction of my life via cocaine." He says he was "well enough to know that I couldn't continue to do that, but too dumb to realize what my problem really was." At the time, he considered that problem to be merely geographical. That belief, combined with a desire to fish more, led him to Key West in 2005.

He got a job at a Key West fly shop that was once owned by the angler and author Jeffrey Cardenas. Four years later, Linville opened The Angling Company. "Then I discovered our old friend, Oxycontin," he says. He founded the new shop in a haze. "I did everything I could to derail it," he says. But Linville somehow made it through that year, and he got clean in 2010. He fished with his cousins, Fitz Coker and Dotty Ballantyne, and through them, he became interested in world records.

Linville set a few shark records on the fly, and then, with O'Hearn in 2018, he caught a sixteen-pound permit on two-pound test tippet (breaking a record held by Del Brown, who was guided by Huff). Linville got so into world records that he had an unusual tattoo inked onto his left leg: two straight, parallel black lines, exactly twelve inches apart, which happens to be the IGFA maximum length for a shock tippet.

Linville's quest to break the six-pound tippet record for tarpon (eighty-eight pounds) has been undertaken in the Everglades. Huff and Linville, usually joined by a third person to handle the gaff, have had some epic fights with tarpon. They battled one fish for twelve hours and forty-five minutes. During that fight, Linville, who is a diabetic, needed an insulin shot, which Huff drew up and administered. They lost the fish at 3:00 A.M. Linville estimates that in the many trips he's made with Huff in pursuit of the six-pound record, they've spent around one hundred hours fighting fish.

Linville's quest came to fruition when, in February 2020, he finally landed one of the hooked beasts. The tarpon turned out to be a mind-blowing 140 pounds, 4 ounces, which obliterated the standing six-pound tippet world record. Huff was the guide, of course, and Huff's older son, Chad, gaffed the fish after a surprisingly quick fight that lasted just under an hour. Given the size of the fish and the tippet, Linville's catch is surely among the greatest in the tarpon record world.

Linville is very aware of the fact that he is something of an anomaly for his age. He believes that the antirecord sentiment of his generation boils down to a lack of knowledge. Record fishing, he says, requires a true understanding of the sport, the quarry, and the gear, as well as an understanding of limitations put on an angler. "I've been on both sides of this," he says. "I've been the guy coming down from the Northeast not really understanding what I was doing on the water, and how I was doing it. And I've been the guy who is totally dedicated to records."

There are dozens of smaller parts that must be mastered to make up the greater whole when you chase records with serious intent, he says. The complexity of an IGFA-approved tarpon leader, with all of its knots and precise measurements—which can take the novice an hour to tie—is just the beginning. All the gear—the rods and reels and lines and flies—must be perfectly squared away. Then there's the guide and the handling of the boat, the cast, the hookup, the fight, the landing . . . everything has to be done exceedingly well, which includes the execution of the world-record application.

But there's more to it than that. "Adhering to a certain established etiquette maintains historical behavior and allows you to take part in the history of the sport and not just the immediate moment," Linville says. The entire endeavor has some intrinsic value, beyond just the record, he believes. "It frustrates me when people say they'd never kill a tarpon for a record, as if the only thing they'd have to reconcile is the killing of the fish, and then they'd do it. Just the process of doing it has total value. It's the same with tournaments. [Linville has won several permit tournaments.] You become a better angler, you learn to fish under pressure, you learn from others. There's so much more to it even when you don't accomplish the end goal. In certain ways, you surrender the desire to catch the fish."

One of the beefs that many have with chasing records on light tippets, like the six-pound that Linville has used, is the amount of time it usually takes to get a fish in. It seems like the ultimate in torture for the tarpon. Linville, as you might expect, disagrees with this take. "I've hooked hundreds of tarpon on six-pound and I've wounded three of them [his world record and two others that were gaffed]," he says. "First of all, you break off most of the fish you hook. But even when I am hooked up to a fish, I'm barely putting pressure on it. They're mostly just swimming slowly, not really fighting, not expending much energy. I would have wounded a lot more tarpon if I had used a much bigger tippet, with all of the thrashing and pulling and energy they use up in those fights."

O'Hearn, not surprisingly, agrees with Linville about world records, even if most of his guiding peers these days do not. "Fishing for records is one of the coolest ways you can spend a day," he says. "On that two-pound permit record with Nat, the process was far more interesting than the actual catch."

O'Hearn says the whole thing—fly fishing the flats—is "ridiculous" anyway. "My job is to push millionaires around with a stick. So why not take that absurdity to its logical conclusion and try to catch world records on the lightest tippet possible? At the end of the day, the only value that exists in the universe is the value you grant something."*

That said, O'Hearn says he does not like killing fish intentionally. "I one hundred percent see the other side," he says. "But I also think it's a bit naïve. I kill fish all the time accidentally. We have to come to grips

---

* O'Hearn has a bumper sticker on his boat that reads TROLLING MOTORS ARE FOR PUSSIES.

with the fact that even with catch-and-release, we are torturing fish for own pleasure."

This torturing of tarpon, for some, is becoming a bigger and bigger issue to confront.

◇

Here is another face of the newer generation. This one is familiar, in both looks and last name. He is, like his father, slim but strong, fishy as hell, and among the premier tarpon guides of his era. His name is Dustin Huff.

Dustin, the younger of Steve Huff's two sons, took out his first paying client when he was thirteen years old. He continued to guide through college at the University of Florida, trailering his boat from Gainesville down to the Keys behind an old Ford Mustang.

Now forty-seven, Dustin lives in Marathon Key, not far from the house he grew up in until the age of ten, when his parents divorced. Dustin guides for permit and, occasionally, for bonefish.* But the tarpon is his favorite fish. "They are just spectacular things, the coolest fish," he says.

World records have not been the focus of Dustin's guiding career. Tournaments have. He and his main client Thane Morgan, an orthopedic surgeon from Amarillo, Texas, have become a formidable pair on the tarpon tournament circuit, winning three Gold Cups, and three out of the five Don Hawley tournaments they've entered. The duo has dabbled in a bit of record chasing, though. In 2011, they set the record for tarpon on six-pound tippet, at 88 pounds (this is the record that Linville broke). Two years later, they caught a 119-pound, 3-ounce tarpon that topped the four-pound tippet category. The latter record is the subject of a twenty-two-page thread on *Drake* magazine's website chat board, in which both Dustin and Morgan are mercilessly disparaged for killing

---

* His older brother, Chad, a trained electrical engineer, has also followed in his father's footsteps in recent years. Apart from serving as Linville's gaff man, Chad has become a highly regarded guide in the Everglades.

the fish. A thread on the chat board on *Saltwater Sportsman* magazine's website, though slightly less vicious than the one on the *Drake*'s site, also gets in on the action.

To Dustin, as for Linville, it's a bit more complicated than the "this is good" or "this is bad" black-and-white line drawn on chat boards and social media. "When people on the internet poo-poo records, they don't know what they don't know," says Dustin. "They have no idea of the abuse these fish take elsewhere. They just don't see it. They don't see the guys on the bridges in the Keys who hook tarpon on live bait and *try* to get a shark to eat them, just for the entertainment."

Dustin has done some serious soul-searching on the subject of tarpon fishing in recent years. "I just love the fish and I feel sorry for them at this point, to be honest," he says. "I'm at the point now where I almost feel bad fishing for them, which sounds crazy even as I say it. They are just getting so abused everywhere they go now, and you can see them changing. I respect these fish more than I respect some people. But I know I'm part of the problem. I'm beating up on them, too."

Increased angling pressure is a big reason for the increased abuse, says Dustin. "And a lot of these newer guys are transient. They come down for the season," he says. "You see license plates from fifteen different states. They don't live here." Dustin says that creates a situation in which the resource—the fish and the flats—becomes merely another commercial item to be transacted, something people just jump into and then out of, which can result in a lack of respect for it. There is a spot near Bahia Honda in the Keys that Dustin once loved and says not many people fished a decade ago. He last went there eight years ago and says he will never return. "It's such a clusterfuck with more than thirty boats out there at any given time. The people have no respect, for the fish or for each other," he says. "They're anchored up. They're using trolling motors. They're cutting each other off. They're all using the same fly [a palolo worm pattern]."*

---

* David Dalu and Scott Collins are credited with the realization that palolo worm patterns can work on tarpon all year 'round, and not just during the worm's annual hatch, which happens sometime in May or June.

Though tarpon are harder for most to catch these days—despite the better gear and technology—the sheer number of anglers means they are harassed now more than ever before. Dustin says it's alarming how few tarpon are found now in the Keys backcountry and in Florida Bay, places that once hosted them by the thousands. "Something is happening. The fish are changing. I don't know what the answer is here. I don't know what to do. But in the end, we may have to be willing to lose something to make this a better situation for the fish. I think something has to change."

Tarpon have always, of course, adapted and changed when the need arises. "I used to have these little bays in the backcountry of the Keys where I was the only one fishing a certain population of tarpon," says Flip Pallot. "And I could tell if I was putting too much pressure on them, if I fished them too hard or too often. And then, as soon as I lost control of the spots and others came in, the tarpon left. They were gone. We manipulate these fish all of the time. The entire population of Florida tarpon has been manipulated."

It also might be the case that we are seeing something more than just manipulation.

I was floored the first time I fished in the Keys and saw all of those tarpon swimming on the ocean side. I saw some giant tarpon on my first day ever in Homosassa and felt the same thing. But I had nothing to compare either situation *to*. I suffer from something that many anglers under the age of fifty do: shifting baseline syndrome. Marshall Cutchin, a guide in the Keys from the mid-1980s until the mid-1990s, who now runs the fly-fishing news website Midcurrent, has been at this game longer than I have. His baseline hasn't shifted quite as far as mine. "The average person goes to the Keys and says, 'This is beautiful,'" he says. "And it is. But it's only ten percent as beautiful as it used to be. If you knew what it once looked like and how much better it was, it's pretty sad."

Perhaps it's as Brooke Jarvis wrote in the *New York Times Magazine*, in a piece about the globe's disappearing insect populations: that "the world never feels fallen because we grow accustomed to the fall." Perhaps one reason we become accustomed to the fall is that we don't want to face up to the facts before us, and because social media and the outdoor industry help us do that by making it seem like it's all fine, that there are plenty of fish out there, that the world is one big beautiful photograph. "Nature is a perfect playground for kids. It provides a range of emotions, from fascination to fear and dread and everything in between," says Cutchin. "It's perfect for kids because innocence is the right way to approach it. At some point, though, you have to grow up and put away the toys and become protectors of the playground, for the next generation. So many adults are stuck in playground mode, something that the industry promotes. We are not thinking about the bigger picture."

Pallot is in agreement. "We are turning over everything we fought to preserve to a generation that has fewer touchstones and that's not prepared to be stewards of these things and doesn't realize what treasures they are," he says. "My generation didn't do a good enough job of preserving it and of helping the next generation to do so. I wish we'd done better."

The bigger picture is that we are currently in a geological age that many scientists suggest naming the Anthropocene—that is, the geological age in which humans, and not ice ages or extreme heat or asteroids, are the major influences on the earth and its environment. We are also in the midst of an enormous loss of biodiversity, a sixth extinction. A lot of that loss doesn't happen in dramatic fashion: though species across the globe are going extinct at alarming rates, much of the damage is what's known as "defaunation," a decline in abundance. The loss of the plentitude of big bonefish in the Florida Keys serves as an example. (It's also a loss that should terrify any serious tarpon angler, since it most likely had to do with the water issues plaguing Florida, which tarpon are certainly not immune to.) Killing fish for records, as senseless as it is to many of us, certainly doesn't help. But, again, it's not the real problem. The idiotic killing that goes on in the Boca Grande Pass is a bigger problem, but that, too, remains secondary. The biggest issues, by far, are the intertwined devastations of the dwindling reserves of freshwater and the loss of rearing habitat. According to Aaron Adams of BTT, these issues have already led to a decrease in tarpon populations, a decrease that will not cease—and, indeed, will only accelerate—unless they are dealt with as soon as possible.

Tarpon are a truly remarkable species that has adapted and adjusted to every adverse condition it has faced so far. But the biggest test for tarpon, and for all species on earth, for that matter (including humans!), may come from the Anthropocene. For if we continue on our current path, in our current ways, the next geological age may be what the biologist and naturalist E. O. Wilson has termed the Eremocene, the age of loneliness.

INTERLUDE 5
CATCH-22

There was one time when the new generation, with its knowledge and biases, mixed with the older generation, with *its* knowledge and biases. It did not go well.

In 2015, Evans and Dopirak had what amounted to a falling out. Evans wanted to book Dopirak not only for the month of May but also for some of June. But that was the month when Dopirak traditionally fished with Brian Tang, and Dopirak, being the principled man he is, refused to cancel one long-term client for another. This angered Evans a bit (he and Dopirak would eventually smooth over their differences and resume fishing together again the following year). So he cast his eye elsewhere, for another place to fish that season for the eight-pound record. He called Huff, who suggested that he give the Panhandle a shot. There were some big fish there (it's believed that some of the Homosassa giants migrate through that area). Huff also suggested that Evans book a guide that he'd fished with a few times in that area. That guide was David Mangum.

Mangum, though he had no interest in world records, was game for fishing with Evans for one main reason: "I thought I could learn something from him." Butler was coming along on the trip, and he would serve as the gaffer if and when the moment came. (Mangum didn't even own a gaff. "I didn't want to be the guy who whacked the fish," he says.) Evans booked Mangum for a week.

Things were rocky right away. Evans didn't like how deep much of the water in the Panhandle fishery was, which made the likelihood of landing a big tarpon on eight-pound tippet much more difficult (the fish could just stay down deep, far away from the gaff, and Evans would be unable to pull it up without breaking the tippet). He didn't like anchoring the boat or fishing for tarpon he couldn't actually fully see in the discolored water. And he didn't like Mangum's hands-on method of guiding. "It was constant noise," says Evans. *"Ticky, ticky, ticky."*

Mangum wasn't enjoying himself, either. He says they hit the fishing just right. There were plenty of tarpon around. "But Evans couldn't catch them. He didn't have the language to speak to the fish. He kept doing what he always did, with the long strips. He didn't want any advice from me." The two personalities were a volatile mix: an innovative, high-strung young guide and an old, stuck-in-his-ways man whose techniques had worked since before his young guide was born.

Butler was caught in the middle. "It was not good, mate," he says. After the first day on the water, Mangum asked to speak to Butler outside the house in which they were all staying. "I told him that I couldn't do this anymore. Evans didn't want me to give him instructions or even speak, and he just talked about Homosassa the whole time. I felt like the boat boy," says Mangum. Butler coaxed Mangum down off the ledge, and they all held it together just long enough to make it through the next few days. "Only because of Dean," says Mangum. Evans hooked one fish during the trip that might have cleared the eight-pound record, but he broke it off. "Mangum never adjusted to me," says Evans. "It was uncomfortable for me the moment I stepped onto his boat."

They left the trip infuriated with each other. Mangum called Evans a "dick." Evans nicknamed Mangum "Maggot." With the passage of time, the tensions have cooled, at least a bit, though it is clear that they will never fish together again. Mangum says now he admires Evans for his dedication to the sport. Evans, for his part, says that Mangum is "clearly a great guide, but it was just a totally different way of fishing." And Evans, unlike his favorite fish, is no longer into adapting. "Maybe I would have changed if I were younger," he says. "But I'm not."

14

THE OLD MAN
AND THE SEA

t ends where it began.

It's May 15, 2019. Evans, Dopirak, Butler, and I are in Dopirak's Mangrove skiff, running on plane up the western side of the Oklahoma flat. It's 10:00 A.M. Evans no longer likes to get on the water too early. Dopirak and Butler, after a morning of restlessly puttering around the poon shack, radiate a sense of relief. The salty spray, the hot sun, the wind luffing their shirts—all of it seems a tonic to these fishing guides. They are back in their element.

We pass Guido Rock, and then a white PVC pipe that juts out of the water. "That's our Bobby," Butler yells over the whine of the motor, as we speed by in one of the gangster's former boats.

The horizon, a commingling of the slightly different blue tints of the sky and the water, is empty and endless until we near Black Rock. There, the outlines of other boats, maybe ten of them, begin to emerge, looking initially like distant oil rigs, and then, as we get closer and can make out human figures and push poles, like a troupe of gondoliers who have somehow been swept over from Venice in a great storm. "The Homo sapiens are in the Cock Hole," Evans growls. Dopirak shuts down the big motor well short of the other boats, setting up his drift, hoping to intercept the tarpon as they begin to take leave of Black Rock. He knows that Evans does not want to take part in the blind-casting to the fish that's being done out there, even though his chances of hooking a tarpon would be improved. Evans wants to actually see his quarry. Old dog. No new tricks.

Dopirak begins to pole ever so slowly while scanning the waterscape. Butler stands, as he usually does, on the bow next to the cage, also looking for the slightest discrepancy beneath the sea's surface. I decide to join the watch. I want to add some value to the endeavor if I can, for I know that my additional weight will make Dopirak's day of maneuvering the boat a little tougher. Evans sits in the lawn chair just in front of the console, unable to see much, relying on his guides, waiting on their command. "Al and Dean take me out there like I'm a baby," Evans had told me the night before. "They will be the ones who catch this fish."

We remain in our positions, "fixed in ocean reveries," as Melville wrote, with very little chatting, and without seeing a single tarpon, for hours.

Sometime in the early afternoon, we move to a spot farther south on the Oklahoma flat. Five boats are already there. Dopirak works his imperceptible magic. Within twenty minutes of joining the other boats, we have somehow gained the pole position, now in the best spot to see, and cast to, any arriving fish.

A thought crosses my mind. Given the tarpon's long life span and the fact that Homosassa remains an annual gathering spot for at least some of its historical run, it's not completely out of the realm of possibility that Evans could cast to a fish today that he also cast to back in 1976. There was a fish nicknamed "Spooner," for the distinctive chrome spot on one of its gills, that Evans and others saw on the flat for two decades. Evans and some of these fish are old acquaintances.

It is Dopirak who spots them first. "Thomas, you better get up there," he says. Evans grabs hold of the rope and, with a loud grunt and a wince of pain, he stands, unsteadily. He takes two labored steps up into the cage and grabs his rod from the stripping bucket and starts pulling out line. "Right there, Tom, at twelve," says Butler, calmly. I finally spot the tarpon—a string of ten or so swimming nonchalantly right for us, their massive bodies black against the glaring white of the sandy bottom. Dopirak moves the boat backward with a slight rightward shift, as if easing into a parallel parking spot, so that Evans has an 11:30 shot into the wind. Evans studies the fish for a few seconds, and then makes a cast, landing his fly just in front of the third tarpon in the string. The fly sinks, momentarily lifeless. Then Evans pulls on his fly line—one long strip, just as he's always done—and the black tail on the fly flutters in the water. The third tarpon in the string peels off from the others, and with a sudden jerk of its head, the great fish takes the fly and then shoots into the air. It's a thrilling sight—all of it taking place maybe thirty feet from the boat. I feel my heart beating in my Adam's apple.

Dopirak hits the trolling motors, moving away from the other boats and toward the tarpon, which is hauling ass for the middle of the Gulf of Mexico. Evans, now leaning back on the railing of his cage, just points the rod at the fish as his line rips out of his reel and through the guides of his fly rod. There is nothing else he can do right now but wait for the tarpon to stop its initial run. When he gets far enough away from the other boats, Dopirak turns off his trolling motors and fires up the big engine. "Start reeling, Thomas," he yells. With his right hand, Evans begins to crank his old Tibor, once a deep red, but now faded pink from decades in the sun.*

With most of his line now back on the reel, Evans begins fighting the fish. He starts off as gentle as he can be, but Butler still reminds him, a few times, that he's using eight-pound tippet. He knows that Evans's natural instinct still is to pull on the fish as hard as he can.

---

* This is another part of light-tippet tarpon record fishing that some within the sport dislike. As with marlin fly angling, much of the fight is done with the boat, running and gunning after the fish (or backing down on it), to help the angler quickly retrieve the line. Doing this helps wear down the fish and allows the angler to retrieve line quickly and maintain a shorter length of it, which reduces the chances of the hook falling out. It is all totally legal under IGFA rules. Whether it's sporting or not depends upon whom you ask.

Soon Dopirak has moved us to within ten feet of the tarpon, which has settled into a rhythm, swimming with the boat—somewhat casually, it seems to me—and coming up for a gulp of air every few minutes. The tarpon looks absolutely enormous, well over the 127-pound mark that Evans will need to break the world record. But I am no expert. Dopirak is, though. "I can't tell for sure, but that fish looks really freakin' close, dawg," he says. With that hint, Butler grabs the gaff and moves in beside Evans.

We follow the fish for another five minutes. Butler hunches over a bit, as if readying himself to apply the gaff. And then, suddenly, there is a slight *pop* and Evans's rod snaps straight. The tippet has broken. "Motherfucker," Evans says, in barely more than a whisper. Butler puts down the gaff and takes the rod from Evans, who is red in the face and audibly panting. Evans grabs the rope and slowly makes his way back down to the lawn chair. After a few moments of silence, Dopirak says, "I thought you fought that fish beautifully."

"No, I didn't," Evans says between deep breaths. "I pulled too hard." It would be the only fish of possible record size that he would hook that season in Homosassa.

∽

Homosassa now, as it has been for a while, is basically hermetically sealed off from the rest of the tarpon world. The fishery is immune to the infusion of youth in the sport, made up of mostly older fishermen. Evans (eighty-two), Cunningham (seventy-two), and Tang (seventy) are really the only true record chasers left. Cunningham, now retired from his law practice, has switched his record focus from eight-pound tippet to sixteen-pound, because he believes he has better odds in that category. "The added bonus is that Evans currently holds that record," he says. "Double your pleasure, double your fun." Tang, like Evans, remains on the chase for the eight-pound record.

But it's not just the record hunters who are aged. Kilpatrick is sixty-seven. Dopirak is sixty-three. Homosassa regulars and semi-regulars, like Ronnie Richards, Gary Merriman, Dan Malzone, Tommy Locke, Tom Mohler, Kent Davenport, and Earle Waters, are all over sixty. A few young guides fish Homosassa—Kyle Staton is thirty and Jonathan Hamilton is thirty-five, and both are well respected—but "you could count the number of young guys out here on Bobby Erra's hand," says one local guide.

In recent years, the fishing in Homosassa has improved a bit from its nadir in the 1990s. But the younger tarpon-fishing generation—and in particular, the young, nomadic hotshot guides from Montana and other places out west, who fish for tarpon every spring—largely avoids Homosassa and heads for the Keys instead. Homosassa is not a weekend-warrior type of fishery. It remains a tricky place to figure out, with its water depth and the plethora of engine-wrecking rock piles. One has to have a certain type of temperament to fish here, has to be comfortable with staring at a vacant sea for hours, days, and sometimes weeks at a time without making a meaningful cast. One has to be comfortable, too, with what others would deem a failed fishing trip. In the Keys, an angler can see hundreds of fish in a day. They are smaller, on average, than the Homosassa fish, and they are not easy to catch. But they are there, and it is exciting and immediately gratifying. Homosassa is an old manual Leica M3 camera. The Keys are the camera on your iPhone.

꿍

Evans's 2019 poon shack is a former health resort located on six acres of land, with a large, plantation-style porch that overlooks an inlet of the Gulf of Mexico. Joining Dopirak and Butler in residence is Dopirak's son Brian, who goes by the nickname "Dope." Dope was once a top baseball prospect before injuries derailed his career, and he has now become a fishing guide and a very good one, at that. Evans has also brought in Eric Wilson, a well-regarded private chef from Jackson Hole, to cook dinners and fish with Dope. (Evans had previously hired Wilson to cook at his Jackson Hole home.) Dinners are an important element of

Evans's poon shacks these days. With the falloff of the action on the water since the late 1980s, dinner "has been the highlight of most days down here," Evans says. Wilson doesn't disappoint. Crispy potato gallete, grilled green asparagus with poached quail eggs, chicken ballontine, leg of lamb . . . all paired with Evans's exquisite wines.

Evans sits in the same chair at a table off the kitchen for each meal. He doesn't talk much while he eats. On most nights, once the plates are cleared and the dishes are done, Wilson and Dope head out to the porch to shoot the shit and watch the sunset. Dopirak hits the couch in the adjacent room and watches television (he likes *American Idol*). And Butler, with a glint in his eye, mixes up massive vodka drinks for Evans, himself, and me, and we sit around the table and talk. At this point in the evening, Evans becomes more animated. The subjects, on various nights, run the gamut . . .

∽

We talk about tarpon, of course, the merits and demerits of certain flies and fly lines, the habits of the fish, Lopez's antics, Erra's former vise grip on the place, and Evans's rivalry, back in the day, with Pate. When Evans tells a story about an individual fish that he has caught, he often mimics the action of the fish coming to the fly, blowing out his cheeks and opening and closing his mouth. When he does this, as Butler has pointed out, he actually looks like a tarpon, his jowls bringing to mind the gill plates of the fish. Perhaps it's like the dog owner who, over the years, comes to resemble his pooch.

∽

Evans often laments the lack of tarpon in Homosassa. "There's no fucking fish here anymore," he says. "I don't know why I do it. I hate the poon now. I hate the fucker because he doesn't come out to play anymore. But when he did . . . shit."

"You love the tarpon, Tom," says Butler.

Butler is right, of course. Huff and Mill have heard Evans say that he hates the poon, too. They don't believe it, either. "He worships that fish," says Huff.

It is perhaps the case that Evans is old and in pain and is deeply saddened by what's happened to the tarpon in Homosassa, and he masks all of this with periodic shots of anger.

∞

"I can't believe the shape I'm in," Evans says one night with a long sigh. "I'm just a three-toed sloth. I'll be gone soon . . ."

"You'll be around a long time, dawg," Dopirak yells from the couch in the other room, the lights from the television flickering on his face. "You're pickled, Thomas."

∞

We broach the subject of politics sometimes, that unavoidable subject these days. Though we are not all politically aligned, the conversations are lifeless and short-lived. Everyone, it seems, no matter which side they are on, is exhausted by the subject. Political talk doesn't mix with the vibe of the poon shack very well, anyway.

∞

Sometimes, the conversations, influenced by alcohol, get a little disjointed.

Evans: "I think we have the team to catch it. I'm the weak link on eight-pound. We just need some opportunities. We started to see some fish today, but it got overcast."
[Silence]
Butler: "That was a spectacular wine we had at dinner, Tom."
Evans: "I got it at auction."

Butler: "Did you tell Monte about your wine cellar at home? The sixteen thousand bottles? You could write an entire book about that."

Evans: "Fuck the wine cellar."

[Silence]

Evans: "It takes no time to get old."

∽

One night, Evans brings up a fish that Mangum had caught almost exactly a year earlier. Mangum was on his home water in the Panhandle, fishing two regular clients who were into tarpon fishing but not so into it that they couldn't have a little fun. They were anchored at one of Mangum's spots that day, chatting and laughing and playing music on the boat. Mangum spotted two tarpon, and one of his clients, a New York City hedge-fund manager, threw his fly at one of them. He hooked the fish, which jumped an estimated fifteen times, exhausting itself quickly. At the boat, Mangum measured the fish. It was eighty-one inches long with a forty-five-inch girth, which, by BTT's formula, meant it weighed around 215 pounds. They let it go.

Mangum had texted me the night they'd landed the fish. He'd wanted to tell Huff about the great fish and send him some pictures, so he'd asked for his email address. I'd told him that Huff didn't have an email address and gave him his landline phone number instead. I'd texted Mangum a few hours later.

"What did Huff say?"

"Busted my balls for not using an IGFA leader . . ." he'd replied.

Mangum had used a straight piece of thirty-pound leader that day, which was obviously not IGFA legal. Huff, like Evans, Butler, Apte, Pallot, Mill, Sandy Moret, and the rest of the old school believed that even if you aren't fishing for records, you should use IGFA-approved leaders and tippet as a matter of principle. Using thirty-pound test allows the angler to get away with more mistakes. Mangum is far from the only guide these days who uses a much heavier leader than the IGFA permits. "It's really disapp{ }inting to me to see this trend," says Moret. "I could probably shoot par in golf if I didn't have to follow the rules." Evans and Butler, as expected, do not like the trend, either. "We've gotten away from the skill needed to land these fish, and from the sporting aspect, where we give the fish a fighting chance," says Butler. "Fly angling, really, is about pulling on a fish as hard as you can on a sporting tippet without breaking them off."

Mangum sees it differently, or at least he did then. "According to Steve [Huff] and those guys, you aren't really fly fishing with that leader size," he says. "That's how they see fly fishing, that you play by a set of rules. But I wasn't fishing for the record, and was just happy to put my hands on a fish like that." But the message, especially coming from Huff—whom he idolizes—was heard by Mangum. He now uses IGFA-approved leaders and tippets for tarpon.

Evans and Butler say they were happy for Mangum and had no problem with the fish. They did have a problem, however, when one of Mangum's sponsors mentioned in a magazine advertisement that Mangum had caught a tarpon that was "thirteen pounds over the world record" with its product. "You just can't say that without weighing it and without it being caught on an approved tippet," says Butler.

For Evans, it all brought back memories of 2008, when a lawyer from Jackson Hole named Peter Moyer caught a tarpon at Homosassa that taped out to well over two hundred pounds, then released it. Though Moyer says he "always acknowledged that it wasn't the world record because I let it go," the tarpon was celebrated as such. That year, Moyer was included in *Outside* magazine's list of "Badasses of the Year," with text that read, "Landed a tarpon conservatively estimated at a world record 210 pounds . . . Released it rather than kill it for the record."

A mount of Moyer's fish, with an inscription that read, in part, "Weight 210 lbs (formula estimate)," was hung in the old Jack Dennis Fly Shop in Jackson Hole. It taunted Evans every time he saw it.

Evans and Butler believe the fishing world has become perverted. Fewer people follow the rules, or even care about them anymore. Even within the membership of the IGFA there is perversion, they believe. There are too many fish species eligible for world records now, and there are certain members who stalk smaller, less glamorous fish just to get their names in the IGFA record book multiple times. "I mean, there's one guy who has a record for what is primarily an aquarium fish," says Butler. There is a schism that's developed within the IGFA membership these days, between the members who focus on the "glamour" records (like tarpon and billfish) and those who go after sheer quantity. The IGFA is caught in the middle of it all, and it's pretty much a no-win situation for the organization and its leadership. No one likes the referees and rule-makers, not these days.

Record chasing, as Evans and Butler know it, has been diminished. And as it has faded, it has become more precious to those who still do it.

∽

Evans thinks that the IGFA problem is symptomatic of a larger one in society. "All of our institutions are breaking down," he says. He may be right about the institutions, but one could argue that some of them deserved to break down and, anyway, what he really seems nostalgic about is the simpler time in which he grew up, or at least how he remembers that time. He frequently tells the story of the day in 1961 when his 12-gauge shotgun needed cleaning, and he walked from Midtown Manhattan to the Abercrombie & Fitch store on the Upper East Side with his gun over his shoulder, "and no one blinked an eye." It was, indeed, a simpler time, with hard-and-fast rules. But times—and those rules—have changed.

∽

We talk about the greenies, who Evans says want to put an end to killing fish and are too sensitive and want to regulate all sorts of things. I tell Evans that I am probably a greenie, at least by some of his definition.

He shrugs his shoulders. I push it a bit and mention that had the state of Florida listened to some of the greenies, Homosassa might not have suffered through its water problems, which means, perhaps, that the Homosassa fishery wouldn't have declined as it did.

"Yeah," he says. "Maybe."

We are all—Evans and me and the rest of us—local relativists.

∽

On most nights, Evans and Dopirak are the first to retire. And when they do, Butler and I usually join Wilson and Dope for a nightcap on the porch. We tell fishing stories and ponder what the next day may bring.

Wilson and I fish with Dope for a few days. We see a decent amount of tarpon, and we each manage to hook and lose one. Evans lands an eighty-pounder one day. The next day and the day after that and the day after that, he blanks. The world-record team shows no outward signs of frustration, though they are all a bit quiet each evening for the few hours before the revelry of dinner begins. The record begins to feel far away, maybe impossible. But as the writer Paul Bruun is fond of saying every time he goes fishing, "You're always just one cast away from greatness."

∽

One morning, we wake up to a massive storm blowing in from the west. Sheets of rain lash against the poon shack's windows. The inlet threatens to rise up over the bulkhead and onto the lawn. There will be no fishing on this day. Butler mixes up a Bloody Mary. He takes a sip. "You can't drink all day if you don't start in the morning," he says. We're back on the water the next day.

∽

One of the most frequent topics of conversation for Evans is Steve Huff. Evans has caught many more world records with Dopirak (four) than Huff (one), but something still gets Evans about Huff. Maybe it's, again, about the nostalgia for those early years. Maybe it's the way their partnership ended. Maybe it's because Huff is one of the few people in the world who has ever told Evans to shove it. Evans still clearly feels some hurt over their parting. In reality, though, the two men never really completely ended their relationship. It just manifested itself differently. "Tom has always been a soft spot for my dad," says Dustin Huff. "Their relationship goes pretty deep."

Evans has called Huff at least once a year throughout the decades. He's also called him every time he set a new world record, for tarpon or billfish. "I get it," says Huff. "I think he wanted to tell someone who understood just how hard those records are to accomplish." Unbeknownst to Evans at the time, Huff wrote letters on two different occasions (in 2013 and 2014) to the IGFA board strongly recommending Evans's candidacy for admission into the organization's Hall of Fame. (Huff himself had been inducted in 2010.) "I wrote those letters because he deserved it," says Huff. In 2015, it finally happened.

Evans invited Huff and his family to the induction ceremony. They accepted. It would be the first time that Evans and Huff had really seen each other in four decades. They would get along just fine, letting any old resentments lie dormant. Their offspring, however, would not show the same restraint, acting out old antagonisms by proxy.

On the evening of November 3, 2015, Evans was inducted into the IGFA's Hall of Fame at the organization's headquarters in Dania Beach. In his acceptance speech, Evans talked about learning how to fly fish at the carefree age of twelve. He thanked Huff, Dopirak, Butler, and the rest of his guides. He mentioned Black Rock at Homosassa, "which I renamed the Cock Hole," uttering those last two words with a relishing smile. He thanked Tania above all.

The after-party was held in a nearby hotel bar. Evans made sure that there was a good bottle of rum on every table. The din in the bar rose as mellow, light buzzes careened into drunkenness. Evans's two sons, Tom Jr. and Mark, were in attendance. Evans had not spent much time at all with either of his sons after his divorce from their mother in the late 1970s. They were little boys at the time. Inviting them to his Hall of Fame ceremony was, it seemed, some sort of attempt at a late-in-life reconciliation.

As the night wore on, some partygoers began to drift off. Huff and Dustin retired for the evening. Tania went upstairs to her hotel room. Maybe two dozen people from the ceremony remained, including Huff's older son, Chad.

Chad, Tom Jr., and Mark had known each other well as children, from the fishing trips their fathers had shared in Marathon and in Homosassa. A lot had transpired in the intervening forty years. Chad began talking to Tom Jr. "Chad was a little ruffled by what happened with my dad and his, and he was also telling me that it sucked that my brother and I hadn't had much of a relationship with our dad," says Tom Jr. "He was touching on stuff that was very real and very true, and his intentions were good, I believe, but he was probably putting his nose somewhere where it shouldn't have been."

Mark was nearby. He overheard bits and pieces of the conversation. "Mark didn't understand the good intentions part of the conversation, or didn't hear it, and he took it all the wrong way," say Tom Jr. At some point, Chad, who is six foot four and around 220 pounds, stood up and started to walk over to Evans. "I was just going to talk to him about his sons and their relationship," says Chad. But just as Chad reached Evans, he was rushed from behind and pushed by Mark. Chad then barreled into Evans, knocking him—bad back and all—over a chair. A brief moment of mayhem ensued. Butler and some of his rough-and-tumble Aussie boat mates jumped into the middle of it all. "There were bodies and tables and chairs all over the place," says Evans. But then it all ended just as quickly as it began. "I meant well, but I probably pushed it a bit too far," says Chad. Mark says the main culprit was simply "too much rum." Butler helped clean up the place and settled accounts with the bar management. He kept the chair that broke under Evans as a memento. He eventually gave it, as a keepsake, to the guide Tim Klein, who still has it in his garage in Islamorada.

The fight did no damage to the relationship of the fathers. In 2018, Huff ventured up to the poon shack one night to have dinner with Evans,

Dopirak, and Butler.* And Evans and Huff still talk on the phone at least once a year.

∽

Fathers. I couldn't help but notice, over the few years that I reported this book, the role that fathers played in the lives of many of the men within it. So many of them had, for lack of a better word, issues with their fathers. For decades, Evans had virtually no contact with his father, even though they both lived in New York City for a time. A good example of how far apart they had drifted happened on May 2, 1981. After a day on the water at Homosassa, Evans returned to his motel room, where Tania was waiting for him. They had planned to go out to dinner. When Evans walked in the door, Tania didn't ask how the fishing was and didn't mention dinner.

Instead, she greeted him with the news that his father's horse had just won the Kentucky Derby. "I was watching it on TV," she said. "Your father and both of your brothers were with the horse in the winner's circle."

Evans knew that his father had a horse farm in Virginia. He had no idea, though, that he had a horse in the Kentucky Derby, and no idea his brothers were involved. (Pleasant Colony was the horse's name, and it would also win the Preakness that year.)**

Evans, at Tania's urging, did eventually work his way back to speaking terms with his father shortly before he died in 1997. But the pain from their relationship—which was emotionally and physically violent—never really receded. "Tom's father was a great businessman who wasn't a good person," says Evans's stepson, Chan Morgan. "Tom

---

* Huff supposedly retired from guiding in 2018, though he can still be found on the water somewhere nearly every day.

** A writer from *Sports Illustrated* called Evans Sr. after the Derby and suggested doing a story on him and his son, the great tarpon angler. Evans Sr. told the writer that "there was no way in hell" he'd do that.

took the brunt of that, and his dark humor, his authenticity, is all a reflection of that."

Huff, as mentioned earlier, swears that his father leaving his family for good when he was ten years old has had no impact on his life. "He probably died in a ditch somewhere," is all he says. But it's not too much of a stretch to view the excellence he attained as a guide, which has been achieved in no small part through the pain he has inflicted on himself over the years, as *some* sort of reaction to it. Butler couldn't stand his father but doesn't like to get into details. "There's something primal with Dean and his father," says Evans. "There was a break, and Dean just said, 'I'll show you what I'm going to do and I'm going to do it better than anyone.'" Dopirak refuses to talk about his father, but, according to Evans, there's a dark history there, too. Dopirak did not attend his father's funeral, and instead guided Evans on that day, despite Evans's pleading with him to take the day off and go. Apte's father gambled the family business away. Ted Williams's father was an alcoholic. So were McGuane's and Chatham's. Lopez's father died in an accident when Lopez was a teenager. Harrison's father and sister were killed in an automobile accident when Harrison was twenty-four. Brautigan only laid eyes on his biological father twice. Pate had a strained relationship with his father.

This is all anecdotal, and I'm wary about making generalizations or playing psychologist from the proverbial armchair, and it might be that there are plenty of other sports or hobbies or industries that also attract men like this, or that it's (primarily) a generational thing. But it could also be the case that the world of big tarpon fishing and all it entails—the pain, the suffering, the fear, the sometimes-infantile machismo, the teamwork, the beauty, the triumph—does an adequate job of filling some hole.

⚭

As his 2019 Homosassa trip nears its end, Evans gets increasingly mellower. He has scruff on his face now. He has only a limited amount of time in which he can stand in any given day, and he doesn't want to waste a second of it in front of a mirror, shaving. On some late afternoons, after fishing, he sits on the porch, his feet up, gazing out over the water, with a look on his face that borders on beatific. He's clearly enjoyed having Wilson and Dope in camp, with all of the youthful energy they bring. Evans laughs a bit more than usual, a giggle that makes him sound like a little boy.

∽

Huff remembers seeing Carl Navarre Sr. in the Keys sometime in the mid-1980s. Navarre was sick by then and knew he did not have long to live. They talked about life and fishing, and eventually got around to their shared time in Homosassa, those magical early years. "All you can ask for in life is that you saw it right once," Navarre told Huff.

Evans saw it that way once, too, and yet he still shows up, having somehow grown accustomed to the fall. There is something that still gets him about the beautiful translucent water here at Homosassa. There is sometimes a window here, one or two days when the big fish swim the flat and provide the illusion that it will all be okay again, some false spring. Maybe that's what keeps him coming down, year after year, in pain, for the suffering.

Or maybe it's something else.

∽

Melville's Ahab saw his quest in grand, symbolic terms. Evans has never been one to view his tarpon fishing, or anything else, really, in that manner. It was never about anything other than doing something at its very highest level. There is symbolism, however, that appears in the things that surround the quest.

Evans's trips to Homosassa each year don't really seem to be about the record itself anymore, though that destination does give shape and coherence to the journey. It's more about everything that the pursuit puts in place, about Dopirak and Butler and about all of the people—friends and foes—and the funky bonds that have taken hold among them. It's about the poon shack, the familiar jargon, the stories told every year, the meals, the wine. It's about being—or trying to find—that little boy again. It's about forgetting about the pain—both physical and emotional—and the wrecked families and lives, at least momentarily. In the end, it's about having something to stay alive for.

∞

On my last night in the poon shack, after another one of Wilson's stupendous meals, Butler mixes up drinks for Evans, himself, and me. We'd already put down a few extra glasses of wine at dinner. Dopirak has gone to bed. Wilson and Dope are somewhere else in the house. Evans moves from his dinner seat to a couch in the kitchen, resting his swollen feet on a small table before him. Butler and I remain at the dinner table. And I ask Evans a question that I'd asked many different times in many different ways for the past two years. I ask him, Why? Why he's come back to Homosassa for more than forty years, and why he's still doing it now. Why he's already talking about coming back.

Evans sits in silence for a few seconds, staring off into some middle distance. Tears begin to collect in his eyes. He finally speaks.

"I can't think of anything else I'd rather be doing," he says, as his shoulders begin to heave. Butler gets up from the table and walks over to him and gives him a giant hug.

"I hate the fucking poon," Evans says, and they both start to laugh through their tears.

ACKNOWLEDGMENTS

This book had its genesis a decade ago when I found myself standing on the bow of Steve Huff's skiff, deep in the Everglades. I was on assignment for *Garden & Gun* magazine, there to do a profile of Steve. During that trip with him and the ones that followed, Steve kept mentioning a word that seemed both enchanted and poetic to me from the first moment I heard it: *Homosassa*.

That Steve Huff article led to another assignment from *Garden & Gun*, this time on Andy Mill. During the three days I spent with Andy and his son, Nicky, in the Florida Keys, I received something akin to a master's degree in tarpon angling, in its art and lore. (I'm still working on that PhD, which may be a long time in coming.)

It was Andy who called me in early 2018. "You *have* to tell the story of Homosassa," he said. He told me about Tom Evans and gave me a phone number. A few months later, I was in the poon shack in Homosassa, with Tom, Al Dopirak, and Dean Butler, and a book was born, one that was an absolute joy to work on, from start to finish.

I'll always be thankful to Steve and Andy for getting the ball rolling, each in their own way. And I remain especially grateful to Tom, Al, and Dean, who generously shared their thoughts and time as I followed them around for many weeks, on land and at sea, with a tape recorder and a pen and notebook in hand.

David DiBenedetto, Tom Bie, and Sid Evans (no relation to Tom) assigned, edited, and published magazine stories by me about some of the characters in this book. All three of them are among the very best at what they do, and I have been incredibly lucky to write for them over the years.

I spoke to a little more than one hundred people for this book. Not every interviewee made the manuscript by name. But each and every one of them helped.

Paul Bruun shared his encyclopedic mind with me for the section on tarpon gear. Jason Schratwieser at the IGFA answered tons of questions and helped me get in touch with a few sources. The late, great Richard Ben Cramer was the first to use "all caps" when quoting Ted Williams, a device I have borrowed here.

Paul, Ruthann, and Olive Weamer put me up on the road as I sought information about tarpon in . . . Montana.

The Olympians continue to encourage and inspire me.

I mention my good friend Charlie Ernst here only because he wants to see his name in print.

First Katie McArver, and then Fabby Theobalds, kept the little girls at bay just long enough for me to complete this book.

Sid Williamson and my uncle Charles Gaines (to whom this book is dedicated) read drafts of this book and offered very wise counsel and encouragement.

My agent, Richard Pine, remains my lodestar in this industry. His guiding principle has always been "Pursue what you love, and I'll help make it all work out."

My sincerest gratitude goes to everyone at Pegasus, but especially to Jessica Case, who made this project come to life and then made it much better.

My father's spirit hovers over everything I do, and I see him often in the eyes and deeds of my brothers, Justin and Chris.

My mother, Hansell, has always showered me with love.

My wife, Heidi, and our three daughters are simply the loves of my life and make everything worth it.

SELECTED BIBLIOGRAPHY

Apte, Stu. *Of Wind and Tides*. Atlanta: Stu Apte Productions, 2008.

Bishop, Bill. *High Rollers: Fly Fishing for Giant Tarpon*. New Cumberland, PA: Headwater Books, 2009.

Bradlee, Ben, Jr. *The Kid: The Immortal Life of Ted Williams*. New York: Little, Brown and Company, 2013.

Burke, Monte. "Pooned: Getting a Grip in the Hands of a Pro." *The Drake* (Winter 2013/2014): 98–9.

Chinnis, Rusty. "The Evolution of Homosassa Tarpon Fishing." *Anna Maria Island Sun* (Holmes Beach, FL), June 12, 2018.

Cunningham, Robert. *Chasing Records: An Angler's Quest*. New York: Skyhorse Publishing, 2012.

Davis, Jack E. *Gulf: The Making of an American Sea*. New York: Liveright Publishing, 2017.

Dimock, A. W. *The Book Of The Tarpon*. New York: New York Outing Publishing, 1911.

Dray, Philip. *The Fair Chase: The Epic Story of Hunting in America*. New York: Basic Books, 2018.

Gaines, Charles. *The Next Valley Over: An Angler's Progress*. New York: Crown Publishers, 2000.

Gibbs, Jerry. "Pioneers and Pioneering: The Allure and Early Days of Saltwater Fly Fishing." *The American Fly Fisher* 38, no. 3 (2012): 14–17.

Gibbs, Jerry. "Saltwater Fly Fishing Comes of Age." *The American Fly Fisher* 39, no. 3 (2013): 2–13.

Henriques, Diana B. *The White Sharks of Wall Street: Thomas Mellon Evans and the Original Corporate Raiders*. New York: Scribner, 2000.

Kelly, Doug. *Florida's Fishing Legends and Pioneers*. Gainesville, FL: University Press of Florida, 2011.

La Valdène, Guy de. *On the Water: A Fishing Memoir*. Guilford, CT: Lyons Press, 2015.

Mangum, David, ed. *Tarpon*. Santa Fe, NM: Talweg, 2019.

McGuane, Thomas. *The Longest Silence: A Life in Fishing*. New York: Alfred A. Knopf, 1999.

McGuane, Thomas. *Ninety-Two in the Shade*. New York: Farrar, Straus and Giroux, 1973.

McKeen, William. *Mile Marker Zero: The Moveable Feast of Key West*. New York: Crown Publishers, 2011.

Mill, Andy. *A Passion for Tarpon*. Mill Creek, WA: Wild River Press, 2010.

Roberts, Jon, and Evan Wright. *American Desperado: My Life—From Mafia Soldier to Cocaine Cowboy to Secret Government Asset*. New York: Crown Publishers, 2011.

Sargeant, Frank. *The Tarpon Book: A Complete Angler's Guide*. Lanham, MD and Plymouth, UK: Larsen's Outdoor Publishing, 1991.

Samson, Jack. *Saltwater Fly Fishing: The Challenge and Adventure of Offshore and Flats Fishing with a Fly*. Harrisburg, PA: Stackpole Books, 1991.

White, Randy Wayne, and Carlene Fredericka Brennen. *Randy Wayne White's Ultimate Tarpon Book: The Birth of Big Game Fishing*. Gainesville, FL: University Press of Florida, 2010.

ABOUT THE AUTHOR

Monte Burke is the *New York Times* bestselling author of *Saban*, *4th and Goal,* and *Sowbelly*, and the co-editor of *Leaper*. He has been the recipient of Barnes & Noble's Discover Great New Writers award and an Axiom Award for biography. His books have been named "Best of the Year" by *Sports Illustrated* and Amazon.com. He is a contributing editor at *Forbes*, *Garden & Gun*, and the *Drake*, and has also written for the *New York Times* and the *Wall Street Journal*. Burke graduated from Middlebury College with a BA in religion. He grew up in New Hampshire, Vermont, North Carolina, and Alabama, and now lives in Brooklyn with his family.

Monteburke.com
Twitter: @monteburke
Facebook: Monte Burke
Instagram: monteburke13